The Veil

The publisher gratefully acknowledges the generous support of Lucinda K. Reinold as a member of the Literati Circle of the University of California Press Foundation.

THE VEIL

Women Writers on Its History, Lore, and Politics

Edited by Jennifer Heath

University of California Press Berkeley Los Angeles London

University of California Press, one of the most distinguished university presses in the United States, enriches lives around the world by advancing scholarship in the humanities, social sciences, and natural sciences. Its activities are supported by the UC Press Foundation and by philanthropic contributions from individuals and institutions. For more information, visit www.ucpress.edu.

University of California Press
Berkeley and Los Angeles, California

University of California Press, Ltd.
London, England

Library of Congress Cataloging-in-Publication Data

The veil : women writers on its history, lore, and politics / edited by Jennifer Heath.
    p. cm.
Includes bibliographical references and index.
ISBN 978-0-520-25040-6 (cloth : alk. paper)
ISBN 978-0-520-25518-0 (pbk. : alk. paper)
    1. Veils—Social aspects.   2. Veils—History.   3. Veils in literature.
I. Heath, Jennifer.
GT2112.V   2008
391.4'1—dc22   2007027035

Manufactured in the United States of America
17 16 15 14 13 12 11 10 09 08
10 9 8 7 6 5 4 3 2 1

This book is printed on Natures Book, which contains 50% postconsumer waste and meets the minimum requirements of ANSI/NISO z39.48–1992 (R 1997) (*Permanence of Paper*).

Contents

Illustrations

Acknowledgments

There are many, many to thank.

The contributors—writers, photographers, artists—for their timely and beautiful work on this book. Their talent and scholarship is immeasurable, as is my gratitude. All went out of their way, above and beyond the call of duty to help make this book as fulsome and rich and enlightening as possible.

My friend Rickie Solinger. My agent, Ellen Geiger. University of California Press editor Naomi Schneider and her assistant, Valerie Witte. Michael Wolfe.

My husband, Jack Collom, and our assorted children and grandchildren.

Shireen Malik for her profound generosity and for listening. Sheryl Shapiro, who has always been there for me with her camera and friendship. Marda Kirn for her dear affection and support across nearly thirty years. My dear cousin Karen Leggett Abouraya. Ghada Elturk. Wahid and

Soraya Omar. Andrew Wille. Father David Denny. Jean Thies. Margot Badran. Daisy Khan. Tom Coburn, president of Naropa University, and Sharada Nayak, founder of the Educational Resources Centre Trust and former director of the Fulbright program in India. Nita Hill and Susan Edwards, for their astonishing patience, enthusiasm, and ideas.

And so many others. Thank you.

Introduction

Invisible and Visible Spaces

JENNIFER HEATH

Vision is through the veil and inescapably so.
—*Ibn al-Arabi*

Veiling—of women, men, and sacred places and objects—has existed among people of countless cultures and religions from time immemorial. Yet the veil is vastly misunderstood. Once upon a time, the veil in all its multiplicity was more or less taken for granted everywhere as, at the very least, an essential expression of the divine mysteries. Today, veiling has become globally polarizing, a locus for the struggle between Islam and the West and between contemporary and traditional interpretations of Islam.

But veiling spans time long before Islam and space far beyond the Middle East. This book attempts to provide a larger picture of veiling by exploring and examining some of its culture, politics, and narrative(s), recalling its universality, great antiquity, uses, and misuses. Twenty-one gifted writers, scholars, and artists—who represent diverse societies, religions, ages, locations, accomplishments, and attitudes—elucidate, challenge, condemn, and/or praise the veil. Contemporary issues and

I

conundrums, such as modesty and security, oppression, liberation, freedom of expression, and worship, are addressed, as are spirituality, the arts, and magic. A collection by exclusively women writers seems appropriate considering that the veil is commonly associated with females and seems to have a kind of feminine pulse.

These contributors' nonfusty, vivacious, sometimes humorous, always perceptive accounts occasionally overlap. In describing the forms and origins of and reasons for veiling in assorted places and times, repetitions naturally and necessarily occur. Thoughts and events echo and intersect, and often the recurrence of an idea serves to underscore how flawed—and ethnocentric—received wisdom can be, how it can slide into wearisome clichés.

Many scholars have considered the veil and veiling in society—past and present—in gender relations, religion, and more. An abbreviated list of the moderns (with titles that are merely samples of their important work) includes Fatema Mernissi (*The Veil and the Male Elite,* 1991), Leila Ahmed (*Women and Gender in Islam,* 1992), Fadwa el Guindi (*Veil: Modesty, Privacy and Resistance,* 1999), Elizabeth Warnock Fernea (*In Search of Islamic Feminism,* 1998), Sherifa Zuhur (*Revealing Reveiling,* 1992), Margot Badran (*Harem Years: Memoirs of An Egyptian Feminist,* 1986), Homa Hoodfar (*Between Marriage and the Market,* 1997), Avivah Gottleib-Zornberg (*The Particulars of Rapture,* 2001), Adrienne Baker (*The Jewish Woman in Contemporary Society,* 1993), Lynne Schreiber (*Hide and Seek: Jewish Women and Hair Covering,* 2003), Haviva Ner-David (*Life on the Fringes,* 2000), Mary Jo Weaver (*New Catholic Women,* 1995), Jo Ann Kay McNamara (*Sisters in Arms,* 1996), Alison Lurie (*The Language of Clothes,* 1981), and Jasbir Jain (*Feminism, Tradition and Modernity,* 2002).

To my knowledge, this book is distinctive in that it brings together, for the first time, within a single volume, manifold—sometimes contradictory—perspectives from numerous traditions, with the intention of displaying how veiling goes far beyond the narrow confines of one group or the prejudices of a moment. My hope is that this unique group ethnography will be transformative and eye-opening and help to alter superficial, exploitative, or hidebound points of view.

Some of the chapters in this book—including the visual essays by graphic novelists Marjane Satrapi and Sarah C. Bell—reflect personal experience with the veil; others take an overarching, investigative approach. The historically and politically based essays are intended to "converse" with the memoir-based chapters—as are the many images ranging from photojournalism to cartoons—so that the mix can enlarge our fields of vision and imagination (the veil has been nothing if not stimulus for the imagination). For example, while Ashraf Zahedi's "Concealing and Revealing Female Hair" provides a concentrated history and analysis of veiling and unveiling in Iran from the Persian Achaemenid Empire (ca. 500–330 B.C.E) to the present, Satrapi's "The Veil," excerpted from her autobiographical graphic novel, *Persepolis,* offers an intimate and poignant look at what Iran's 1979 Islamic Revolution meant to a little girl when the veil was imposed on all females, including children. In "Going the Whole Nine Yards," Roxanne Kamayani Gupta speaks to, among other things, her own lyrical voyage of discovery in India, in the world of the sari, while in "Purdah, Patriarchy, and the Tropical Sun," Jasbir Jain considers the segregation of Indian women from a pragmatic, literary, and sociological angle. These and other exchanges between the passionate and the detached are intended to balance and widen our understanding of the veil's vast significance for individuals and in larger social and spiritual contexts.

As much as the veil is fabric or an article of clothing, it is also a concept. It can be illusion, vanity, artifice, deception, liberation, imprisonment, euphemism, divination, concealment, hallucination, depression, eloquent silence, holiness, the ethers beyond consciousness, the hidden hundredth name of God, the final passage into death, even the biblical apocalypse, the lifting of God's veil, signaling so-called end times. When veiling is forced—then *en*forced—it is repression. Yet, as we see increasingly today, the veil is also a symbol of resistance—against ethnic and religious discrimination.[1] When the veil is forcibly stripped from its wearer, that too, is subjugation, not emancipation.

This book is divided into three sections that are simply numbered and not titled. The nature of these essays and the collection's objective make it nearly impossible to organize by, for example, region, chronology, or studies versus personal accounts. These and other options seem contrived and unbalanced here, whereas mixing it up, without boxing it too tightly, helps provide freshness, rhythm, and harmony, and, I hope, will bring to bear the rhizomic and multiple truths inherent in the veil. The essays within each grouping have commonalities meant to be seen very broadly. In the first section, the essays generally speak to the veil in its sacred aspects, not as some immutable entity (or sacred cow), but as that which is cherished as an ancient custom or signifier of devotion. Here, writers consider various ways in which, from the beginning of human time, the veil has played a part in sacred activities and thought. Yet all things sacred, in order to finally *become* so, are accompanied by internal and external conflicts. How is the veil employed as a sacred vehicle? Does it liberate the wearer on the journey to the divine? Change is a requirement if the sacred is to *remain* so; to be truly sacred, a thing or idea cannot be transfixed, trapped in fundamentalisms—it becomes meaningless if it mesmerizes and paralyzes. Writers speak not only to Islam but to Hinduism, Judaism, and Christianity—which all taught submission through veiling (variously, and including that of men and objects)—and also to veiling in pre-Abrahamic traditions, as well as to masking and magico-religion, for there is much more to sacredness than is necessarily found in institutionalized faiths.[2]

The second section addresses the veil in its sensual aspects, not as "profane" (the irreverent opposite of sacred), but as it relates to the physical, to body/spirit, and to feelings. The chapters here stretch from Shireen Malik's "She freed and floated on the air," a scrutiny of how the story of Salome's dance of the seven veils developed into a notorious icon of carnality and the Oriental woman (and then the belly dance), to Michelle Auerbach's memories of her struggles with Jewish orthodoxy in "Drawing the Line at Modesty," and to Rita Stephan's "Virtue and Sin," describing the social, moral, and cross-cultural pressures (and pleasures) of growing up in mostly Muslim Syria as an Arab Christian.

Finally, the third section touches on the veil in its sociopolitical aspects. Here, writers by and large look at some of the current diseases of veiling, as well as its history as a prize in the push-me-pull-you of internal and external strife. Muslim veiling is at the center of turmoil today—in the media, in the courts—an item of clothing whose impact on our culture is tremendous. Unfortunately, contexts are often left out of the debates. Unless we consider how veiling is perceived and employed everywhere—in Abrahamic, pre-Judaic, as well as Hindu and other traditions, along with male covering and various metaphysical, mystical, or erotic aspects of the veil—these fierce flurries can have no real relevancy, except as they might limit individual choices and cause social discord.[3]

These three loosely themed assemblages are layered and coincide: sacred meets sociopolitical, for example, in Pamela K. Taylor's "I Just Want to Be Me," where she argues for, among other things, a feminist reading of the Qur'an. In Eve Grubin's "After Eden," where the poet considers modesty and union, the sacred and sensual are woven tight as newlyweds.

The idea of veiling likely started when humans began observing Nature's mysteries. Consider the veiled nebula, eclipses of sun and moon, the shedding by animals of an outer bodily layer (feathers, skin, horn), or the ocean's waves that might eventually have inspired, for example, the veiled Orisha called Yemaya, the West African creation goddess, associated with moon and sea, who was transplanted to Brazil and the Caribbean with the African diaspora. Ancient Greece gives us the primeval goddess Nyx (Night), drawing the veil of darkness across Earth, while Selene (Moon) rises wearing a veil. (Although Odysseus's waiting wife, Penelope, tells her suitors that she is creating a shroud for her father-in-law, Laertes, the cloth that she weaves and reweaves each day might also be her own veil, for she finds sanctuary and is untouchable at her loom, within the shuttling of the threads and the emergent fabric.)

The "whens" and "whys" of veiling are mostly speculation and certainly subject to argument (as are the "whethers," which writers Taylor and Auerbach, for example, ponder in their essays). Throughout history, the veil has signified rank, religion, and marital status or indicated that the wearer belongs to a specific ethnic group. Headdresses—hats, head wraps, and so on—often serve similar purposes, from displaying class (e.g., crowns or the church hats of African American women) and belonging (e.g., the red cap of the eighteenth-century French revolutionaries) to practical functions of protection from the elements.[4] But the veil is more than emblem, shield, or decoration (although it is those, too). The word veil comes from the Latin *uelum* (or *velum*), a sail, cloth, or standard.[5] The verb *velare*, to veil, means to conceal. Revelation comes from *revelatio*, an act of drawing back the veil, to reveal.[6] To qualify as a veil, the scarf, the bonnet, the turban, or the cloth usually requires a mystique, and religious or magico-religious significance. The veil is itself mystery, even as it is also the shroud that guards the mystery. To be veiled is, to some degree, to be hidden. And right there we have a condition of both great attraction and great repulsion.

In the West today, the veil is rarely treated as a traditional or sacred custom but is perceived almost entirely politically. The practice of veiling has long been the subject of conflict, though now in the early twenty-first century arguments grow louder and more combative than ever. As we learn from Zahedi and from Mohja Kahf, in "From Her Royal Body the Robe Was Removed," the custom of veiling has historically been a source of political manipulation, from the British treatment of it in Egypt in the nineteenth century to Atatürk's and Reza Pahlavi's forced unveilings in Turkey and Persia in the early twentieth century. It was a colonial and imperial football. It still is. First lady Laura Bush mimicked old colonialist patterns when she boasted of the "liberation" of Afghan women to justify American foreign policy in the Middle East. Ironically, this policy sent the once-*unveiled* women of war-torn Iraq scurrying for cover,[7] and in fact, most women in Afghanistan continue to seek the refuge of the veil, not only for safety's sake, but because veiling is a venerable tradition. Everyone is acquainted with the Taliban's imposition of the veil on Afghan women during its brutal reign of terror; abuse of the veil was rampant and continues to be. But in "That (Afghan) Girl! Ideology Unveiled in *National Geographic*," Dinah Zeiger has taken an expanded approach to veiling in Afghanistan, probing ways in which the Western media have colluded with Western political agendas.

Battles about veiling are by no means restricted to Muslims. Not all people who veil are Muslims, nor do all Muslims veil. As Laurene M. Lafontaine writes in "Out of the Cloister," disputes regarding the unveiling of Roman Catholic nuns in the mid-1960s, after the Second Vatican Council, were ferocious and painful. Until Vatican II, laywomen customarily wore head coverings at Mass. There are still those adamantly in favor of the veiling of Catholic women religious and some who even advocate the continued veiling of Christian women generally.[8] In Germany, in 2004, when a court in the state of Baden-Württemberg passed a law forbidding Muslim teachers to wear head scarves, it barred Roman Catholic nuns from wearing their habits in public schools into the bargain.[9] All this is déjà vu: Roman Catholic nuns were banned during England's Reformation in the sixteenth century and not reinstated until 1840.

Principles of modesty and humility before God are maintained by other Christians, as well. Jana Hawley's "The Amish Veil" describes practices among the Amish in Pennsylvania, where veiling is manifested in women's bonnets and quiet dress. Mennonites, Hutterites, and even Mormons, who wear special undergarments,[10] honor a symbolic connection between clothing and faith and can also be said to "veil." Indeed, the black scarf worn for centuries by women in Greece, Corsica, Sicily, Sardinia, and other nations of the Christian Mediterranean is nearly indistinguishable from that of rural Turkey, Egypt, or Iran and "is a vestige of what was once a very widespread accoutrement."[11] In the nineteenth and early twentieth centuries, Jewish, Muslim, and Christian women veiled in Egypt, but "Lucie Duff Gordon, a perceptive Englishwoman who lived in Egypt in the 1860s, remarked that the Christians she saw in Upper Egypt were more fastidious than the Muslims in veiling."[12] Is the Spanish mantilla originally Christian—a religious compulsion, as some claim—or did it begin with the practices of Arabs who ruled much of Spain from 711 to 1492, and whose women in various periods were the most liberated in Europe?

Borders shift, empires come and go, customs interconnect. In *Muhammad: Biography of a Prophet,* Karen Armstrong suggests that "when the wives of the Crusaders saw the respect in which Muslim women were held, they took to wearing the veil in the hope of teaching their own menfolk to treat them better."[13] It's an arguable notion. Yet however it was introduced, the veil is ubiquitous in European history. In "He hath couerd my soule inwarde," Désirée G. Koslin considers the veil's prominence and permutations for churchwomen in medieval Europe.

As a number of writers in this book note, there is evidence of veiling in ancient Mesopotamia, the Iberian Peninsula, and in ancient Greece and Rome. Inanna, Sumerian goddess of heaven, Ishtar, chief goddess of the Babylonians and Assyrians, and her Phoenician counterpart, Astarte, as well as Isis, Egyptian goddess of fertility and motherhood, are often found veiled, their wide, all-seeing eyes framed in black. "Various considerations suggest that the veil is in origin rather an *affirmation* of the face, as a human and particularly a sexual glory, than a concealment, though the emphasizing of maidenly modesty comes in as a secondary and still more prominent factor. The veil also serves as an expression of the head and the hair."[14]

Statues of the ancient goddess—Sumerian or Babylonian or Phoenician or Egyptian—were frequently covered during processions on holy days, as were priestesses, and as are figures of the Virgin Mary today. Gupta notes in her chapter that goddess figures in India are dressed in saris. Such covering indicates profound, hidden, divine knowledge. Thus the veiling of sacred objects and icons: the Old Testament tells of the veiled tabernacle on Mt. Sinai; the Christian Eucharist is veiled; Mecca's central shrine, the Ka'aba, is veiled. "In the [Tibetan Buddhist] shrine room, there are two *mandalas* that are always veiled. There are certain statues in the *stupa* that can't be seen except by certain practitioners with certain levels of understanding."[15] The veil is used universally in ritual and dance as a channel leading to the Mysteries, to wisdom, and healing of mind or body.

In ancient Rome the vestal virgins entered service as children—offered up by their families—and were consecrated, like later Roman Catholic nuns, by cutting their hair. When performing sacrifices, they wore veils of white cloth bordered with purple and clipped under the chin with a brooch.[16] In Nepal, little girls are still given as Buddhist *kumaris*, sequestered and adorned as goddesses. A child is allowed to see the world and be seen on rare ceremonial occasions and is finally dethroned when she begins to show signs of humanity, such as the loss of her baby teeth, a signal that the goddess has vacated her body. She is then returned to her family and a new girl is chosen. On nearly all continents, there have always been holy wanderers and hermits (male and female) who isolate themselves. Seclusion goes by many names, has many manifestations, and offers many justifications. It is not, however, a synonym for polarization, though this tends to be the belief in the West, which is obsessed with penetrating the veil and obfuscating the lines between public and private spaces.

Elite women of ancient Greece were deeply secluded, rarely emerging from their homes and solidly swathed when they did. In Athens, in the fourth century B.C.E., slaves, courtesans, artists, musicians, and tradeswomen were free to move about publicly, while highborn women were not.[17] In the third century C.E., Tertullian reported the substantial veils of Jewish women.[18] Indeed, a biblical tale says that Rebecca veiled herself before Isaac, her bridegroom-to-be, and that their son Jacob—as Bell notes in her graphic essay, "Nubo"—married the wrong woman, so heavily veiled she was unrecognizable. (Figure i.1) Tamar veiled to disguise herself as a prostitute in order to get pregnant.[19] Jewish women into the twentieth century in Iraq or Tunisia or Turkey dressed and veiled much as their Muslim sisters did. In "Shattered Vessels That Contain Divine Sparks," Barbara Goldman Carrel recalls her studies among Hasidim in Brooklyn, revealing how dress codes affect a community and its spiritual identity.

Moses veiled his "radiant" and "frightening" face when speaking to the Hebrews after spending forty days and forty nights alone with God.[20] Peter the Deacon tells of Pope Gregory the Great (ca. 554–605), who dictated his homilies from behind a veil drawn between himself and his secretary. The pope was silent for such a long time that the curious secretary made a hole in the veil. He saw a dove seated on Gregory's head with its beak between his lips. When the dove withdrew its beak, the holy pontiff spoke.[21] In these accounts, the veil conceals and vouchsafes wisdom.

Before the coming of Islam, the noblewomen of Mecca, like those in myriad other places, veiled to distinguish themselves from the rabble. The Prophet Muhammad's first wife, Khadija, a wealthy woman in her own right, wore a head covering to display her social position many years before the advent of the Qur'an's controversial "Verses of the Curtain."[22]

The Moroccan traveler Ibn Battuta (1304–69) journeyed for twenty-six years throughout the Muslim world writing extensive journals. He was shocked and dismayed when, at a ceremonial event, an Ozbeg sultan welcomed his unveiled senior wife by advancing toward her, greeting her respectfully, taking her by the hand, and seating himself only after she had mounted the couch. Upon encountering an unveiled Turkish woman entering a bazaar with her husband, Ibn Battuta remarked scornfully, "Anyone seeing [the husband] would take him to be one of her servants."[23]

Figure I.1. A double wedding in Turkmenistan, 2005. Photo by Sheryl B. Shapiro.

Tribeswomen Tertullian encountered in Asia Minor appeared in public totally enveloped in their mantles, with only one eye left free. Such styles of dress still exist here and there but are disappearing fast. Islam is far from being a monoculture, yet, as Aisha Shaheed notes in "Dress Codes and Modes," there has in recent decades been a push toward a Muslim monolith that is articulated at least visually in women's dress and veiling practices. Technology and education, immigration, globalization, and war have also contributed to rapid changes and cultural defense mechanisms, which have sometimes resulted in forced veilings.

I regret that this book does not offer more about veiling in Muslim areas of sub-Saharan Africa, Malaysia, or Indonesia (figure i.2).[24] Nor have we ventured into Buddhist-majority regions of the Far East, where—with exceptions such as the Confucian *jangoui* in Korea—the use of personal veils seems to be rare.[25]

Fashion designers and clotheshorses have always appreciated the veil. In "On the Road," Maliha Masood recalls the trendy veiling she encountered among the young, hip fashionistas of Cairo, Damascus,

Figure I.2.   Studio portrait of an
Acehnese woman, ca. 1908. Islam
first entered Southeast Asia through
Aceh in the eighth century. It is now
a province of Indonesia.

Amman, and Beirut. The veil has been equally trendy among Western
women. In the 1950s, for example, modish ladies would not think of leaving the house until they had donned their veiled hats. These chapeaux
with fishnet face screens—also worn in some veiling societies as tran-
sitional garb during periods of modernization—seem to have been most
popular between the world wars when European and American men re-
claimed the workplace, sending women back to the kitchen, hearth, and
nursery.

   An era of artistic tolerance in Afghanistan in the 1970s, during the reign
of Zahir Shah, was celebrated by Hamida Sekander, who transformed the
chadri (also called *burqa*) into an exquisite, carefree, pleated dress, its
square bodice tailored from the veil's crocheted eyepiece and cap (figure
i.3). Alas, that heyday (which, as Zeiger writes, first stuttered into being
when Afghan Queen Soraya unveiled in the 1920s) has passed. And as
Zahedi notes, the anxiety of the Islamic Republic's current regime about
the increasing liberties the irrepressible women of Iran take with their
appearance is such that the government now sponsors fashion shows.
Models tripping along runways show off exquisite colors and fabrics in

Figure 1.3.   A model, *left,* displays a variation on the burqa dress origi-
nally created by artist Hamida Sekander in 1970s Afghanistan. Photo by
Jennifer Heath. A woman, *right,* wears a *chadri* or *burqa* in Pakistan.
Photo by Sheryl B. Shapiro.

a gorgeous chadri, niqab, or *abaya* (figure i.4).[26] In "From Veil to Veil," Zuhur
describes her experiences with, among other coverings, the abaya—
oppressive despite its potential beauty—recalling unpleasant encounters
with Saudi Arabia's self-appointed male monitors of morality.

Veiling has a huge impact on our psyches . . . and our pocketbooks. The
image of the veiled woman has been exploited for generations to sell
cigarettes, coffee, perfume, jewelry—the list goes on. In 2001, Reebok
advertised its shoes on a completely veiled woman with the caption, "A
Hidden Classic." In 2004, Forex used the image of a woman wearing *niqab*
to market condoms.[27] Islamic dress, especially since the tragedy of September 11, 2001, is also a favorite of newspaper cartoonists, as contribu-
tor Kecia Ali observes in "Burqas and Bikinis."

Early in this project, Jeni Allenby, curator of the Palestine Costume
Archive in Canberra, Australia, wrote, "I'd suggest [writing about] veiling in Palestine, but . . . they didn't veil. [Nevertheless], Europeans in-

Figure I.4. A woman wearing *niqab* in a fashion show in Tehran, 2005. The face veil is unusually sheer. Photo by Satyar Emami. Courtesy of the Iran Times International.

variably posed Palestinian women for their Christian imagery pictures veiled."[28]

This, from the flip side, recalls *turcmania*, which hit France in 1704, when Antoine Galland's translation of *Arabian Nights* was published and all things Oriental suddenly became fashionable. In 1714, the French ambassador to Turkey published costume plates with paintings by Jan Baptiste Vanmour that kicked off a craze for Turkish dress. All Paris's rich and powerful became pseudo-Turks, commissioning portraits in which men and women wore caftans, pants, and turbans. (Later, Marie Antoinette and her ladies took up a dress called *à la sultane.* Nineteenth-century suffragists wore pantaloons that originated with women in the East but were named for Amelia Bloomer, who advocated less restrictive clothing for European and American women.)[29] Lady Mary Wortley Montagu accompanied her husband to Constantinople on an ambassadorial visit in 1716 and became the first to introduce Turkish dress to England. She sported local styles during her two years in Turkey, much to the bemusement of her hosts. She did not, apparently, go so far as to adopt the Turkish *yashmak*, the sheer face veil.[30]

The vogue for portraits in costume waned after awhile, although the interest in Oriental art stayed steady, thanks to increasing colonialist intrusions in the Near and Middle East and India. In 1885, Sir Richard Francis Burton's unexpurgated, titillating version of the *Arabian Nights*—published under the title *The Thousand Nights and a Night*—appeared. Scheherazade's influence (like turcmania) was felt in all the arts: painting, theater, fashion, ballet, literature.[31] In "She freed and floated on the air," Malik follows the similar trajectory of Salome.

Edward Said defined Orientalism in his seminal book as "an accepted grid for filtering through the Orient into Western consciousness . . . a product of imaginative geography and history."[32] Orientalist art was popular from the 1700s through the 1950s, with Western artists taking inspiration from Islamic miniatures, architecture, and design for their paintings, household furnishing, fabrics, book illustrations, and more. With the invention of photography, studio portraits such as those in Malek Alloula's *The Colonial Harem*[33] were produced in Algeria depicting women, many attired (some not) and staged in much the same way Edward Curtis costumed Native Americans without regard to their tribal affiliations or authentic traditions. The Western artist's gaze fell on invented interiors of harems, where strange men could never enter. Thus, they often employed prostitutes, street musicians, and dancers as subjects for their whimsies— and unveiled them, offering them up to Western viewers as symbols of an erotic, fabricated East, where every capricious desire was welcomed with languid hospitality. Manet, Renoir, Matisse, Picasso . . . nearly all the usual suspects made Orientalist paintings, exploiting the veil for design as much as for its exoticism, as in Mario Simon's 1919 painting *Odalisque*, in which a bare-breasted woman in bloomers is framed by two shapes in flowing white niqab, triangular, generic specters not unlike lampshades. Paul Klee's *Arab Song*, a 1932 abstraction, "exists simultaneously as portrait and not-portrait, for it is impossible to say who is pictured."[34]

Klee's painting seems to blur the categories of art about veils and art that is veiled, like the abstract expressionist work of, for example, the painter Mark Rothko or the films of Stan Brakhage, notably, *Text of Light*, shot through a glass ashtray, which becomes the veil through which we see distorted and imagined objects and landscape. In 1988, Cyril Christo, son of Christo and Jeanne-Claude, wrote of his parents' works *Running Fence, Surrounded Islands,* and *Wrapped Pont Neuf:*

> Under the guise of veils
> you cannot return to the embodied vein.
> . . . .
> What you conceal is the form
> of our inquiring gaze.
> Being is the ghost
> Of selected mystery.[35]

An exhibition produced in Great Britain in 2003, "Veil: Veiling, Representation and Contemporary Art," was "designed to show how the heterogeneous use of veiling, as dress act and visual trope, is endlessly repositioned by changing world events and constantly reframed by the nuanced shifting responses of veiling communities."[36] Artists featured in the exhibition, among them Shirin Neshat, Emily Jacir, Zineb Sedira, and Jananne Ali-Ani, as well as others who were not represented, such as Lalla Essaydi, Tasmina Bouziane, Fatma Charfi, or Susan Hefuna, might be labeled new anti-Orientalists. Their lives are or have been affected by the veil and by Western perceptions and depictions of it, which ultimately define and/or misrepresent them. They make art "within loaded social and (sometimes) personal conditions . . . their work and its reception are bound to be positioned in relation to existing visual conventions in the depiction of the veil."[37]

In Clea T. Waite's 1999 video sculpture, *What Was Lot's Wife's Name?* a veiled figure—a woman encased in a pillar of salt—absorbs the tirades of patriarchal Christian fundamentalists. In 1977, Los Angeles performance artist Suzanne Lacy created *In Mourning and In Rage,* seven-foot-tall veiled women in black carrying a banner reading Women Fight Back. The first performance occurred at Los Angeles City Hall to protest the murder of women by the Hillside Strangler. It—and subsequent "mourning women" performances (including those by other groups who adopted Lacy's imagery)—signified not only grief, but the unveiling in public of such taboo subjects as rape, violence against women, incest, prostitution, and agism.[38]

A paradox of veiling is that it can reveal what is denied and it can deny or censor. In August 2002, U.S. Attorney General John Ashcroft "veiled" the art deco "Spirit of Justice" statue (a Works Progress Administration project of the 1930s, nicknamed Minnie Lou), which stands proudly with one breast bared in the Great Hall of the Justice Department. In February 2003, in the press area of the United Nations building, a tapestry reproduction of Pablo Picasso's brutal masterpiece *Guernica*, his response to the horrors of the Spanish civil war, was veiled as U.S. diplomats made their case for invading Iraq. There's a sort of reverse irony in a cartoon by an artist calling himself "Tignous," published during the 1990s in the French magazine *Télérama*, highlighting the social condition of Algerian women. A viewer—looking quizzically at a statue of a veiled female figure labeled "Tribute to Algerian Womanhood"—asks, "When is the inauguration?"

Not surprisingly, an Amazon.com search for books with the word "veil" in their titles yields thousands. "Lifting the veil," "beyond the veil," and "behind the veil" are just three of the most popular for poetry, novels, histories, travelogues, memoirs, biographies, exposés, how-tos, advice for brides, or tomes about the occult. Hundreds are about finance or covert operations: the veiled spy; veiled illicit corporate schemes.

In her essay, Grubin wrestles with questions of modesty in the company of fellow poets William Blake, John Keats, Emily Dickinson, Walt Whitman, and others. The veil has been considered by hundreds of versifiers for hundreds of years in hundreds of cultures: Ibn al-Arabi, Rumi, Zeb un-Nissa, Byron, and Gerard Manley Hopkins are a mere few.[39]

Veils naturally play prominent roles in folklore, fairy tales, and mythology. As Jain notes, the veiling of Sita, wife of Rama, in the great Sanskrit epic Ramayana, is one explanation for the applied practice of purdah in India.

In tales everywhere—Indian, African, Turkish, Persian, Arabic, Central Asian, Japanese, Chinese, Native American, and European—djinn, fairies, sprites, goblins, and other invisible beings of many names pop in and out of the lives of humans through veils of smoke or the roots of hawthorn trees, the blooms of peonies, wells or tides, mists or fog, dreams or wishes. Sometimes they are invisible and make their mischief or accomplish their good deeds unseen. They live in concealed places, where supernatural acts are commonplace but hidden from human eyes. The world is full of hidden caves or indiscernible isles, such as Avalon, the misty Island of Women in Arthurian legend (in which the "dark veil" dominates many adventures). The lands of mythologies, of fairy and folk tales are veiled in silence or veiled in thorns for a hundred sleeping years until the prince arrives. Or veils are escape routes—as when Hans Christian Andersen's little match girl meets a wall, which becomes "transparent as a veil," so that she sees into other possibilities. There are veils of illusion *(maya)* and cloths and cloaks that make the wearer invisible and immune from harm. Odysseus is given a veil by the sea nymph Ino, so that he can return home to Ithaca. And sometimes the skin veils another being, like the selkie, the fur seal who sheds her coat in order to love a human and to walk, for a time, upon the earth.

These wonder stories and variations show up in film as well, thoroughly Disneyfied and Hollywoodized, minus their spiritual power. However, early avant-garde cinematographers such as Marcel Duchamp, Luis Buñuel, and Jean Cocteau understood how film itself can be enchanted visual poetry, a vehicle that carries us through the veil and into the surreal. Further enriched, their lineage continues with postwar experimental filmmakers like Brakhage, Maya Deren, Kenneth Anger, Marie Menken, and Gregory Markopoulos, who also contemplate the veil's many metaphors.

Salome with her seven veils, as Malik points out, was thoroughly limned in movies from silents to talkies.[40] In his book *Reel Bad Arabs: How Hollywood Vilifies a People*, Jack Shaheen exposes the awful stereotypes—and outright lies—promulgated about Arabs and Arab culture (and therefore the veil) by the movie industry from its earliest beginnings.[41] Gillo Pontecorvo's 1965 *The Battle of Algiers* describes how, during the revolution in Algeria against French occupation, the veil was transformed into "a technique of camouflage," as Frantz Fanon put it.[42]

It can be disconcerting for Westerners to watch Iranian films (where women must be veiled by law) when women wear a head scarf in some of the most intimate situations (as intimate as the law will allow). "Veiling is the armature of modesty. . . . In Iranian cinema modesty necessitates that men and women treat each other at all times as if they are in public, even when they are in the privacy of their own home or bedroom." Out of this situation a vivid, reflective, and unique women's cinema has arisen.[43]

.   .   .   .   .

Standing as a beacon of tradition or an emblem
of progressive modernity, the veiled or unveiled,
de-veiled or re-veiled woman has been a feature
of divergent struggles over decolonization,
nationalism, revolution, Westernization and anti-
Westernization. . . . In all these developments,
women's agency has been central.[44]

As several writers here note, an exchange in September 2005 between U.S. envoy Karen Hughes and Muslim women exemplifies profound mis-understanding of Eastern women's lives. To non-Muslim Americans and Europeans, the practice of veiling describes suppression and obedience to absolute male and religious authority and is the principal symbol in the West of supposed Muslim backwardness and ignorance.

During a "listening meeting" held in Ankara, Hughes faced loud crit-icism from women of Turkey, Egypt, and Saudi Arabia for her inaccurate assertions about their condition. They informed Hughes, in no uncertain terms, that the veil does not make them inferior. War, poverty, lack of edu-cation, and neocolonialism, not the veil, the women noted, are the greatest enemies of women's rights worldwide. Women who veil are by no means mute ghosts. Many are educated, feminist elite, putting the lie to those who wish to equate veiling with complete lack of self-determination. Cer-tainly the veil was a source of contention among early Muslim feminists, as it is among Muslim feminists today. Misrepresentations of the veil and the political, social, and psychological disruptions created by colonialism and subsequent diasporas are the roots of frustration, anger, bigotry, and internal strife. They can and do lead to extremes and contribute to the im-position of the veil where it may not be desired.

Whether the women writing in this book are "for" or "against" veiling is not the point. What is germane is that none are ideologists and all are concerned about women's choice and their well-being and rights to full humanity worldwide. To that end, a clear grounding in the history and context of veiling is vital.

Veiling is an enormous and complex topic, lately reduced to a one-dimensional screen onto which we project our stereotypes and misgivings. "The veil is a persistent symbol of [contemporary] Europe's struggle to come to terms with cultural diversity and social inclusion."[45] The United States—politics and prejudices (on all sides) notwithstanding—has been, so far, relatively free of the public veiling disputes that have in current years besieged Europe.[46] Despite occasional references to recent clashes, the writers in this book have tried to avoid joining today's wars of cultural relativism or allowing this book to become a hijab battleground.[47] Events occur rapidly and each uproar—from the banning of head covering, whether hijabs, turbans, wimples, or yarmulkes in schools and public places to the firing of workers for wearing crosses—has only a short shelf life in the news media. This latest veil fetishism will pass, and the veil, which has existed from time immemorial, in one or another of its aspects of beauty and mystery, will continue to be with us.

NOTES

1. It has been suggested that for some African American women, the veil represents a shield against the shame their ancestors suffered as slaves stripped for sale. It may also occasionally act as a "flag"—an identifier, like gang colors in the 'hood—and protection. "No one fucks with me," a young, veiled African American convert in Atlanta, Georgia, told me in 2004. "They know my Muslim brothers are watching out for me."

2. Some scholars believe that Islam borrowed veiling from Christianity, which in turn borrowed it from the Greeks. The custom of separation or sanctuary—the *harām*—is thought to have been adopted by early Arab Muslims from elite Zoroastrian Persians.

3. In October 2006, Britain's archbishop of Canterbury, Rowan Williams, joined the religious symbols fracas by saying that everyone should be free to wear visible religious symbols and that "aiming for a society where no symbols such as veils, crosses, sidelocks or turbans would be seen was 'politically dan-

gerous.'" In such a society, he said, the state would become a "'central licensing authority' which creates public morality." *BBC News*, "Williams Joins Faith Symbols Row," October 27, 2006, http://news.bbc.com.uk/go/pr/fr/2/hi/uk_news/6089988.stm.

4.   Of interest here is Georgia Scott, *Headwraps: A Global Journey* (New York: Public Affairs, 2003).

5.   In Walter W. Skeat, *A Concise Etymological Dictionary of the English Language* (1882; repr. Oxford: Clarendon Press, 1972), s.v. "veil," which continues: "Lit. 'propeller' of a ship; from *uehere*, to carry along."

6.   In personal correspondence, January 18, 2007, Margot Badran—coeditor with Miriam Cooke of *Opening the Gates: A Century of Arab Feminist Writing* (Bloomington: Indiana University Press, 1990)—mused on the connection "between veil, cloth and paper [vellum]. . . . Unveiling (face) and writing were thickly associated with each other in the late 19th and early 20th centuries with the rise of women's published writings (i.e., new women's Arabic press and various books). . . . Egyptian feminist Huda Shaarawi . . . with Zaiza Nabarawi, unveiled in public in 1923. . . . I see her memoirs (committed to paper—actually dictated to a male secretary cum administrative figure not published in her lifetime) as her final unveiling."

7.   Much has been reported about the reveiling of Iraqi women, including Jackie Spinner, "Head Scarves Now a Protective Accessory in Iraq," *Washington Post*, December 30, 2004; and Terri Judd, "For the Women of Iraq, the War Is Just Beginning," *Independent*, June 8, 2006.

8.   Outlooks about veiling (and reveiling) of Catholic and Christian women can be found on the Internet on sites such as www.catholicplanet.com/women/headcovering.htm and www.bibleviews.com/veil.html.

9.   *BBC News*, October 10, 2004, http://news.bbc.c.uk/1/hi/world/europe/3731368.stm.

10. Jean A. Hamilton and Jana Hawley, "Sacred Dress, Public Worlds," in *Religion, Dress and the Body*, ed. Linda B. Arthur (Oxford: Berg, 1999), 43.

11. Juliette Minces, *The House of Obedience: Women in Arab Society*, trans. Michael Pallis (London: Zed Press, 1982), 49.

12. Lucie Duff Gordon, *Letters from Egypt* (1865), as quoted in *Harem Years: The Memoirs of An Egyptian Feminist (1879–1924)*, by Huda Shaarawi, trans. Margot Badran (New York: Feminist Press, 1987), 10.

13. Karen Armstrong, *Muhammad: Biography of a Prophet* (New York: HarperCollins, 1992), 198–99.

14. Ernest Crawley, *Dress, Drink, and Drums: Further Studies of Savages and Sex* (London: Methuen, 1931), 136; emphasis added.

15. Conversation with scholar and American Buddhist Susan Edwards on November 4, 2006. Edwards went on to say, "Things are veiled based on your

personal understanding. There are layers of understanding to accomplish in order to get the sense of that allegorical journey toward enlightenment—that you went through each gate." The Sanskrit *mandala* is a ritualistic geometric design symbolic of the universe, used in Hinduism and Buddhism to aid meditation; a *stupa* is a dome-shaped monument, used to house Buddhist relics or to commemorate significant facts.

16. François Boucher, *20,000 Years of Fashion: The History of Costume and Personal Adornment* (New York: Harry N. Abrams, 1987), 435.

17. Elise Boulding, *The Underside of History* (Boulder, CO: Westview Press, 1976), 259.

18. As quoted in Boucher, *20,000 Years,* 235.

19. Genesis 24:67, 38:14 (New Revised Standard Version).

20. Exodus 24:18.

21. *Catholic Encyclopedia,* s.v. "Peter the Deacon, Vita," www.newadvent.org (accessed 18 July 2007).

22. A. J. Arberry, trans., *The Koran Interpreted,* Surah 24.

23. As quoted in Ross E. Dunn, *The Adventures of Ibn Battuta: A Muslim Traveler of the Fourteenth Century* (Berkeley: University of California Press, 1986), 168–69.

24. For an interesting, if somewhat dated article, see Marion Bowman, "Islam, Adat and Multiculturalism in Malaysia," *Diskus* 2, no. 1 (spring 1994): 15–27.

25. Excavations indicate that Confucian men and women in Korea wore identical *jangouri* until the eighteenth century, when women used *jangouri* "to cover their heads like long veils when they were going outside of the home." Inwoo Chang and Haekyung L. Yu, "Confucianism Manifested in Korean Dress from the Sixteenth to the Seventeenth Centuries," in *Undressing Religion: Commitment and Conversation from a Cross-Cultural Perspective,* ed. Linda B. Arthur (Oxford: Berg, 2000), 108.

26. Of interest here is Leela Jacinto, "The Veil Is Not Oppression, It's Chic, Say Muslim Women: The Bush Administration Cares About Women's Rights (as Long as There Aren't Any Pesky Women Around)," *ABC News,* March 7, 2002. And from personal correspondence with Riem Farahat in August 2005: "I think you will be surprised about the abaya market in Saudi Arabia. It all depends on how much you want to pay. You can find an abaya for 50 Riyals (about $15) very plain and bad fabric. Then you can find one that is a few thousand Riyals—yes, you read correctly! Type of fabric and ornaments play a big role in the price. The ornaments can be anything from colored patches and shiny stars to drawings of flowers and writings. One teenager had an abaya with "go for it!" written on the back. If her mom only knew what it meant. . . . My aunt is very fashionable. For her granddaughter's wedding, she had an abaya custom-made from the same fabric as her strapless dress. . . .

Weddings are not mixed. When the men came in, she wore the abaya and still looked elegant. Moral of the story: the abaya says a lot about the female wearing it and differs from one place/family to the other. It also depends on where one is going. I would never wear a colored abaya to a conservative shopping mall. But in Jeddah, it is normal to wear a colored one."

27.   On September 28, 2004, *Al-Jazeera News Service* reported that, in response to an Italian demand that the burqa be banned as a "symbol of death," fashion designer Giorgio Armani disagreed, adding that it was "no crime" to wear it. "To see a veiled woman on the streets of Paris used to have exotic appeal. Now they are seen as terrorists and people take fright," he said. "You can be packed with explosives even with your face uncovered."

28.   Personal correspondence, April 2005.

29.   Lynne Thornton, *Women as Portrayed in Orientalist Painting* (Paris: ACR-PocheCouleur, 1994), 4–19.

30.   Thornton, *Women as Portrayed,* 12. Of interest here is Lady Mary Wortley Montagu, *Letters* (New York: Knopf, 1992).

31.   Thornton, *Women as Portrayed,* 16.

32.   Edward Said, *Orientalism* (New York: Vintage Books, 1979), 6, 83.

33.   Malek Alloula, *The Colonial Harem,* trans. Myrna Godzich and Wlad Godzich (Minneapolis: University of Minnesota Press, 1986), focuses primarily on postcards—which Alloula calls "comic strips of colonial morality"—made across thirty years for French colonialist trade.

34.   Dinah Zeiger, "Unusable Faces" (spring 2005).

35.   Cyril Christo, *The Whispering Veils: Poems on Christo's Art* (Westport, CT: Hugh Lauter Levin Associates, 1988).

36.   Reina Lewis, preface to *Veil: Veiling, Representation and Contemporary Art,* ed. David A. Bailey and Gilane Tawadros (Cambridge, MA: MIT Press, 2003), 10.

37.   Lewis, preface to *Veil: Veiling,* 14.

38.   To view Clea T. Waite's *What Was Lot's Wife's Name?* see www.khm.de/~clea/works/works.Lots_Wife.html. For more about Suzanne Lacy's mourning women, see Lucy R. Lippard, *Get the Message? A Decade of Art for Social Change* (New York: E. P. Dutton, 1984).

39.   For a provocative and comprehensive look at veiling in European literature from the medieval period to the mid-nineteenth century, refer to Mohja Kahf, *Western Representations of the Muslim Woman: From Termagant to Odalisque* (Austin: University of Texas Press, 1999).

40.   Of interest here is *Hollywood Harems,* a short 1999 documentary by filmmaker Tania Kamal-Eldin.

41.   Jack G. Shaheen, *Reel Bad Arabs: How Hollywood Vilifies a People* (Northampton, MA: Olive Branch Press, 2001).

42. Frantz Fanon, "Algeria Unveiled," in *Veil: Veiling,* 74–85.

43. Hamid Naficy, "Poetics and Politics of the Veil, Voice and Vision in Iranian Post-Revolutionary Cinema," in *Veil: Veiling,* 138–39.

44. Lewis, preface to *Veil: Veiling,* 10.

45. David A. Bailey and Gilane Tawadros, introduction to *Veil: Veiling,* 19.

46. In Canada, a television show called *Little Mosque on the Prairie,* which began in 2006, features veiled and unveiled Muslim women and with its universal sitcom humor goes a long way toward acceptance and assimilation.

47. Of interest here, Karen Armstrong logged in during a high point in Britain's recent niqab battles, with an article in the October 26, 2006, *Guardian Unlimited,* titled "My years in a habit taught me the paradox of veiling: If ministers really want a proper debate, they must learn that where the veil is forbidden, women hasten to wear it," www.guardian.co.uk/comment/story/0,1931544,00.html.

ONE

Shall any gazer see with mortal eyes,
Or any searcher know by mortal mind?
Veil after veil will lift
but here must be Veil upon veil behind.

—Edwin Arnold

1 From Her Royal Body the Robe Was Removed

The Blessings of the Veil and the Trauma of Forced Unveilings in the Middle East

MOHJA KAHF

It is like a second skin to me. It is supple as a living membrane and moves and flows with me. There is beauty and dignity in its fall and sweep. It is my crown and my mantle, my vestments of grace. Its pleasures are known to me, if not to you.

Veiling—covering the head with a piece of fabric, and sometimes the face as well—predates Islam. Christian women in the Near East veiled long before the advent of Islam and continued to veil in Europe until the twelfth century (they did not unveil because of an increase in gender equality; in fact, medieval scholars regard the Gregorian reforms of that era as a nadir for European women's rights). Before them, Jewish women veiled, as did Roman, Greek, Zoroastrian, Assyrian, and Indian women, among many of whom veiling was a privilege belonging to women of the upper classes and aspired to by lower class women. Women veiled in the ancient pagan Near East. Statuettes of veiled priestesses date back to 2500 B.C.E., long before any of the three Abrahamic religions (figure 1.1). In the city-state

Figure 1.1.   Statuette. Gypsum, 2500 B.C.E. Temple of Ishtar, Tell Hariri, Ancient Mar. 23 × 14 cm. National Museum, Damascus, M2072 (M2308/2368) BAAL 98.

Figure 1.2.   Funerary bas-relief of a woman. Hard limestone, 137 C.E. Breiki tomb, Tadmor, ancient Palmyra. 60 × 43 × 23 cm. Palmyra Museum B 2667/8968.

of Palmyra, where the pagan Arab queen Zenobia would rule in defiance of Rome, bas-reliefs ca. 137–150 C.E. depict elegant veiled women, whose high status is evident from their jewelry, servants, and commemoration in limestone. In figure after figure, the woman's right hand touches the edge of her veil where it drapes over her shoulder, as if in the act of drawing the curtain that defines her personal space (figure 1.2).

One way to interpret this long historical presence of veiling is to believe that men have always tried to control women's bodies. This may be true, and it is true that Islamic as well as Christian and Jewish authorities have asserted their own definitions of veiling, but it doesn't tell half the story of the veil. Men have also tried to control women's bodies through the institution of motherhood and continue to do so through laws governing reproduction but, as Adrienne Rich points out, this does not make motherhood conform to patriarchal prescriptions.[1] Rich distinguishes motherhood prescribed by male definitions from experiences of motherhood springing from women's lives, and there is a similar distinction between institutions of veiling defined from above and women's own multivalent practices of veiling.

There is also, in the West, the ubiquitous assumption that a Muslim woman is made to veil by her husband. While St. Paul appears to require head covering of woman as a sign of her being created in subjection to male authority, or at least in relation to her status compared to man (1 Cor. 11:4–10, NRSV),[2] Muslim veiling is not posited in terms of women's spiritual status in relation to men. Instead it is framed as part of a sexual ethics that ought to govern the social life of men and women. In the Qur'anic verse usually cited as the main impetus for modest dress (33:59),[3] the reason given for the practice is that women "may be recognized and not harmed," and the subsequent verse describes the kinds of people in the world who represent the potential harm: "hypocrites and those whose hearts are diseased." The other Qur'anic passage cited as calling for modest dress, 24:30–31,[4] frames the practice within a commandment to chaste behavior for both men and women, positing veiling as part of a personal morality. Veiling, in Islam, does not begin at marriage and has nothing to do with marital status; donning it is a rite of passage for a girl at puberty (and laying it off is, theoretically, a rite of passage for women at menopause when, presumably, the temptation to unchaste behavior has passed); it is something between a woman and God, or a woman and herself.

Just because my veil blocks your *senses, doesn't mean it blocks mine. The veil is no blindfold. I see out; you are the one whose vision is obstructed. My senses are alive and have a field wherein to play, away from where your eye can penetrate. My sex is alive—what on earth makes people think that women who veil do not take pleasure in eros? Veiling—with us—has nothing to do with asceticism and self-denial. My sense of beauty is alive. I comb out my hair and put on the rouge and the silk, among friends, in a women's culture curtained off from you, an outsider. Is that why you find the veil frustrating from your male-identified viewpoint, you who are used to women putting out for your gaze? Because its aesthetic is the opposite of strut, is that the secret reason why you take it as such an affront?*

In *The Epic of Gilgamesh,* the oldest written literature in existence (ca. 2000 B.C.E.), Siduri, the young woman in the garden at the edge of the sea who guards the vine and makes the sacred wine, wears a veil. She bars the gate against Gilgamesh, and the hero must listen to her wisdom before he continues his search for immortality. At its physical essence, stripped of any religious or ideological definition (if that is possible; grant it for a moment), to be veiled is to partake in a primal power: *I see without being fully seen; I know without being known. I shore up an advantage over what I survey. Like a goddess, like a queen of unquestioned sovereignty, I declare this my sanctuary, my* haram, *from which I impart what I will, when I will.* The French playwright Racine knows this power; he keeps the king veiled in his sixteenth-century dramas, wrapped in a mystique almost divine. The Prophet Muhammad (peace be upon him) is depicted face veiled in Persian miniatures, to preserve his visage from becoming a thing of common consumption in the world's exchange of images (and it works: even after fourteen hundred years, he is neither lowered by association with any recognizable graphic, nor venerated in the form of any icon). Ereshkigal, queen of the underworld in Sumerian myth (her name and title are inscribed on tablets ca. 1750 B.C.E.), knows the power of the veil when she forces her sister, the goddess Inanna, to disrobe on her descent through the seven gates, making her remove one layer at a time until Inanna arrives naked and powerless into her sister's clutches in the pit of hell. She is like one skinned alive.

When she entered the seventh gate, from her body the royal robe was removed. . . . Inanna asked, "What is this?" She was told, "Quiet, Inanna, the ways of the underworld are perfect. They may not be questioned." Naked and bowed low, Inanna entered the throne room. . . . The judges of the underworld surrounded her. They passed judgment against her. . . . Inanna was turned into a corpse, a piece of rotting meat, and was hung from a hook on the wall.[5]

In the Bible's Book of Esther, Queen Vashti refuses the command of her husband to unveil before his court. Vashti's insistence on her right to veiled dignity is taken up in a poem by African American writer Frances E. W. Harper in the nineteenth century, in which context the biblical story may be a comment on the trauma of forced exposure experienced by enslaved women on the auction block. In the Americas, slaves of Muslim origin tried to keep up modest dress, a residue of Afro-Islamic heritage; their preferences were ignored, and often criminalized, by life under slave conditions.[6]

Being stripped of their veil is a trauma masses of women in the twentieth-century Middle East know.[7] In country after country, from Turkey to Tunisia, from 1925 to the present, Muslim women have been yanked, coerced, and coaxed out of their veils by governments and social elites. The story of the forcibly unveiled woman almost never makes the cover of *Time, Ms.*, or the Arabic weeklies *al-Majalla* or *Sayyidati*. We hear story after story of the poor woman forced to veil, and she exists, yet forced *unveiling* has been the experience of the last century for far greater masses of Muslim women. If two countries, Saudi Arabia and post-1979 Iran, plus Afghanistan during the very brief (horrendous) Taliban era, mandate veiling, far more countries prohibit veiling. But *this* violation of women's freedom usually draws no protest from the West, or from secular Muslim feminists. Indeed, it is often applauded in the same quarters that purport to advocate women's rights.

It is 1965. We are traveling through the Middle East and North Africa. It seems not to be common knowledge in the West that the veil has been banned in much of the Middle East for much of the twentieth century. The veil has been forbidden in Turkey since Mustafa Kemal's edict in 1925. This means employees in public sector jobs cannot wear it, nor can students at government schools and universities. *Hijab* (head cover and modest dress) is similarly outlawed in Iran, which is ruled by the Pahlavi dynasty. Wearing hijab is illegal in public schools under the Baath in Syria and Iraq. And in this heyday of Arab secularism, veiling is discouraged with such overwhelming pressure by the elite classes in most other Arab populations, including Palestinians, that it amounts to a social, if not legal, prohibition. Hijab is definitely passé by this time in Egypt, where it had been subject to condemnation since the nineteenth century by the British colonizers and by influential Muslim liberals such as Qasim Amin.[8] In Algeria, where the French waged war against veiling for decades,[9] their efforts have born fruit in the nation's largely unveiled postcolonial culture, at least in cities. Upper-class women across the Middle East and North Africa are unveiled, as are most middle-class women, and even among the lower classes and in the countryside, the rising generations are joining the tide of unveiling.

Hey, I'm glad it's happening. Who cares if it came from above, from the state. I'm a Lebanese teenager, it's the '60s, and a new door is opening—it's exciting! I like going out with my hair flying, and swimming in a bikini like in the Egyptian beach movies starring Shadia and Abdul-Halim. In real life, people are more conservative than in films, and you still get raised eyebrows when you're out in a mini-jupe. But yes, the old world is getting swept away. Good riddance. Stupid Westerners think we all go around in heavy shrouds. Most of us don't anymore! And then on the other side, I resent stupid conservative Muslims who think just because I don't veil means I don't believe in God or have morals. I'm still Muslim. Let's hear it for unveiled Muslim girls—we're the majority now!

There are holdouts. In Damascus University, my young mother and a small group of veiled science majors cover their hair with *écharpes* and wear tailored long-sleeved outerwear with modern touches: cuffs and lapels, brass buttons, Peter Pan collars. They are quite distinguishable from the peasant women who clean classrooms wearing traditional country *ghatwehs*[10] and caftans with britches peeking beneath. Still, my mother and her modern-style middle-class hijabed friends get snickers from unveiled coeds. Hijab is not hip, not in the 1960s. Everyone else on campus is wearing sleeveless sheath dresses with hemlines above the knee. Like Jackie Kennedy—or Suad Husny, the beautiful Syrian-Egyptian movie star.

The Arab states of the Gulf are another holdout. They never experienced direct European colonization, so their traditions have never been under direct assault by a Western power. Still, they are part of the Arab world, and its cultural impetus toward unveiling is felt there. Without state intervention on behalf of unveiling, however, there is a slow Burkian evolution toward loosening veiling customs, rather than the stark top-down model happening in other Arab lands, and in Turkey and Iran. To varying degrees in the Gulf states, with Kuwait on the quicker-to-unveil side of the spectrum, hijab customs begin to overlap with options of partial unveiling as new generations rise.

I am an Emirati woman, leathery and fierce—I came up before oil made everyone soft and fat and lazy. Men were men then, and women were women! We call the face mask of metallic cloth a burgu. *Hell, I don't even let my husband see my face most days! I take pride in that. "But you veil more than Islam even requires," my son says—he got religion yesterday, Mr. Preachy. So what if it's not religion, it's tradition. Those are our customs, here, in my tribe, my place. Or they used to be: my daughter is starting to drop the burgu, although she still wears the abaya and the shayla[11] covering her hair. And her own daughter's shayla barely covers the crown of her head. Fine, times change: but stretch your hand to* MY *burgu and I'll break your arm for your insolence.*

The exception to the slow evolutionary shift in veiling in the Gulf states is Saudi Arabia where, because of strategic intertribal alliances formed at that nation's birth in 1932, the state must appease the ultraorthodox or "Wahhabi" sector of its society, creating a unique situation that is more stridently religious and insistent on making the veil part of what the nation-state enforces. Until Iran's Islamic Revolution in 1979, Saudi Arabia was the *only* Muslim country with legally enforced veiling. Even there, veiling is not a monolithic practice and has subtle shadings in different geographic areas (as it does in Iran as well, where veiling is not as uniformly enforced as outsiders tend to assume).[12] Women doing farmwork in the Saudi countryside, for example, do not veil their faces (face veiling is not generally practiced by rural women in any country) but otherwise carry on traditions of modest dress. In other Gulf states, veiling remains practiced by the overwhelming majority but is not pursued as a legal matter and not imposed on foreign visitors, be they Muslim women from other countries or otherwise.

Outside the Gulf, the mainstream culture of the Middle East and North Africa sets its face against the veil during this period. In Egyptian cinema's golden age from the 1950s to the 1970s, there is nary a hijabed woman to be found, unless it is a poor old farmwoman. Even after hijab begins to make a comeback in the 1970s, Arab media refuse to recognize it. To look at books, school texts, magazines, newspapers, and television from the

1940s to the 1980s, or at any imprint of pop culture or government-approved text, in Syria, Egypt, Lebanon, Iraq, and other formerly colonized Arab countries, as in Turkey and Iran, you'd think veiling is alien to these lands.

It is 1978. We are in Iran. Urban middle and lower middle classes, including the *bazaari* class of small merchants, suffer under the shah. His long-standing ban on Islamic hijab has become symbolic of the violence his right-wing Persian nationalist ideology perpetrates through brutal state apparatus such as SAVAK (the secret police). Women who endured the hijab ban and want to veil as an expression of their values are joined in anti-shah protests by some unveiled upper- and middle-class women who take up the veil only as a symbol of resistance to the shah's regime.

Much has been written about how betrayed these women felt after the success of the Islamic Revolution when, instead of freedom of choice about the veil, the shah's ban was neatly turned into its mirror image, a ban on unveiling. But who made it a political issue in the first place? Neither regime can be exonerated: if postrevolution Iran is to be condemned for forcing veiling, so is pro-Western, Pahlavi Iran for forcing unveiling.

We are in Damascus again. It is September 28, 1982. The state war against hijab continues unabated here in Syria and has had no sudden reversal as in Iran. One thousand young female paratroopers in boots and camo are dropped into the city by the Baathist state. Each young representative of the socialist dictatorship is backed by a young male soldier, armed. They begin their task: stopping veiled women and forcing them to unveil at gunpoint. Veiled women walking by are grabbed by the elbow. Cars are stopped if veiled women are drivers or passengers in them. Trooper girls accost and soldier boys point rifles at the women or, if they are accompanied by husbands and fathers, at the men's heads. Women are forced to peel off their head covering, hair in disarray, hands shaking.

To try to enter into their feelings if you do not wear hijab, imagine having your blouse removed while passersby watch, or your underwear. Such a parallel is a realistic translation of a hijabed woman's mortification at being unveiled in public. Several heart attacks from this section of the city are reported in hospitals that day.

My hijabed aunt takes shelter inside a building, heart pounding, and avoids the public strip down. It is one her daughter faces at school every day, where the guard at the gate makes her remove her scarf. If she manages to slip by him with hijab intact, the Baathist civics teacher will report her to the principal for wearing it. My aunt and her husband eventually locate a free religious private school that allows their daughter to veil; they are unwilling to sacrifice her schooling for her values, or her values for her schooling. Many are not lucky enough to find a way out of the bind the state forces on them. Some girls from religious households lose their education. Those willing to forego the veil lose something too, something less tangible, a part of their autonomy and dignity.

The September hijab rape in Damascus epitomizes the story of forced unveiling: the state, a leftist one advocating ostensibly "progressive" secular ideology, uses its police powers to rip what it regards as the sartorial sign of reactionary religion from the bodies of women. *You will be liberated from hijab, even if we have to rape you into enlightenment.* How many people have even heard of this incident? It did not make news on *CNN, Nightline,* the *Phil Donahue Show,* or any other program, Arab or Western. Nawal El Saadawi did not issue a protest, nor did NOW. Jean Sassoon did not whip out a quickie paperback about it.

Even the Baathist regime realized that it had gone too far. The following week, paratroopers were sent again into Damascus, this time with roses, in an elaborately staged "apology" to hijabed women, and Syria's president Hafez Asad blamed the incident on his brother Rifaat, a handy scapegoat for the brutal regime.

Hijab is just as stringently punished in Tunisia, where, after the 1984 ban, police will pull you off the street for wearing it.[13] Not until the 1990s, after it had become clear that veiling was making a massive comeback across Arab societies, did Egyptian film grudgingly include an image of a woman in hijab, and at first only on villainous characters.[14] By then, studies examining "the new veiling" began to appear.

For in the Arab world, Turkey, and Iran, it is a *new* veiling, distinctly modern in both tailoring and ideological trappings. The *jilbab* or *manteau* (terms for tailored outer garments that resemble trench coats), matched with a sleek modern head cover, is a veil tailored for getting out *into* the modern world, not one designed for retreating from it like the older, more formless abaya, *milaya*, or *burqa*.[15] Homa Hoodfar points out that by adopting the new veil, young working women in Cairo are able to have the cake of modernity and eat the prestige of tradition too.[16] They make a choice that marshals the best of both value systems for them, an empowering choice that *works*, that offers pragmatic *advantages*, for these particular Egyptian women in their specific set of "givens," just as unveiling offered pragmatic, empowering advantages for an earlier generation.[17]

My mother doesn't understand why I want to veil. Her generation, even her mother's generation, threw off hijab, like Huda Shaarawi.[18] Don't waste their struggle, she says. It's the 1990s, for goodness sake! She and my fiancé are aghast. I'm twenty-eight, I have a PhD, I should be able to do what I want. It has nothing to do with fundamentalists; it's spiritual for me. It's what my body is comfortable in, more than the pretentious way she wants me to look, all glossy lips and bouffant hair. I'm embarrassing her, she says. We're too high class to veil. And he's threatening to break off our engagement. Hijab doesn't fit his idea of himself as a modern, successful Muslim man. It doesn't fit my boss's idea of an employee in the Cairo tourist industry either; I've just been fired for hijab. But I have a job interview next week at a television studio where two of my friends are technicians, one in hijab, one without, and I hear it's a work environment that respects both of them.

The upsurge in hijab began to be visible in the 1980s and crested in the 1990s. Mothers who were reluctant at first began to join their daughters in veiling. Today, in 2006, the hijab enjoys a new plurality (not a majority, even now, in most Arab cities outside the Gulf). Syria's ban was finally lifted after the death of Hafez Asad and the coming to power of his son Bashar, with his erratic gestures toward conciliating Syria's long-brutalized populace.

I am against the hijabed girls getting browbeaten, but the new hijab makes me, a Christian Jordanian, nervous even though veiling has been part of Christian tradition too. While I am conservative in dress, unlike a lot of Muslim girls you can see all over west Amman malls who bare their midriffs down to the pubic bone, I think hijab today underlines the difference between Christian and Muslim Arabs and allows people who want to discriminate to do so. My coworker, who doesn't wear hijab herself but has a sister who does, assures me that it's not

about discrimination or fanaticism, just pride in your heritage, like when I wear
a cross necklace. Easy for her to say—she's not a minority.

Many Americans have the bizarre idea that Iraqi women under Saddam faced forced veiling, as Afghan women did under the Taliban. Whatever other horrors Saddam perpetrated, his regime spouted a so-called progressive, socialist gender policy of equal employment and education for women, and women in Iraqi cities were mostly unveiled.[19] In fact, a hijab ban remained on the books, even though the Baathist regime stopped enforcing it during the Iran-Iraq war, what with internal and external pressures threatening the regime. The ban certainly was not enforced after the United States invasion in 1991, when Saddam began mouthing Islamic rhetoric to boost his popular support. This means veiled women could at last go to school and college without harassment; it does not mean the majority of women started veiling. With the 2003 U.S. invasion of Iraq releasing populist Islamist forces suppressed under Saddam, and unleashing anarchy and rapine, Iraqis have seen an upsurge in veiling—a lot of it out of the fear created by these conditions and by the rising influence of Islamists, a little of it—this cannot be denied—out of women's beliefs long prevented from public expression.

I'm twelve and I've been wearing hijab since I was nine and a half. Duh, of
course I wear it. All my friends wear it. Salma thinks she's so grown up because
she wore it a month earlier—give me a BREAK. Just because she goes to 'slamic
school in Paterson and I go to public school in Clifton, she thinks she's fly, but
really she's so '90s. Mom said I should wait a few more years, but I didn't want
to. Mrs. Bundy next door said it was a shame. Mom goes, "Oho, my Hana's veiling is a shame? I tell you what, Joan, it's a shame you put your Tammi out in
that tiny two-piece swimsuit and she's only nine, dressing a little girl like the
women at that strip club your boyfriend goes to. You teach your daughter what
to wear and I'll teach mine."

The veiling scene that plays in the Western media is this: poor oppressed Muslim woman, forced to veil. Here come Americans to free her from this tragic victimhood. This actually happened: in Afghanistan, where the Taliban really did impose brutal misogynistic laws on women. But the story ends with a twist that doesn't fit the white man's burden narrative: many Afghan women, it turns out after the "liberation," want to keep wearing the burqa. Some do because there is still a prevailing atmosphere of war, rapine, and fear in the country; but there is no denying that others who have always worn the burqa will continue to do so because it is their tradition.

Likewise the five hundred women, including Saudis, who met U.S. envoy Karen Hughes in 2005 and startled her, Western news sources reported, by informing her they didn't see themselves as oppressed and were tired of Americans telling them they were.[20] Some might argue that such an event may have been orchestrated. Maybe. Yet elsewhere other Saudi women have voiced similar opinions. Novelist Raja Alem, for example, says veiling is at worst a mild annoyance for some, not the gigantic oppression that the West thinks it is.[21] "I'm a Saudi woman; I like my veil," says Mai Yamani, Saudi feminist and author of *Feminism and Islam*.[22] And a recent poll of Arab-world Muslim women concurred that most do not consider themselves oppressed.[23] None of these things seem to register with Western audiences.

The classic Western and secular Muslim feminist answer to this sort of thing is condescending: women who aren't bothered by veiling just don't know any better, and one day, with guidance and continued freedom, they will be enlightened and stop veiling.

They may. Then again, they may not. In the Arab world, it is becoming apparent that with every step toward democratization, women help vote in more Islamic candidates, not fewer, and with many a step toward liberalization in Arab societies, more, not fewer, women seem to be adopting the veil. Are these women just stupid? Religious nuts? Brainwashed? Controlled by men? This is what some progressive Muslims seem to believe.

Am I the only one here who thinks this whole essay is bull? Veiling in the Middle East today has nothing to do with Inanna and goddesses. How come you aren't talking more about forced veiling? What about the Islamist pressure on women to veil in the Gaza Strip? As a secular Arab feminist, I know my own society and I tell you: it's not women who want it; it's being pushed by Islamo-fascists who want to take power away from women, plain and simple! Don't tell me I have to account for Islamist women and their mentality—I don't think they're worth talking about, or talking with, and I don't have to include them in my feminism. Any woman who wants to veil is just a self-hating woman.

There are other possibilities. It is possible that power is not given or taken away from Muslim women by the absence or presence of the veil, but by the presence or absence of economic, political, and family rights. It is possible that women who want to veil have their own reasons, stemming from their own priorities and not those of patriarchal authorities. Yes, there is an Islamic revival movement going on and yes, parts of its ideology are appallingly backward steps for women. But first, there are women who veil for reasons unrelated to any Islamic movement. And second, there are women who experience the modern Islamic revival as a step forward from traditional status quos and double standards. For them, sexist customs, not progressive or liberal ideologies, constituted their prior options and secular feminism is not, to them, a viable alternative. Just as American women embraced and led the conservative, moralistic temperance movement a century ago, with its demands that men not drink or frequent prostitutes, many Muslim women today see religion as leveling the playing field and giving them the spiritual authority to demand that men adhere to moral codes, thus making them more accountable to their wives, mothers, and children. Women's embrace of the veil cannot be understood only in terms of their being "controlled" by male-defined religious ideologies. For some, it is a step toward greater power.

I am a committed Muslim, and I, too, don't understand what the author is trying to do by diluting the issue with goddesses and how women feel about their bodies. It's not about politics, or tradition for that matter: It's about religion. I veil to show my commitment to God's law. It's in the Qur'an and Sunna,[24] plain and simple!

It is possible, too, that many Muslim women see their liberation differently from how secular Muslim feminists or the Eurocentric media see it. Maybe, rather than argue over veiling or unveiling, women in oil-rich Gulf states want, for example, to solve the marriage crisis by gaining the equal right to give their spouses citizenship. Maybe Palestinian women want to see the Wall come down and the occupation cease. Maybe people in the Arab world, both Muslim and Christian, ought to fight for Christian wives' equal right to custody of their children with Muslim men. Maybe there are more important gender issues than veiling.

Progressive and liberal women and men, Arab or Muslim or Western or otherwise, should be free to argue against veiling, a freedom they unfortunately don't have in the two most conservatively Muslim countries, Saudi Arabia and Iran. But when they join the state and its repressive apparatus in supporting bans on veiling, they resemble the Baathist paratroopers in Damascus. When they assume that Muslim women who veil have no agency or choice in the matter, they do violence to women's lives. Like Ereshkigal, they strip away their sisters' robes.

Conservative Muslim women and men who see hijab as an integral part of faith are entitled to contest other views that have long held sway in Arab societies. When they try to create a society in which wearing it will be not just a community value encouraged through educational and cultural means, but a requirement enforced by the state and a cause for harassment of women who do not veil, then Islamists will have become just as tyrannical as the secular powers that have dominated much of their world for the last five decades. Islamists should be careful to avoid a mirror-image reversal of the hijab-banning policies of secular regimes, the way the Islamic Republic of Iran reacted to the shah. After all, if last century's hijab bans spurred the current Islamic hijab reactions, what counterreactions would a move to hijab enforcement cause in the future? Is the tiresome cycle going to keep repeating itself?

One veil is lifted; another drops. Women's veiling practices predate and will outlast the current political pull-and-tug over them. Veiling is far more a matter of women's body life than surface debates. In some lands it is a physical fabric; in others it exists in makeup, married names, and other masking practices. The veil is not one thing; it shape-shifts. The veil has so many meanings that it is an empty signifier. When we come to accept that (generations hence?), we will—at last!—be able to let go of our era's obsession over the presence or absence of a veil.

I am wearing a long, loose overgarment, burqa, sari, abaya, jilbab, milaya, haïk, chador, manteau, tobe, safsari.[25] Call it by its beautiful small name in each land, for it is many garments, not one overarching. I am wearing a foulard, *shayla, ghatweh,* khimar, dupatta.[26] *In this little mobile sanctum, my body is free. My limbs swing loose; each leg is not stuffed sausagelike into a pant leg. Nothing cinches my waist. Nothing holds my belly in. Nothing demands that I conform to a certain shape or size. It is supple as a living membrane and offers a depth of layered meanings.*

Without it, I walk differently, and this too is a kind of knowledge, a new understanding of the surfaces of my body. Without it, I learn how to manifest my spirit with a balance more outward than inward. Indeed, "the Manifest" (al-Zahir) *is among the divine Names as well as "the Hidden"* (al-Baten).

Sometimes I love to cast it off, layer after layer, like a revelation of my heart. And sometimes I love to draw it around me and gather its folds like insights. The play of veiling and unveiling, neither possible without the other. How blessed is each to each!

NOTES

1. "Motherhood and Bondage," in *On Lies, Secrets, and Silence* (New York: W. W. Norton, 1979), 195–97.

2. "For a man ought not to have his head veiled, since he is the image and reflection [or glory] of God; but woman is the reflection [or glory] of man. Indeed, man was not made from woman, but woman was made from man. Neither was man created for the sake of woman, but woman for the sake of man. For this reason a woman ought to have [a symbol of] authority on her head, because of the angels."

3. "O Prophet, tell thy wives and daughters and the believing women that they should draw their outer garments closer over their persons; that is better, that they should be known and not harmed, and God is ever forgiving, merciful."

4. "Say to the believing men that they should lower of their gazes and guard their private parts; that will make for greater purity for them; and God is ever aware of all they do. And say to the believing women that they should lower of their gazes and guard their private parts; that they should not display their ornamentation except what appears of it; that they should draw their veils over their bosoms, and not display their ornamentation, except to their husbands, their fathers, their husbands' fathers, their sons, their husbands' sons, their brothers, or their brothers' sons, or their sisters' sons, or their women, or the slaves whom their right hands possess, or male servants free of physical needs, or small children who have no notion of the nakedness of women. And that they shall not stamp their feet to draw attention to what they hide of their ornamentation. And O you who believe, turn all together toward God, that you may attain success."

5. Diane Wolkstein and Samuel Noah Kramer, *Inanna, Queen of Heaven and Earth* (New York: Harper and Row, 1983).

6. See Sylviane A. Diouf, *Servants of Allah: African Muslims Enslaved in the Amer-*

icas (New York: New York University Press, 1998), 72–82 for a full discussion of Muslim slaves' frustrated attempts to keep their distinct sartorial practices.

7. I mostly limit my comments to the area where I have some expertise, i.e., the Arab world, but have allowed myself some extension into Turkey and Iran. There are similar patterns in Pakistan, where the very few middle- and upper-class urban women who veiled in the 1980s were harassed for doing so, but I will refrain from trying to extend my analysis into South Asia, Southeast Asia, or sub-Saharan Africa.

8. Leila Ahmed's chapter on "Discourses of the Veil" is the best discussion of this history in Egypt. *Women and Gender in Islam: Historical Roots of a Modern Debate* (New Haven: Yale University Press, 1992).

9. See Frantz Fanon, *A Dying Colonialism,* trans. Haakon Chevalier (New York: Grove Press, 1965) for an early analysis of the French colonial assault on veiling in Algeria.

10. *Ghatweh* is what Arab village women in Syria and Palestine call their big white cotton head covers, which are much wider than Gulf *shaylas* or Pakistani *dupattas* and larger than a Syrian city woman's *écharpe.* See the cover photo of Naomi Shihab Nye's *Words Under the Words* (Portland, OR: Eighth Mountain Press, 1995) for an example of a *ghatweh.*

11. In the Gulf Arab states and Iraq, *abaya* (or *aba*) is the traditionally black long loose open cloak (used for both women's or men's cloaks), often embroidered at the edges and with tassled tie cords. *Shayla,*also used in the Gulf Arab states, is a long narrow scarf worn wound around the head that now comes in haute couture designer models and has experienced fringed, monogrammed, embroidered, and other trends in its fashion history.

12. Teun Voeten, "This is Iran, Too," *LA Weekly,* January 3 2007, with photographs showing how, for example, "Dress codes are relaxed for the skiers at Mt. Tachol, 30 minutes from downtown Tehran."

13. The bans continue to this day, 2006.

14. Thanks to my colleague Dr. Joel Gordon for the insights on Egyptian film and television. Thanks also to Dr. Ted Swedenberg and Nadine Sinno.

15. *Milaya* is a long loose cloak worn by women in Egypt and Syria, especially in premodern eras. Both the abaya and milaya require separate headgear, whereas the *burqa,* used in Afghanistan, covers head, face, and body at once. Traditional burqa color is sapphire blue.

16. Homa Hoodfar, *Between Marriage and the Market: Intimate Politics and Survival in Cairo* (Berkeley: University of California, 1997); also see her article in *Working Women: International Perspectives on Labour and Gender Ideology,* ed. Nanneke Redclift and M. Thea Sinclair (New York: Routledge, 1990).

17. See also Sherifa Zuhur, *Revealing Reveiling* (Albany: State University of New York Press, 1992), an important empirical record of the experiences of veiled Muslim women she surveyed.

18. It is a popular misconception that Huda Shaarawi took off hijab. She actually took off the face portion of the veil but continued to observe hijab (head cover and modest dress), relative to social contexts, throughout her life. See Mohja Kahf, "Huda Shaarawi: The Memoirs of the First Lady of Arab Modernity," *Arab Studies Quarterly*, winter 1998.

19. See http://riverbendblog.blogspot.com for remarks on being unveiled from a young female Baghdad resident who worked in the computer industry before the war and does not wear hijab.

20. Steven R. Weisman, "Saudi Women Have Message for U.S. Envoy," *New York Times*, Sept. 28, 2005, accessed online.

21. Interview with Raja Alem published with her novel *Fatma: A Novel of Arabia* (Syracuse: Syracuse University Press, 2002).

22. "Women of Saudi Arabia," *National Geographic*, October 1987.

23. Helena Andrews, "Muslim Women Don't See Themselves as Oppressed, Survey Finds," *New York Times*, June 8, 2006, www.nytimes.com/2006/06/08/world/middleeast/08women.html.

24. *Sunna:* the traditions and teachings of the Prophet Muhammad, peace and blessings be upon him.

25. The *haïk* is traditionally white, a long loose cloak/wrap worn over clothing by lower-class women in Morocco and Algeria. The *chadri* is worn over clothes by lower-class women in Iran; black in the city, it is often of light-colored cloth with tiny print patterns in the countryside. *Manteau* is the French word for "coat," by which Syrian, Iranian, and Lebanese women have referred to their Islamic overgarment for decades. The *tobe* is a traditional wrap-around garment for women in Sudan; it is similar to the Indian sari, but the wrapping method and length of cloth differ. The *safsari* is an outergarment for lower-class women in Tunisia.

26. On the Indian subcontinent, the *dupatta* is a long scarf often worn draped over the bosom. And I haven't even begun to exhaust the marvelous variety of local terms for specific head-covering and body-covering garments.

2 Shattered Vessels That Contain Divine Sparks

Unveiling Hasidic Women's Dress Code

BARBARA GOLDMAN CARREL

As a graduate student in anthropology at New York University, I enrolled in a class that explored the rich cultural life of New York City. On one class excursion, we visited Hasidic Borough Park to witness the celebration of Purim. I was quite surprised by the overt displays of "fashion" in the clothing of the women who gathered at the Bobover Beis Medrash (house of study and prayer).[1] There seemed to be a striking incongruity between the dress of the men and women, echoed in and further pronounced by the partitioned seating from which they viewed the Purim play. The men were uniformly dressed in black *bekechers,* the long robelike coats Hasidic men wear on ceremonial occasions.[2] *Peyes* (long side curls) dangled under their black hats or fur *streimels* (emblematic hats reserved for ritual). Their appearance implied the suspension of time and an intentional otherness, both of which indisputably identified these men as members of the Hasidic community.

The fashionable clothing of the women seemed more closely to mark the pulse and passage of time. In contrast to their male counterparts' monotone and seemingly uniform mode of dress, these women revealed diversity and individual expression through the creative manipulation of color, design, fabric, and style. Although most Bobover women were dressed in classically styled designerlike clothing with straight, formal lines in fabrics of solid dark colors, others were dressed in robust prints or brave plaids or ornamentally extravagant outfits. Some women sported the latest styles in elegant footwear: high heels or pumps trimmed with clip-on bows, gold buttons, or fancy beading.

These blatant "fashion" displays challenged my rather ethnocentric notion of how Hasidic women would be, and perhaps *should* be, dressed. My understanding of the religious prescriptions that regulate their dress promoted an image of dark, matronly, outdated clothing. When I voiced this frequently held misconception to a twenty-year-old, newly married Hasidic woman named Suri, she responded, "[The Jewish laws] say we have to be *modest*. That doesn't mean we have to be *backwards*."

This experience led to a personal fascination and scholarly exploration of Hasidic women's fashion.[3] In researching Hasidic women living in New York City and elsewhere, I was unable to find published discussions either wholly dedicated to or appreciably attributing cultural significance to Hasidic women's clothing. Their dress code and clothing practice have been virtually dismissed by both the academic literature and popular media as presenting no distinctive forms and/or meanings (other than modesty) because of the outward appearance of mass-produced fashion.[4] Descriptions have often been reduced to "modestly dressed" or "heads covered with wigs or scarves," with little if any discussion of cultural details (figure 2.1).

My research, however, reveals a much more complex reality filled with culturally meaningful principles, practices, and distinctions unknown to many outside the Hasidic community. Despite the incorporation of mass-produced fashion, women of the Hasidic community do infuse the clothes that cover them with religious and cultural significations. They perceive their mode of dress as the symbolic expression of Hasidic spirituality and modesty, which not only promotes a distinctively feminized Hasidic identity but also ultimately serves as a protective shield against the larger (non-Jewish) New York City secular society in which they live.

First and foremost, dress for the Hasidic woman represents more than fashion or a form of material self-expression. Her clothing operates as a culturally distinct method of covering as well as a veil of sanctification. Although she may incorporate secularized fashion into her wardrobe, the clothing of a Hasidic woman is believed to confirm the sacred status of human beings. Chaya (figure 2.2), a Bobover Hasidic woman, explains the overall religious significance of dress within the Hasidic community:

> A person . . . is in the image of God. And you have to give respect to yourself and to anybody that's created in the image of God. This is something great . . . [A person] is not just an animal walking around. He has something there and he's supposed to dress accordingly.

For the Hasidic woman, this sacred status is inextricably bound to modesty. Hasidic girls are taught at a very young age the importance of dressing in a manner that reflects the inner soul rather than any external manifestation of feminine physicality—sexual or otherwise. Miriam Grossman, in her book for adolescent girls, *The Wonder of Becoming You: How a Jewish Girl Grows Up,* outlines the desired symbolic result of being dressed in Hasidic fashion—stressing spirituality—in opposition to non-Jewish or American secular fashion statements, which she presents as accentuating the female anatomy:

> One responsibility we have as Jews is to remind people of the holy and unique status of man. . . . One way to do this is to dress and behave in a modest manner. Dressing in a revealing way draws attention to the body, but modest dress de-emphasizes the body. It permits the attention of others to focus on our non-physical qualities, for example, on our thoughts or our personality. A girl who dresses modestly is making a significant statement. She's sending out a message which says, "My body is important, but it is only the vessel for the real me—my soul. I think of myself that way, and I want people to relate to me with that in mind."[5]

Modesty is considered a Hasidic woman's unique and honored contribution to the world. This paramount feminine distinction is, however, interpreted and overwhelmingly celebrated as being "concealed" or "hidden" in the Hasidic religious ideology. It asserts, "The Honor of a Jewish Daughter Is Inside."[6]

Figure 2.1. Hasidic woman wearing a *tikhl* over her wig on Borough Park's 13th Avenue, the Bobover community's main shopping district, 2006. Photo by Barbara Goldman Carrel.

Figure 2.2. Chaya dressed for a family celebration, 1999. Photo by Barbara Goldman Carrel.

Judaism believes that women were created to bring a number of qualities into the world. One of these qualities is modesty. Eve was purposely created from Adam's rib—a part of him that was concealed and internal. Perhaps this was done so that we would have the capacity to bring "innerness" (modesty) into the world in a greater way than could Adam and his male descendants.[7]

Therefore, the clothing of Hasidic women is meant to embody this divinely designated "innerness" where "covering your body . . . is the most fundamental way of using your outside to tell others who you are on the inside."[8]

The Hebrew word for modesty, *tzniuth*, comes from *tzanua*, which means "to conceal." Modesty, therefore, "means keeping concealed that which should not be revealed."[9] The proper form and manner of coverage for Hasidic women's dress are explicitly detailed in and regulated by *halakhoth*, or laws of the Torah. Tzniuth halakhoth not only direct a Hasidic woman's selection of clothing and manner of appearance, they constitute a way of life for the religious Jewish woman in general, and for the Hasidic woman in particular. Tzniuth informs the entire spectrum of thoughts, conduct, and social interactions of the Torah-observant woman, especially with males, both within the community (e.g., the prohibition of singing in the presence of certain males) and outside it (e.g., appropriate modest behavior for visits to hairdressers and doctors).[10]

Rav Yitzchak Yaacov Fuchs, in his halakhic guide, *Halichos Bas Yisrael: A Woman's Guide to Jewish Observance*, delineates the tzniuth clothing prescriptions for the Torah-observant Jewish woman. He states that the law requires that the neck (below and including the collarbone), the upper arms (including the elbow), and the thighs and knees (when sitting or standing) of a married or unmarried woman's body be covered both in public and within the confines of her own house.[11]

In addition to the halakhoth that determine which parts of a woman's body must be covered, Fuchs outlines the specific halakhoth that identify the types of "immodest" clothing proscribed for the observant Jewish woman:

1. It is a serious transgression for a woman to dress immodestly. If clothing oversteps propriety in even the smallest detail, it is a violation of the Torah injunction, "You shall not walk in their statuses" [that is, adopt the clothing, appearance, or behavior of non-Jews or nonobservant Jews].

2. A woman may not wear clothing intended specifically for men (including pants, even if they are specifically manufactured for women).

3. Immodest clothing may not be worn including bright, red, and tight-fitted clothing.[12]

Last, according to Jewish law, a married woman may not appear in public with her hair uncovered. She is "required to wear a head-covering that hides all her hair from view. It is proper to ensure that no hair protrudes from it."[13] The head covering not only symbolically distinguishes a Torah-observant Jewish woman in New York City but also differentiates the married from the unmarried woman within the religious community. Chaya explains that "A [married] woman has to cover her hair. . . . Because she's married, [a wig] is to tell everyone, 'I'm not available. I'm married and I'm not looking for a husband. . . . I'm out of bounds. '"

According to Jewish law, a woman's hair is an *ervah*, or erotic stimulus, which must be covered just as the other ervah parts of a woman's body mentioned above must be covered. Ella, a Torah-observant Jewish woman living in the Borough Park vicinity, interprets the prescription for hair covering this way:

> The whole idea is that technically, the hair of a woman is a very, very sensual part of a woman. No matter how ugly the hair is. It could be the frizziest, ugliest hair. Really bad. Straggly. But it's her hair, coming out of her head. And it's nature. Anybody that studies people, that understands nature [knows that] any man that's attracted to a particular woman, no matter what he likes about her, he will be attracted to her hair. Her hair . . . It's her. So we don't let our hair be seen by other men.

Fuchs identifies the importance attributed to tzniuth in the life of the individual Hasidic woman when he states that the "laws on this subject are so important that in certain situations a man is *actually required* to divorce his wife if she insists on disobeying them."[14] Moreover, all persons in the global Hasidic community are charged with the individual responsibility of "uplifting the sparks" of the divine by sanctifying the whole of their everyday physical activity and material property; the earthly world is saturated with spiritual opportunities because the *Shekhinah,* or presence of God, is everywhere. This responsibility stems from the kabbalistic belief that the earthly world is composed of "shattered vessels," each containing "sparks" of the divine. For the Hasidic woman, tzniuth dress is not only the "uplifting" or "hallowing" of her clothing but also the material means through which she infuses her physical being with godliness and holiness.

Tzniuth dress, however, is considered to be much more than a personal mandate. The repercussions of not complying with the halakhoth related to modest dress, attitude, and behavior (all of which are symbolically represented and asserted in Hasidic women's mode of dress) extend far beyond the personal safeguarding of marriage and individual spirituality. One of the critical responsibilities assigned to Jewish women is that of "redeemers of the Jewish people," as exemplified by the lives and actions of the original matriarchs of the Torah—Sarah, Rebecca, Rachel, and Leah.[15] For each individual Hasidic woman, maintaining the signification of tzniuth dress is considered a crucial part of her obligation as a "redeemer" of the Jewish people. Her dress is believed to affect the whole of the collective soul and destiny of the entire Jewish nation and the coming of the *Meshiekh* (Messiah). Ella reflects on the monumental spiritual outcome of each and every Jewish woman adhering to the halakhoth on tzniuth dress for the entire Jewish nation:

> Do you know the reason that we were [freed from bondage in] Egypt when we were slaves? This is not a fairy tale. This is written down in history. [It] was because we didn't change our names. We kept our Hebrew name. We didn't change our language. We spoke our Hebrew language. And the women did not change their clothing. They remained dressed the way they should be dressed. . . . And this is something to remember constantly. Like right now, we're not in Egypt. We're not slaves. Many rabbis speak that the redemption will come, that we'll be brought back to Israel. And we will once again be the Chosen Nation when the women of Israel are dressed properly according to all the Laws [of the Torah].

The Jewish laws of tzniuth are derived from two sources: the *dath Moshe*, or those requirements specified in the Torah itself, and the *dath Yehudith*, or generations of rabbinic interpretation and commentary that represent variations in customs established through time and across space by different Jewish communities. The interpretive struggle among Torah scholars, rabbis, *and* female practitioners of tzniuth to define appropriate material expressions of the intangible modesty continues today.[16] The elusive nature of tzniuth, coupled with substantial precedent given to community norms or tradition in defining appropriate representations of this paramount feminine attribute have produced dress distinctions in practice and form that reveal a woman's level of religiosity, both within and between Hasidic communities.

It is significant to stress that the dath Moshe provides the non-Hasidic Orthodox Jewish woman and the Hasidic woman with identical laws on covering and immodest dress. However, the Hasidim are often characterized as *ultra-Orthodox* due to their zealous adherence and extra fulfillment of Jewish law. In this sense, the Hasidim "hyperbolize" Jewish precepts to construct "protective fences" around custom, behavior, and interactions in order to guarantee a safe distance from either conscious or unconscious transgression of Jewish law.[17] Community interpretations and restrictions related to Hasidic women's means and methods of coverage have, therefore, created dress distinctions that reveal not only stylistic traditions and preferences but also meaningful hierarchies of religiosity.

For example, most Hasidic women will cover their heads even within the confines of their own homes (though perhaps not alone with their husbands). The feminine Hasidic hyperbolization of Jewish precepts is probably no more pronounced than in the custom whereby the women of Hungarian, Ukrainian, and Galician Hasidic communities shave their heads entirely the day after their weddings. This custom is repeated monthly "to ensure that not a single strand of hair would ever peek out from beneath a covering and also that, when immersing in the *mikvah* [ritual bath that purifies a woman after her menstrual cycle], a woman need not worry about her hair rising to the water's surface, rendering the immersion unkosher."[18]

Although there are many covering practices of the Brooklyn Hasidic dress code that distinguish a Hasidic woman from a non-Hasidic, Torah-observant woman, Ella discusses one of the more recognizable ones:

> It's little details. It's called customs. . . . The Law is the Law. We all agree on the same Law. . . . They [Hasidic women] just will be much more strict. Like in the summer, although I will not uncover my legs, or anything like that, I would wear bobby socks and a longer skirt. So my whole leg is not covered with a stocking, let's say. But if my skirt is long enough . . . But they would never. Even if their leg is covered [by a skirt]. They wouldn't take off [their stockings].

Thus, while a non-Hasidic, Torah-observant woman is content with covering the ervah parts of her legs with a skirt only, the Hasidic woman will fortify her coverage by wearing stockings (no matter how long her skirt) to zealously guard her modesty and "doubly" guarantee her Torah observance.

Dress distinctions and levels of religiosity are not only revealed by means of clothing practice. Levels of religiosity are also displayed through distinctions in the material used to construct a tzniuth appearance. Hasidic women's head covering provides an excellent illustration of how form expresses distinct levels of Hasidic religiosity both between and within Hasidic communities.[19] Hasidic women wear a variety of head coverings depending on their community's customs, preferences, and level of religiosity. The most hyperbolized display of a female Hasidic identity and religiosity is evidenced by those women who wear a *tikhl* (scarf) without a wig and thus reveal no hair whatsoever. Although generally found among the more traditional women of many Hasidic communities, this level of covering is predominately associated with the women of the Satmar Hasidic community in Williamsburg, Brooklyn.

A *sheytl* (wig) is considered less religious than the tikhl due to the appearance of hair. Even though her own hair is not revealed, a wig is less religious because it conveys ambiguity in coverage and too closely approximates a religious woman's uncovered head. An obvious-looking synthetic wig is, however, considered more religious than one made of human hair. The women of the Bobover Hasidic community employ a variety of head coverings though most wear wigs with or without a hat. A hat over a wig increases a modest appearance, thus raising a woman's level of observance and religiosity. Many Bobover women claimed to greatly admire those women in their own and neighboring Hasidic communities who wear a tikhl only. However, they confessed that they felt more comfortable when wearing a wig—they were too hindered by their vanity to present a hairless image in public—because they haven't yet arrived at the tikhl-only level of spirituality. Most Hasidic women have more than one wig and an assortment of hats and scarves from which to choose. A varied wardrobe provides a considerable amount of control and flexibility in dress (different levels of acceptable hyperbolization) for different social contexts. Suri provides an illustration of how a woman may symbolically assert a particular religious position by adorning a certain form of head covering. She explains that although she customarily wears a sheytl that is 50 percent synthetic and 50 percent human hair (as does her own mother), when she visits her husband's family, she "upgrades" her head covering by adding a tikhl in order to please her more religious mother-in-law. "Why offer a rose with the thorns showing?" she says.

In addition to the signification of religious observance of the laws on modesty, a Hasidic woman's discriminating manipulation of clothing serves as the symbolic expression of her Hasidic identity and her non-compliance with the values of the larger New York City culture. Clothing is deliberately manipulated into expressive forms through which the community as a whole symbolically distinguishes itself from the larger secular world of Gentiles (non-Jews), as well as from the non-Hasidic and irreligious Jewish populations. "Clothes are there to tell the person who I am," Chaya declares, "It speaks for me. It's telling me I'm trying to be a religious person and trying to serve God. And this is what I represent." Grossman parallels Chaya's statement concerning the demarcating intentions of Hasidic dress, defining a Hasidic girl's modesty as serving to distinguish her as being Jewish in opposition to non-Jewish:

> Because we follow the laws *Hashem* [God] gave us in the Torah, our lives are unlike those of other people. . . . [One of] the activities in our lives which identify us as Jews . . . [is that] we dress and behave in a modest, or *tzanua* way.[20]

This opposition to American (non-Jewish) secular culture is over-whelmingly expressed in terms of a spiritual/material dichotomy, with dress at the very core. Hasidic teaching awards great value to living a spiritually driven life. Chaya provides a biblical foundation for opposing materialism owing to its potential to thwart one's ability to reach the spiritual objectives of Torah:

> All through the Torah you'll find that in almost every portion. . . . Go out from your materialism and then you will learn. How can you retain and hear and understand what you're learning and keep it within you? By going out of your materialism. In other words get rid of it. Don't want it. I've seen it over and over. . . . [When God appeared to Moses for the first time,] He said to him, "Take off your shoes." At the burning bush, the first thing God said

to him [was], "Take off your shoes, because the place you're standing on is holy." I saw in a beautiful commentary that shoes are a symbol of materialism. So the first message was, "Don't be caught up in your materialism and then you will be able to understand and be a spiritual person."

Fashion, the ultimate symbol of secular materialism in opposition to Hasidic spirituality, is often translated as the *yetzer hora*, or evil inclination. From the perspective of Hasidic religious and cultural ideology, the American fashion system represents the epitome of a materialistic secular influence that threatens to infiltrate Hasidic communities through the female segment of its population.[21] Chaya explains, "For us this is a terrible thing. For us, for somebody to dress like that or . . . just to have her whole head in fashion. . . . To us is a terrible thing." Describing the distress experienced in her community due to this seemingly uncontrollable decay, Chaya boldly continues, "You're [mainstream American society] having a drug epidemic. We're having a fashion epidemic."

Solomon Poll, in his ethnography on the Satmar community, found that the Hasidic male dress code provided a symbolic barrier against the foreign influences of American secular culture.

> [The Hasidic man] feels that by wearing garments identifying him as a Jew he will be helped to refrain from coming into contact with sin. "Looking like a Jew in the image of God upon one's face" will serve as a barrier against acculturation and assimilation. As one Hasidic Jew expressed it, "With my appearance I cannot attend a theater or movie or any other places where a religious Jew is not supposed to go. Thus, my beard and my side locks and my Hasidic clothing serve as a guard and shield from sin and obscenity."[22]

Exactly the same dynamic may be found in a Hasidic woman's mode of dress. Even though she may incorporate mass-produced items from the American fashion system, her deliberate selection and manipulation of clothing to construct a modest appearance not only serves to distinguish her as a member of the Hasidic community, it also protects her against the oppositional values of the secular society in which she lives. As Bobover sewing teacher Rifka Glazer explains, in a handout to her female students on how to combat enticing fashion trends in clothing stores, dress that embodies the female aesthetic of Hasidic modesty functions as a "symbolic armor" protecting a Jewish girl's spirituality or "innerness" against foreign—dominant American secular or non-Hasidic—infiltration:

> The way we clothe our *guf* [body], has a direct effect on our *neshome* [soul]. The Gaon Rav Elijah teaches that *tzniuth* is the woman's defense against her *yetzer hora*. Certainly, were she to attire her *guf* in modest clothing, her *neshome* likewise, would be protected from alien winds.[23]

Chaya's comments mimic Glazer's depiction of dress as a divinely mandated protection against the sin, temptation, and indecency of American secular culture. She sees the Hasidic tradition of modesty in dress as necessary for preserving the "precious gem" of her Torah-observant way of life in the face of powerful infiltrating "outside influences."

> I'm going to quote a verse in the Bible that says it all. "You will turn aside and you will serve strange gods or idols." If you just turn aside . . . [and] . . . let go of one little commandment that's called serving strange gods. 'Cause the rabbis, in their wisdom, and their foresight, they had . . . divine revelation. They saw that if you start turning slowly, it will evolve slowly. It doesn't mean that day you will serve strange gods but you'll wind up doing things that in their youth they couldn't image themselves seeing. Or their children dressing like this. This is an evolution of something that somebody turned [away from the Torah's commandments].
>
> There's an expression, *Azoy Kristelt zikh, azoy Yidltzikh.* [It means,] "Those [Jews] who are trying to be like the Gentiles, so then they'll start being like them." The same that's going on by the Gentiles is happening to us. And of course we're on a bit of a higher level of spirituality. We're more modest. But proportionately, it's sort of the same. It's happening because we're letting go. The influences of the outside world seep into the Jewish culture. That is the root of the problem. . . . The forces are so strong. The outside world is so strong . . . that it can just grab you and take hold. Do you know how hard we're working? But it's worth it. I don't mean working hard physically. I have to be on guard. *It's like a war from all sides.* . . . Judaism is a gem that has to be so guarded.

In conclusion, overt displays of fashion do abound in the clothing of the Hasidic women in Borough Park. Hasidic women cover their bodies with ready-made garments and accessories from the American fashion system, adopting the latest dominant fashion trends *as long as styles are modestly appropriated be modesty-appropriated.* Moreover, their mode of dress is neither conspicuous nor atypical in the context of the secular society in which they live. It's not the uniformed "folk costume" of their male counterparts, or the iconic Roman Catholic habit of women religious, or one of the various exotic (to many Westerners) forms of veiling by women in Muslim cultures worldwide. Perhaps it is the lack of uniformity and an obvious otherness coupled with the appearance of modesty-appropriate mainstream fashion that has omitted the clothing of Hasidic women from Western academic literature, in both ethnographies on the Hasidic community and discussions on the cultural significance of dress.

Yet Hasidic women's mode of dress does in fact signify culturally specific meanings and distinctions. There is no distinction between the sacred and the everyday in the clothing of Hasidic women. The everyday, mass-produced clothing that a Hasidic woman wears—her sacred covering—is one of the means by which she fulfills the obligation to sanctify her worldly existence. Rather than mere self-expression, the value of Hasidic women's dress is ultimately appraised by its reflection of tzniuth, that is, how she simultaneously covers and promotes—concealing ervah body parts as specified by halakhoth and, at the same time, symbolically promoting that which is concealed or hidden, her *kedusha* or neshome. Ultimately, it is her tzniuth clothing, her sacred covering, which not only publicizes her religious intentions and identity but serves as the primary symbolic protection against the dominant and unwelcome outside influences of the non-Jewish secular society in which she lives.

The multivocal nature of Hasidic women's mode of dress does not render her clothing symbolically insignificant. On the contrary, the female Hasidic dress code is a language through which religious and cultural distinctions are declared and revealed to those fluent in its meanings. Differences in clothing practice and form reveal the variety of cultural traditions established through time and across space. Distinctions in dress also articulate a hierarchically ordered system of religiosity that not only distinguishes a Hasidic woman from a non-Hasidic, Torah-observant woman but also positions women both within and between Hasidic communities on different levels of Hasidic spirituality. The more a woman's

clothing and/or head covering hyperbolize her tzniuth coverage—the more comprehensive and unambiguous her coverage—the more religious it is considered.

The following account of an early nineteenth-century Eastern European Hasidic woman was proudly offered by Chaya. It demonstrates the utmost importance of tzniuth and the commitment held by the most zealous of Hasidic women to defend and preserve their precious Torah prescriptions for covering, even in the face of extreme danger, in order to assert their religious identity and protect their religious tradition:

> There was a woman. She was Jewish and she was being persecuted for her religion. They dragged her through the town. They tied her to a horse and dragged her through the town. She knew that this was going to happen so she stuck pins in her skin [so that her dress would not separate from her skin], so [as] not to be immodest. This shows how important tzniuth is.

NOTES

1. The class, "The Aesthetics of Everyday Life," was taught by Barbara Kirshenblatt-Gimblett. And the Bobover are one of many Hasidic sects living in the predominantly Hasidic neighborhood of Borough Park in Brooklyn, New York.

2. Hasidic men's clothing and appearance do vary and undergo change both within and across the different Hasidic communities. Distinctions in Hasidic men's dress exist through differences such as length, quality of material, and decorative patterning of *bekechers*; styles of *streimels*; and stylization of *peyes*. See Solomon Poll, *The Hasidic Community of Williamsburg* (New York: Schocken Books, 1962); and Yonassan Gershom, *Hasidim.info*. 2005, www.pinenet.com/rooster/hasid2.html#HASID2-Q1 (accessed July 12, 2006) for a discussion of the meaning of distinctions in Hasidic men's dress.

3. I conducted my research on Hasidic women's dress mainly among the Bobover Hasidim from the spring of 1991 to the fall of 1992 while a graduate student at New York University.

4. This deficit is in striking contrast to numerous publications issued from the religious Jewish community, some of which I presented in this paper, which discuss the importance of Hasidic women's and girls' mode of dress in relation to modesty. In the past few years there have been numerous works both from the religious community and in the academic literature, most specifi-

cally in the journal *Judaism,* discussing, in minute detail, the religious prescription for head coverings.

5. Miriam Grossman, *The Wonder of Becoming You: How a Jewish Girl Grows Up*
    (New York, Feldheim, 1988), 55.
6. "The Honor of a Jewish Daughter" is the title of a handout on modesty I re-
    ceived from a granddaughter of the third Bobover rebbe, Shlomo Halber-
    stam (1905–2000), written by Mrs. Rifka Glazer, a sewing teacher at Bnos
    Zion, a Bobover school for girls.
7. Lisa Aiken, *To Be a Jewish Woman* (Northvale, NJ: Jason Aronson, 1992),
    130–31.
8. Gila Manolson, *Outside Inside: A Fresh Look at Tzniut* (Southfield, MI: Targum
    Press, 1997), 28.
9. Grossman, *Wonder of Becoming You,* 51, 57.
10. Jewish law is continually being revised and updated in order to apply ancient
    Jewish regulations to the circumstances of the modern world. For instance,
    Rav Yitzchak Yaacov Fuchs, in his *Halichos Bas Yisrael: A Woman's Guide to
    Jewish Observance* (New York: Feldheim, 1985), 116, includes mention of con-
    temporary practices such as excessive dieting and cosmetic plastic surgery
    in his discussion of *tzniuth* behavior.
11. Fuchs, *Halichos Bas Yisrael,* 71–72.
12. Fuchs, *Halichos Bas Yisrael,* 101–4.
13. Fuchs, *Halichos Bas Yisrael,* 88.
14. Fuchs, *Halichos Bas Yisrael,* 69; emphasis added.
15. Aiken, *To Be a Jewish Woman,* 43–63.
16. The most pronounced example of this struggle centers on the wig. There are
    divergent interpretations concerning whether the head or hair needs to be
    covered, how much of a woman's hair should be covered, and what is the
    best form of covering. Most recently, the global Hasidic community was up
    in arms over discovering that many of the wigs made of human hair pur-
    chased by religious women were made from hair obtained by the Venka-
    teswara Temple in Tirupati, where Hindu women cut off their hair as a
    sacrifice to their gods and goddesses. The rabbis have temporarily ruled
    against women wearing wigs of human hair, recommending synthetic wigs
    or scarves. Satmar women, who are among the most religious Hasidic com-
    munities in Brooklyn, took to the streets to burn their banned wigs.
17. Barbara Kirshenblatt-Gimblett, personal communication, 1992.
18. Lynne Schreiber, *Hide and Seek: Jewish Women and Hair Covering* (Jerusalem:
    Urim Publications, 2003), 23.
19. See Barbara Goldman Carrel, "Hasidic Women's Head-Coverings: A Femi-
    nized System of Hasidic Distinction," in *Religion, Dress and the Body,* ed. L. B.
    Arthur (Oxford: Berg, 1999), 163–79 for a detailed discussion on distinctions
    in Hasidic women's head coverings.

20. Grossman, *Wonder of Becoming You,* 51.
21. At the time of my research, there were many lectures in the Hasidic community directed at women in an attempt to combat the influx and presence of American secular fashion. The late Bobover rebbe Shlomo Halberstam himself was said to be extremely concerned.
22. Poll, *Hasidic Community of Williamsburg,* 65.
23. Glazer, "Honor of a Jewish Daughter," 1. Gaon Rav Elijah is a Hasidic rabbi.

REFERENCES

Aiken, Lisa. *To Be a Jewish Woman.* Northvale, NJ: Jason Aronson, 1992.
Carrel, Barbara Goldman. "Hasidic Women's Head-Coverings: A Feminized System of Hasidic Distinction," In *Religion, Dress and the Body,* edited by L. B. Arthur. Oxford: Berg, 1999.
Fuchs, Rav Yitzchak Yaacov. *Halichos Bas Yisrael: A Woman's Guide to Jewish Observance.* New York: Feldheim, 1985.
Grossman, Miriam. *The Wonder of Becoming You: How a Jewish Girl Grows Up.* New York: Feldheim, 1988.
Manolson, Gila. *Outside Inside: A Fresh Look at Tzniut.* Southfield, MI: Targum Press, 1997.
Poll, Solomon. *The Hasidic Community of Williamsburg.* New York: Schocken Books, 1962.
Scholem, Gershom. The *Messianic Idea in Judaism and Other Essays on Jewish Spirituality.* New York: Schocken Books, 1971.
Schreiber, Lynne. *Hide and Seek: Jewish Women and Hair Covering.* Jerusalem: Urim Publications, 2003.

3 Going the Whole Nine Yards

Vignettes of the Veil in India

ROXANNE KAMAYANI GUPTA

In memory of anthropologist Chantal Boulanger

Until I spotted them, during that very first ride from the airport back in 1973, I couldn't really believe I'd arrived. But there they were: women draped in bright orange, yellow, and chartreuse walking barefoot under a clear blue sky. I was only nineteen and had traveled alone to India to study classical dance. The sari had long conjured the India of my fantasies—a land of exotic and graceful femininity, temple dancers, and goddesses (figure 3.1).

But here was the reality I was to spend my life exploring: millions of women in millions of saris, from workers in the rice fields and maidservants in the kitchens, to bank clerks, social workers, doctors and engineers, all the way up to Prime Minister Indira Gandhi herself. Indian women work, sleep, bathe, marry, have sex, give birth, and are carried to the cremation pyre wearing the sari. If all the saris in India were tied end to end, they would encircle the globe twice, with enough left for a decorative bow.

Where else on earth is an entire civilization or ethnicity associated with

Figure 3.1.   In India, deities are often draped and dressed
in a sari, an outer garment worn chiefly by women, 2007.
Photo by Vijay Kutty.

a style of dress, a piece of cloth? In the early twentieth century, the world
watched as Mohandas Gandhi traveled to England and challenged colonial rule dressed in a dhoti, the male equivalent of the sari, which Winston
Churchill disdainfully called a "diaper." Today the world can't take its eyes
off the sari or, in light of India's emerging economic role as the world's
largest democracy, deny its power and fascination. This contrasts greatly
with the fear projected upon the *burqa,* the Muslim veil.

One of the most popular stories in the Indian religious epic Mahabharata is that of Draupadi, a virtuous wife. When Draupadi's husband loses his kingdom and forfeits her in a game of dice, his evil cousin attempts to humiliate her and the whole family by undressing her. Draupadi prays to Lord Krishna and miraculously, the villain pulls at her sari only to find that the more cloth he removes, the more appears. However, this is no simple story of female chastity, for Draupadi is married to not only one, but all five heroes of the epic, the Pandava brothers. The Pandavas, according to the tradition, represent the five senses, and Draupadi's condition is our own: her modesty reflects the inviolable nature of the naked truth, the sari the "covering" that saves us.

As Arjuna the warrior hero discovered later in the same epic—in the section called Bhagavad Gita, or Song of the Lord—unveiled reality is terrifyingly immense. After Arjuna beseeches Krishna to grant him a mystical vision of all that is, he begs him to take it away and return him to his normal consciousness.

The sari attracts because it is a veil that covers but does not hide. In the Hindu worldview, nature is maya or illusion, insofar as it is limited. Yet through this limited form the infinite reveals itself. This understanding works against the notion that Hinduism and Buddhism are world denying. In both religions, divinity appears in both male and female forms and nature holds a sacred status. The feminine is conceived as, and conceives, nature. At the core of the tantric worldview, common to both religions, is the secret that—metaphysically understood—the body, embodiment itself, is feminine: all souls, insofar as they are embodied, veiled in matter, one with and born of the Mother, are themselves originally feminine. All matter is feminine.

The spiritual arts of India, painting, sculpture, dance, and literature all express a preoccupation with the feminine, the body, and the erotic as a mode of mystical awareness. If spirit is imaged as masculine, then in relation to the divine, all creation is feminine. Sri Vidya, India's preeminent tantric tradition, expresses this most profoundly in its elevation of the divine feminine. Focusing on the phenomenal world, the entire cosmos takes the form of Sri, the goddess as embodied nature.

The act of veiling becomes a metaphor for the feminine itself, and for the way we enter into nature, into bodies, into life. The *Bhagavad Gita* says, "As a [human being], casting off old garments puts on ones that are new, so the dweller in the body, casting off worn-out bodies enters into ones that are new."[1] If our endless cycle of rebirth casts us into a state of separation from the undivided whole, tantra and the yogic traditions teach that the body is nonetheless its own universe, a microcosm that reflects the macrocosm. The body becomes the means by which inner subjective consciousness projects its experience and then observes its reflection in the objective world. The body is a veil of senses, a delicate curtain dividing the inner and outer worlds. One and many, embodied consciousness contains within it the wholeness and multiplicity of the universe.

This metaphysical sense of the sari as veil may subtly underlie its value and the important role it plays in Hindu society for defining individual and social identity. An eminent scholar in New Delhi recently told me, "A few years ago I met a colleague at a party. Though Indian, she was dressed in Western style and asked me how I liked her new dress. I didn't want to be rude, but she pressed me for a comment. Finally I told her, 'Please don't assassinate me. My earliest memories were of my mother wearing a sari. My entire life I have seen my wife, my sisters and even my maid-servant dressed always in the sari. Seeing an Indian woman in these clothes destroys my world. '"

Although dramatic, this story is not unique and aptly expresses the deep psychological attachment that Indian men hold for the sari, despite the fact that since independence, most educated men in India wear Western dress. The double standard is based on the classic division between home and the world, between inner and outer realities, which plays out in traditional gender roles. Men work outside the home where social change requires at least superficial adaptation. In contrast, the home, the psyche, and women's bodies are still seen as sanctuaries in which the sari equals tradition.

Yet Indian tradition is multiple and by reflection, the sari is its own material reality: countless designs, fabrics both natural and synthetic and more colors than the rainbow. Saris are typically six yards, or five and one-half meters in length, but temple dancers wore the whole nine yards, not only wrapping it, but drawing it back between the legs. The *palu*, or decorative end that drapes over and hangs behind the left shoulder, is the sari's center of attraction. Worn Rajasthani style, the palu is brought from back to front where it shows itself off.

The palu displays the sari's color scheme, motif, and theme, if any. For example, elephants on the march, peacocks dancing, or a village scene complete with women carrying jugs on their heads. Colors are highly symbolic, relating to the substance of religious ritual—white for purity, red for fertility, and yellow for prosperity. Metallic silver or gold threads are woven into the palu and border, making them shimmer or shine. The palu's length is another variable, worn long or short, cyclically changing, like skirt lengths in the West. Sequins, mirrors, embroidery, roping, traditional weaves, hand painting, and countless other modifications lend infinite variety in a land where the goddess is one but her forms are many.

Wearing a sari offers our body a unique sensation of security: a feeling of being wrapped, tied, hemmed in, our experience fastened within safe boundaries, our power bundled, concentrated. Yet unlike the burqa, there are certain key openings that can be contracted or expanded. The space between the bottom of the sari blouse and the top of the sari can expose anything from a couple inches of skin to a navel or healthy little roll of fat. The neckline of the *choli,* or sari blouse, can be high or low in front or back, with short, medium, long, or no sleeves. The free end of the sari can be long or short, loosely draped to modestly cover the breasts, or drawn tightly across them to expose shape and size. It can stay up or it can fall down (sometimes quite "accidentally," thus "nice" women pin it up). The limbs are free under the voluminous pleats. A woman can squat on the ground, sit cross-legged, spread her knees, stretch her legs, assume nearly any posture necessary for daily life this side of standing on her head or running a marathon.

Unlike the burqa, the sari offers choice. It is both revealing and concealing, about showing and not telling, the feel and the look, the objective gaze and subjective experience intricately interwoven. The power, how much to show, how much to hide, even how much to feel its sensuality lies in the individual woman, prescribed only, though never completely, by her family, culture, and nearest male kin.

Dress in India sends strong messages about a woman's family's social location: caste, class, religion, sexuality, and last but not least, sophistication. Since ancient times, sophistication has had to do with the cultural gap between rural and urban cultures and has been highly influenced by contact with other cultures, most recently European colonialism. Today postmodern transnational consumerist values add a new layer of "coolness" to what's hot and what's not. After the Indian economic liberalization of the 1990s—a shift from a mixed economy to today's deregulated techno-boom capitalism, Indians who have settled in America tend to be far more conservative in their tastes and lifestyles than the jet-setters of Delhi, Mumbai, or cyber cities like Hyderabad.

The rules of the sari game are complex and subtle. They vary from region to region, each with its own language, culture, and aesthetic. For example, since the 1980s, it has been fashionable for middle-class women throughout India to tie the sari Rajasthani style, showing off rich palus, but only for parties and weddings. To do so everyday would be considered gauche, unless the women are living in Rajasthan or Maharasthra, where this style is traditional.

Only a prostitute, a low-caste woman on her way to a marriage party, or a rich Bollywood sophisticate at a disco would dare don a metallic or shiny sari. Yet saris covered with sequins, mirrors, and glitter, which only ten years ago would have been considered gaudy, are now worn by younger women to less formal parties and functions. Traditional gold-bordered silk remains the classic standard for those attending weddings and other religious ceremonies, especially in the south, although colors today are brighter. Brides nonetheless still wear red in North India and cream-colored saris for the ritual ceremony in the south. In a country where wedding celebrations can go on for days, marriages are the main stage on which saris play their most dramatic role.

At the other end of the social spectrum, a village peasant or urban laborer is immediately identifiable by her inexpensive printed cotton sari, with bright color combinations and designs in which a woman of any sophistication would never be caught dead. While blue jeans still largely spell spoiled middle to upper class, I guarantee that any Indian woman can still assess the cost of another woman's sari, judge the carats of its gold border, sum up the woman's personality, and instantly pinpoint her community of origin.

As a young American woman in the early 1970s, I was first coached in the lore of saris by Bharathi, the mother of the Brahmin family that "adopted" me. Thirty years later, I remember her advice. I still have most of the silk and cotton saris I purchased then, tucked in a trunk with more than thirty others from all the eras of my life in India. When I open the trunk, the distinctive aroma of India flows out with the memories, each sari its own story. From Bharathi I learned the right way to choose, wrap, sit, stand, and walk in a sari. I also learned how to wash, starch, iron, and fold different fabrics. I had to wear up to three saris a day—one to walk to and from class, one to dance in, and an everyday sari to change into when I got home. If I went anywhere special at night I had to put on a fresh one appropriate to the occasion. As for the laundry, I did what Indians do and sent my saris to the *dhobi* (washerman).

The sari is part of a larger matrix of tradition that teaches a Hindu woman how to decorate herself, especially after marriage. In North India, a newly married woman is instantly recognized, not only by the bright colors of her sari, but by the pile of bangles on her arms and the red vermilion powder along the part of her hair. In South India, flowers are worn in the hair. Bangles, black *kajal* (kohl) outlining the eyes, and of course, the *tilak* or *bindi*, the red mark on the forehead, are all necessary accessories to a sari. It is also traditional in the north to decorate the feet with *alta*, a red dye. In the south, henna is used to decorate both hands and feet.

While many of these cosmetics have medicinal properties, their religious significance transcends their therapeutic qualities. The arts of decoration reflect Hinduism's love of beauty and positive embrace of nature, the feminine, life itself. But Hindus also recognize the danger that beauty attracts to both individual and society. They call it *dristhi* or, roughly translated, the "evil eye." I learned of this during my first few months in India when I proudly showed up in a new sari for an evening outing with Bharathi and her husband. I was surprised at their reaction—they complimented me but warned I should be careful of dristhi. I laughed it off as superstition but sure enough, later that night I came down with a fever.

Dristhi may be understood as the shadow side of the concept of *darshan*, "to see and be seen," the positively transformative experience that happens in a temple or in the presence of a holy person, place, or thing.

Darshan is a spiritual interchange in which the eyes are particularly powerful, but also vulnerable when on the receiving end of a powerful gaze.
If the gaze projects thoughts of jealousy, desire, and other negative feelings, it becomes dristhi. This is the primary reason that women wear the
tilak or bindi on the forehead and kajal around their eyes (also applied to
children's eyes from infancy) and why in North India, women literally
cover their heads and hide their faces under their saris.

I was told that in the north, hundreds of years of Muslim rule posed a
threat to Hindu women's security, so the sari came to play a role somewhat analogous to the Muslim burqa. Unlike South India, where a woman
does not cover her head, even for religious ceremonies, in the villages of
the north women keep their heads covered even at home in the presence
of men. In North Indian homes as well, a curtain divides the inner, private area of a home and the space where those outside the family may be
received. In either case, the private sphere is veiled and should not be pen-
etrated, even by a gaze.

By the end of my first year in India, I was hooked on saris and felt un-
comfortable in anything else. I got so attached to my favorites that I could
not bear to throw them out even after they became old and torn. In fact,
old saris rarely become rags. They are passed down to servants, sewn into
shirts or door curtains, or cut up for patchwork. New saris are purchased
at festival times, exchanged at weddings (when every female member of
the groom's family receives a new silk one), and presented as ritual offerings to Brahmins, gurus, and deities in a temple. They also work well
as political bribes—one South Indian chief minister won the election after his campaign workers handed out free saris to huge crowds of village
women.

And while saris can be all about status, hierarchy, and social location,
they are also a means of transcending boundaries, a language spoken by
Indian women in general. Early on I had no patience for all that "sari talk,"
but as my friendships with Indian women grew, I came to realize that when
a woman opens her sari cupboard, she is really offering you an intimate
glimpse into the many sides of her personality, the color palette of her
world.

The choice of covering is especially important in a culture where nakedness carries a loaded significance. As soon as a baby is born, male or female, a thread and small amulet are tied around the waist so that the child will never be naked. I was told that traditionally even a husband and wife would not appear naked in front of each other. Even the highly erotic, dancing figures sculpted on the walls of Konarak and Khajuraho temples wear ornaments and veils.

I relearned the meaning of modesty during my first year in India when at the dance school we had to change our clothes before and after class, being careful not to expose our bodies even to members of the same sex. Once, during a dance tour in Rajamundry, one of the hottest places on earth during the summer, I created a stir when I felt I was being forced to choose between cultural norms and sheer survival. The women in the troupe were resting on some straw mats the afternoon prior to an evening performance. Without a fan, I felt I would suffocate. Wanting to rip off all my clothes and run wildly about in search of air, I took instead the risk of removing my blouse, covering my breasts with the end of the light cotton sari. Somewhat relieved, I lay down to rest. I woke up an hour later to find that in my sleep I had rolled over and exposed my breasts. There sat the other young women staring and whispering in shocked disbelief.

Living by the banks of the Ganges I saw hundreds of people bathing in the river and changing their clothes without ever exposing themselves. Indian women are proficient at changing in public: They wrap a dry sari around themselves, holding it in front with their teeth as a screen. Behind this they remove their wet clothes and don a blouse and petticoat before neatly tying the dry one, the whole process taking no more than three or four minutes.

Hindus often refer to the world as *samsara*, a word that captures a chimera of experienced pleasure and pain that sooner or later the individual soul outgrows. Yet even when Hindus have had enough, are ready to get off the wheel, the carousel does not easily stop. Trapped as humans are by rebirth, the quest for liberation is complex. It involves sacrifices and rituals, the renouncing of unconscious habit in favor of conscious awareness. The archetype of the naked sadhu (holy man) reflects the belief that humans in a natural state of divine grace need only to depend on nature for their sustenance. In a religious sense, to remove one's clothes is to remove the veil from one's eyes, to remove the illusion that humans are somehow separate from nature. While there are many sects like the Hindu Nagas and the Jain Digambaras that engage in ritual nudity (males only), in general it is considered very inauspicious or "unlucky" for everyone else, especially women.

So what do women on the quest for liberation wear in India? Saris, of course. The pleats of the sari fully cover and provide ample legroom for sitting cross-legged during meditation. Widows wear white for sexual purity. Women undertaking *vratas*, or religious fasts, wear yellow for the earth. *Sadhvis*, female holy women, wear ochre for detachment, and tantric yoginis wear red for shakti, or power. The single color signals that the mind is now focused on a single goal, choice has been relinquished, variety has been transcended, the senses have been withdrawn from the external world of illusion in favor of an inner path.

Sari shopping, on the other hand, is the exact opposite of meditation! While meditation requires inner one-pointed focus and slows the heartbeat, sari shopping involves a one-track mind and has been known to induce adrenal rush and cardiac palpitations. I have seen women dive into oceans of fabric and not come up for hours, elbow each other as if boarding a commuter train and even try to snatch a sari out of the other's hands. Today's malls heaped with tables of saris to plow through are feeding the frenzy and literally cheapening the sari, unlike traditional shops where a customer still gets the full treatment I came to know and love.

Entering, you must remove your shoes to sit on the floor spread with clean white sheets. The salesman's first question will be, "What will you have—tea or a cold drink?" His demeanor suggests you might as well write off the rest of the afternoon. Shelves of stock line the walls from where the salesman tosses onto the sheet in front of you saris of various colors, fabrics, and price range, and he will gladly open out for you any number of them. Before you know it, you will be swimming in a sensuous heap of color, increasingly confused and conflicted about how many, what kind, and how much it is going to cost. You finally get to bargain with the salesman, bickering back and forth, using good humor to mask just how much you really want that sari, until one side or the other gives in. If all else

fails, just walk out—the salesman, whose name you will know by now—
will likely follow you with a final offer you can't refuse.

The whole experience is such a dizzying feast for the senses, it is easy
to become totally disoriented. A few years ago, I quickly ducked into a
sari shop in South India with a French girlfriend "just to look." We entered in broad daylight and emerged in total darkness at closing time, five
hours and four cups of tea later, laden with brightly printed bags of saris
neither of us have worn since.

While women in the affluent West purchase the dream of sexual attractiveness through cosmetic surgery, in India the sari, both revealing and
concealing the body it covers, conveys the full gamut of sexual expression: From holy woman to prostitute, dancing girl to Mother Theresa, the
sari equals female sexuality, either its renunciation, control, or exploitation. In Bollywood films, the wet sari scene became a standard feature
from the forties on, illustrating in the midst of any plot how nature can
sabotage the good intention of the most modest of heroines. The attraction of a thinly veiled body fuels lucrative forms of entertainment in India. During British colonial rule, *nautch* dancers, prostitutes with veils over
their heads, entertained maharajahs and British officers alike. After World
War II, Western cabaret replaced nautch dancing (a cheap cousin of classical *kathak* dance) in popularity and greatly influenced the dance choreography of Indian films.

Cabaret and "filmie" dance in India reflect the projection of supposed
Western values onto the uneven backdrop of traditional values, bent
through a lens of guilty desire. Giving full reign to the imagination of all
that would be forbidden in the highly prescribed rules of classical Indian
dance, nearly anything goes in the symbolic realm of the Western-
influenced "nonclassical" performance. The result seems almost designed
to capture the danger of a world that runs amok of tradition.

My single live experience of Indian-style cabaret was a bizarre show
in a nightclub owned by some friends of ours in Nainital, the Himalayan
hill station. The cabaret consisted of a single dancer performing vulgar
moves to some loud Hindi music. I watched in horror as she relentlessly
teased a turbaned man in the front row sitting beside his mortified wife.

The man's face turned bright red as the dancer gyrated in front of his table, encircled him, and nearly sat on his lap. The dancer used the end of her sari like a veil that slowly began to unwind, transforming performance into striptease as the music grew louder. The dance reached its climax with the dancer pulling off her sequined top—false breasts and all. The lady was a man!

While the dancer in Nainital may or may not have belonged to such a category, India has its own transsexual community in the *hijras*, men who live their entire lives as women. Colonies of hijras are found in all major Indian cities. Comprising their own caste, traditionally hijras made their livings performing music and dance, and by prostitution. Hijras were invited to religious ceremonies celebrating the birth of a son where they were called upon to inspect the genitals of the child to make sure he was "normal." It is said that if the child exhibited hermaphroditic genitalia, the hijras took the infant away with them. Otherwise they danced and sang vulgar songs as a ritual of good luck to remove the evil eye from the beautiful newborn. Today such customs have largely fallen by the wayside, but the hijras remain and still can be seen moving in groups in cities, using a particular threatening form of humor to beg for alms.

One afternoon during the season of Diwali, the festival of lights, I was sitting at the Bengali jeweler's shop in Varanasi (in Banaras) when all of a sudden I heard a raucous voice and tambourine. Into the shop danced a strange-looking woman. Her blouse did not match her sari and a plethora of bangles and gaudy jewelry instantly identified a hijra. An electric charge of shock and suspense made the other women in the shop sit up and take notice, but they all gave disapproving looks before lowering their eyes. Not me! I flashed a grin at her as she strutted over to the jeweler's counter. The shopkeeper's expression was one of disgust as he opened the cash box and placed some bills on the counter. With dramatic feminine gestures the hijra petulantly refused the money. "No! That's not enough and you have to put it in my hand!" The jeweler refused and told her to get out. Unfazed, the hijra then commented upon the jeweler's masculinity, which made some people titter, and the jeweler's face turned bright red. The hijra started singing again and nonchalantly began removing her sari. At that threat, the jeweler, flushed now with anger, motioned her closer, and placed some bills in her hand. As she turned, she winked at me and danced out the door.

In Banaras, I came to know another hijra, known to the local neighborhood as Mausiji (Aunty). She lived alone in a small house where she performed tantric rituals for those who came to her with problems. Mausiji was eighty but looked remarkably younger. She dressed in a sari and was so feminine a stranger would never guess she was biologically male. Born in an upper-class family in Bombay (now Mumbai) and educated as a young man, he ran away from home to join the hijras after discovering his homosexuality. Mausiji once told me that hijras were superior prostitutes because "being men, we know better what men like."

When Mausiji was younger, she danced on the stage during festivals. Once, a group of *gundas* (hoodlums) kidnapped her and took her to a lonely place to have their way with her. When they removed her sari and realized she was really a man, they beat her up and left her by the side of the road. The sari is that which both hides and reveals. The archetypal image of the sari coming off to reveal a different reality beneath the surface appearance is central to its attraction. Sometimes what is revealed is an indication of what lies below. At other times, just as in the Hindu myths and philosophies, appearances are shown to be quite deceiving.

The sari makes quick work of cross-dressing in India precisely because it is so immediately identified with the feminine—both human and divine. India is one of the few cultures where transsexuality, always from male to female, is an integral part of religious life. The Ramandandis, a Vaishnava male ascetic order headquartered in the region of the North Indian city of Brindaban, involve the spiritual practice of men dressing up in saris and bangles to imagine themselves close to Lord Krishna. They may adopt the guise of Radha, Krishna's favorite consort, or one of her female *sakhi*s, who attend the pair's divine lovemaking sessions. Like the Hare Krishnas, who also imagine themselves the beloved of Krishna, these men are not homosexuals. Most are married and have children, but they practice cross-dressing as a way to disassociate from their social identity and participate instead in a cosmic myth, a religious drama of symbolic significance. Like the goddess-centered tantric sects, Sri Vaishnavism places primary emphasis on the feminine. But unlike tantric traditions, where the feminine principle is primary, the consort model adheres to the *sa-guna* (qualified) form of God and the relationship between male and female, God and man, the divine and the human, becomes central.

Many of India's most revered saints, especially in the modern period, engaged in transsexual behavior to emphasize that transcendent unity includes and goes beyond gender difference. Ramakrishna Paramahansa, who also "tried on" other religious traditions, was photographed in a woman's sari in the mid-1800s. A century later, Avadhut Bhagwan Ram, an *Aghori* saint of Banaras, referred to by his followers as "Ma Guru," was worshipped as Sri Sarveshwari, the goddess of all beings, incarnate in a male body.

Women and goddesses alike wear the sari, so it is not always easy to distinguish between the two in a country where men brag, "We worship all women as our mothers, as goddesses," and human women are sometimes literally worshipped as living goddesses. Sri Anandamayima was India's most famous modern female saint and today is succeeded by Ammachi, Mother Meera, Sri Ma, and many others. In addition, many of the classical dance traditions of India—*kuchipudi, odissi,* and *kathakali*—involve male characters dressed like females, and females dressed like goddesses. Because the dance was seen as a religious practice, this was in keeping with other rituals involving male characters who become "possessed" by female spirits or divinities. In each case, the sari is that which transforms male into female, female into the divine. In shorthand, the sari communicates a timeless, essential "feminine" that goes way beyond biology.

During the monsoons, the city streets turn to muck. Indian women must wear their saris so they are barely touching the ground and walk as if their feet don't. I have looked down and seen delicately decorated feet peaking out beneath pleats of pale pink chiffon, stepping gingerly over sludge, garbage, and feces. A lotus blossom remains untouched by the mud from which it grows. All that cloth between body and world creates a boundary, a consciousness of the relationship between the inner subjective reality, our place of concealment, and the outer world of objective experience, the locus of the seen.

This boundary, between inner and outer worlds, is the original veil. We may recognize it from our earliest beginnings, floating in the amniotic waters, when through transparent eyelids, our unfocused gaze dimly registered a filtered light, separated from a world where every bright light casts an equally dark shadow.

NOTES

1. Annie Besant, *Bhagavad Gita* (Wheaton, IL: Theosophical Publishing House, 1961), 2:22.

4 Out of the Cloister

Unveiling to Better Serve the Gospel

LAURENE M. LAFONTAINE

"We are so much more than the habit!" exclaimed Sister Vicky as she described her interaction with a hospital patient's family. "They asked me if I was a real nun because apparently only real nuns wear a habit. Why don't they get it? It's been twenty years since Vatican II." (Figure 4.1)

Sister Vicky, a Benedictine nun for twenty-five years, was training to be a hospital chaplain. She was burned out from teaching middle school and frustrated with the current state of the Roman Catholic Church. It was she who introduced me to the deep personal concerns facing feminist nuns. As a young Presbyterian seminarian, my experience with women religious was limited to the classroom; I simply assumed that nuns could choose how they wanted to dress and live. After all, it was the 1980s. But Vicky's personal and professional ordeal gave me a clearer picture of the challenges faced by women religious within the Church, particularly in the development of pastoral authority as "unveiled" women.[1]

There seems to be a common belief—shared by people of every faith in

Figure 4.1. "At Vespers." Sister Linda, at Colorado's Abbey of St. Walburga, an order of contemplative Benedictine sisters, wears the veil of a postulant nun, one who hasn't yet made formal vows to the order. Photo by Valari Jack.

American society—that nuns are clad in long robes, wimples, and veils. The stereotype is still prevalent four decades after Pope Paul VI—on December 8, 1965—concluded the Second Ecumenical Vatican Council, one of the most groundbreaking and historic congresses in the history of the Church. Among other things, it directed women religious to update their manners of living, governance, and religious habit and highlighted a pervasive and implicit understanding of the habit as the defining symbol for women religious.

In 1959, Pope John XXIII called for an ecumenical council of bishops "to help renew and update the church."[2] Three years later in Rome, 2,500 bishops gathered from around the world for the opening of the Vatican II Council. During his commencement address, Pope John XXIII expressed his hope for the work of the council and the Church:

Illuminated by the light of this Council, the Church—we confidently trust—will become greater in spiritual riches and gaining the strength of new energies there from, she will look to the future without fear. In fact, by bringing herself up to date where required, and by the wise organization of mutual co-operation, the Church will make men, families, and peoples really turn their minds to heavenly things. . . . God grant that your labors and your work, toward which the eyes of all peoples and the hopes of the entire world are turned, may abundantly fulfill the aspirations of all.

John's vision for a renewed and revitalized Church shaped the scope of the council's work, which addressed the "modern conditions of faith and religious practice, and of Christian and especially Catholic vitality."[3]

In 1962, Belgium's Cardinal Leo Josef Suenens, in his newly published book, *Nun in the World,* stunned the still highly structured religious communities by calling for women religious to become more involved in people's lives, acting as "animators" for groups of men and women whose everyday lives need evangelization. A vital protagonist for women religious, he went on to challenge the 1963 Council of Bishops by pointing out that half the members of the Church were unrepresented.[4] As if those challenges were not enough, Cardinal Suenens was quoted in the November 1964 issue of *Time* magazine attacking the "ridiculous complications" of nuns' flowing habits, "which give the impression that the church is growing old rather than trying to renew itself in order to meet the needs of the day."[5] His leadership, in a male-dominated organization, was essential in raising the issues of women.

From 1962 to1965, the decrees adopted by the Church reflected a dramatic shift from traditionally structured medieval institution to a relevant and engaging living embodiment of the Gospel of Jesus Christ. "The Church as the people of God"[6] described the inclusive spirit of the Vatican II proceedings. Its focus on the dignity of human beings, the renewal of the Roman Catholic Church, and ecumenism enabled the shift from separation to activism.

It was within this context that the "Decree on the Adaptation and Renewal of Religious Life" was written. No one could have predicted the profound impact it would have upon the lives of many women religious and the Church universal.

Religious life, prior to Vatican II, meant living in cloistered or semi-cloistered and highly regimented communities. "The old ideal that governed convent life was that of the medieval monastery."[7] Community leadership was hierarchal and often autocratic. A mother superior had absolute authority. "Every small detail of life was regulated, not in the name of community order which surely they served, but in the name of the vow of obedience."[8] Daily events and tasks were closely controlled: silence, prayer, work, recreation, sleeping, and meals. Many women religious were ready for the progressive actions of Vatican II.

The "Decree on the Adaptation" encouraged religious congregations and orders to take ownership and leadership of their own communities, adapt their modes of living, provide opportunities for education of members, recognize the importance of social justice, and adapt their religious habits to "be simple and modest, poor and at the same time becoming . . . meet the requirements of health and be suited to the circumstances of time and place and to the needs of the ministry involved."[9] They were empowered to explore new and relevant ways to live their lives in order to live out the Gospel. Women religious were given the opportunity to define for themselves what it meant to be a nun in the twentieth century.

As the religious orders and congregations began to change, "many lay Catholics were outraged or upset about the updating of habits. Of all of the changes to religious life, the habit was the most dramatic because it was so visible."[10] For most people, religious experience is deeply rooted in symbols.[11] For many, the Catholic faith meant that nuns wore traditional habits, as they had since the medieval period. Neither the council nor the religious congregations and orders seemed to have anticipated the reaction of those with strongly held beliefs about the traditional habit as definitive and women lacking the religious authority to make significant changes to centuries-old practices for the "greater good to the Church."[12]

These beliefs are rooted in Pauline theology as expressed in sacred scriptures. With his letter to the Christians at Corinth, the apostle Paul instructs the congregation, which was in chaos, on several specific issues, including the necessity of head coverings for women within worship:

> I commend you because you remember me in everything and maintain the traditions just as I handed them on to you. But I want you to understand

that Christ is the head of every man, and the husband is the head of his wife, and God is the head of Christ. Any man who prays or prophesies with something on his head disgraces his head, but any woman who prays or prophesies with her head unveiled disgraces her head—it is one and the same thing as having her head shaved. For if a woman will not veil herself, then she should cut off her hair; but if it is disgraceful for a woman to have her hair cut off or to be shaved, she should wear a veil. For a man ought not to have his head veiled, since he is the image and reflection of God; but woman is the reflection of man. Indeed, man was not made from woman, but woman from man. Neither was man created for the sake of woman, but woman for the sake of man. For this reason a woman ought to have a symbol of authority on her head, because of the angels.[13]

Significant in his commentary is the emphasis he placed on the importance of social customs—"maintain the traditions just as I handed them on to you"—and his dramatic theological shift regarding humanity—"woman is the reflection of man" and not created in "the image and reflection of God."

These two major points contradict Paul's theological understanding as expressed in an earlier letter to the congregation at Galatia, "there is no longer male and female; for all of you are one in Christ Jesus." Paul's recorded words of encouragement to several women leaders within the early church also supported this theological understanding of equality.[14]

Unfortunately for women, the Corinthian passage has been the primary rationale for the subjugation of women throughout the history of Christianity. Most problematic is that Paul equates the veil with a symbol of authority: not God's authority, but man's authority over woman. Paul's own belief in women's natural inferiority informed his insistence that women veil. Being veiled in worship served as a public reminder of their inferiority and subordination.[15]

The early church fathers endorsed the practice of veiling consecrated virgins. "For wedded you are to Christ," Tertullian (155–230 c.e.) admonished young virgins, "to Him you have surrendered your flesh; to Him you have espoused your maturity. Walk in accordance with the will of your Espoused. Christ is He who bids the espoused and wives of others Veil themselves."[16]

Saint Scholastica, sister of Saint Benedict, founded and governed a monastery of nuns in the early sixth century, which followed the Rule of Benedict. Upon entering the monastery, a woman was given a habit, a cowl, scapular for work, and stockings and shoes to cover her feet.[17]

In the late ninth and early tenth centuries, the habits of women religious began to be comprised of a tunic (a long, loose fitting outer garment), a head veil, a coif (a hoodlike cap, often worn under the veil), and a linen wimple arranged in folds about the head.[18] The habit was a significant symbol to express a personal commitment to Jesus and the Roman Catholic Church. Depending on the style and color of the habit, it allowed the wearer to be identified with a specific congregation.

During the twenty-fifth session of the Council of Trent in 1563, all aspects of women's religious life were codified into canon law. The council's decrees placed strict parameters on entrance into religious life, made vows permanent, required all vowed women to be cloistered in convents, instituted the pope's governance over the convents, and required that every woman who made vows be given a habit.[19] The rigid cloistered environment completely separated the nuns from the outside world, thus negating their ministries of compassion and care. In response to the council's actions, new orders began to establish themselves purposely outside the boundaries that the Council of Trent had set up.[20]

From Trent until the 1917 Code of Canon Law, women religious throughout the world wore extremely distinctive and diverse dress. With their founding in 1633, the Sisters of Charity adopted the country dress of French peasant women, which by 1750 included the white cornette with starched, folded wings. The American Holy Cross sisters wore a white cap, black habit, long apron, and short veil.[21]

A congregation or order's religious dress was at times influenced by circumstances beyond its control: in 1843, the Sisters of the Holy Family, a congregation of African American sisters, were banned from wearing their habits by the diocese of New Orleans, which bowed to the racism of other Catholics. In 1887, New York's State Board of Education ruled that sisters could not wear religious habits in public schools.[22] Inadvertently, these religious communities were able to determine their own manner of dress, until the reinstitution of papal jurisdiction over women religious as dictated by the Code of Canon Law. The code required women religious to be veiled and modestly dressed and to sit separately from men.[23] Neither were women allowed to preach, even within their own congregations.[24]

The 1917 declarations signaled a dramatic return to the Middle Ages and reinforced to Catholic laity and society at large that the Church's male leadership absolutely controlled the lives of women religious, determining how they would live and defining what constituted a "good" nun. Once again, the requirement of the veil by papal fiat served to remind women, religious and lay, of the Church's theological position regarding women as inferior and subordinate.

The roots of patriarchal definition and oppression of women are deep and have been nurtured throughout the history of Christianity. Intense reactions to women religious as they implemented significant life changes have served to expose profound sexism and misogyny and have challenged the commonly held belief that the habit or veil defined a nun's value in society. By returning the locus of the decision-making power to the specific congregation or order, Pope Paul VI subtly prompted the Church to address the pervasive sexism present within Christianity since the ministry of the apostle Paul.

Vatican II did not impose a specific directive regarding the updating of religious life, it gave the responsibility to the congregations and orders. "We discovered before long that the responsibility to develop these wider perspectives could be carried out only by our own creativity—by our own best efforts and energies—spurred on by new hope in the Spirit's presence among us and around us,"[25] Sister Mary Luke Tobin, a member of the Sisters of Loretto, recalled. After much reflection and discussion, individual religious communities decided how they were going to define themselves as women religious in light of the liberating and empowering Gospel of Jesus Christ and how they were going to share this good news with the rest of humanity.

This willingness to explore religious identity behind the veil allowed many women to realize themselves, but it overwhelmed others. Writing in 1967, Sister Jeanne Reidy revealed some of the sentiments of her colleagues:

> Many sisters expressing disapproval have feared the loss of respect, . . . loss of vocation, trouble with hair, vanity, expense, unsightliness of figure, too

much attention to dress. One said, "I know it's right to change, but I'm afraid."[26]

Certainly, it was a moment of enlightenment. The unmasking of a woman who had been hidden behind a habit, an assumed name (usually a masculine one), and a regimented lifestyle often revealed a woman with a newly realized sense of maturity who felt called to make a different life choice.[27]

Sister Joan Chittister described what many women religious experienced:

> It was 1968, I think. The community had been in turmoil for years. Religious had begun leaving in droves—not after Vatican II was over as people so often now glibly assume—but long before it ended, not only in my own community but all over the country. The women who stayed were plunged into both uncertainty and excitement . . . in a group that hadn't changed much for centuries, anything was suddenly possible . . . by 1970, uniform dress had been discarded and even the veil was optional. . . . [A]ll the old absolutes had blurred.[28]

One of the first American communities of women religious to abandon the traditional habit was the Sisters of Loretto. Its mother general, Sister Mary Luke Tobin, was the only American nun to be invited to audit sessions during the Vatican II Council.[29] In the spring of 1966, the nuns adopted business suits. "Throughout many congregations, minor alteration of the habit became major tailoring, sometimes quickly, often gradually. By the late 1960s, New Jersey's Sisters of Charity agreed to permit both blue suits and full habits. By the early 1970s some sisters had dropped the veil."[30]

Not all the changes within the congregations were welcomed. When a bishop determined that a congregation within his diocese went beyond his limits of acceptable change, he sometimes took action to prohibit the implementation of their decisions. One of the most painful of these experiences occurred in 1967, when the Immaculate Heart of Mary (IHM) sisters in Los Angeles determined to adopt modern dress or modified habit, no longer require communal prayer, and govern the community based upon a shared responsibility model. The congregation also decided that community members needed to return to college for further education.

In response, Archbishop Cardinal James McIntyre, a traditionalist, removed all the IHM nuns from the archdiocese's parochial schools. The cardinal also objected when the congregation formed an affiliate program for laywomen and men wanting to work with the sisters. He then complained to Rome, prompting an investigation of the order in June 1968.

Meanwhile, fifty members broke away from the main group to continue living as a traditional religious community. At the 1969 Conference of Major Superiors of Women (later renamed Leadership Conference of Women Religious)[31], a Vatican representative demanded that women superiors refrain from passing a resolution supporting the IHM because of alleged "deviations," referring to the changes made by the order. The motion for a supportive resolution lost by one vote.

In August 1969, conference president Anita Caspary—formerly Mother Mary Humiliata, who had been the IHM mother general since 1963—went to Rome to petition Pope Paul VI to consider the community "a new form of religious life." She was met with silence. "We worked hard to stay within the church structure, but apparently they felt there was no place for us," said Sister Helen Kelley, now president of Immaculate Heart College. "We thought we were the best qualified to make judgments about our lives, and we thought that was the message of the Vatican Council. But they didn't like it."[32]

In December 1969, more than three hundred Immaculate Heart nuns voted to become a noncanonical community, freeing themselves from Rome's control.[33] "The change gave us the freedom to be self-determining and to make more choices on the basis of conscience without leaning on the authority of others," Caspary said. "This is the same struggle for feminist values that continues for women in all walks of life today, especially for women in the church."[34] The sisters were following the directives of Vatican II, but their efforts were squelched by a hierarchy fearful of powerful women. Fear destroyed a religious community.

Two years later, in Raleigh, North Carolina, a bishop ordered the sisters within his diocese to stop wearing secular clothing, which prompted eight teaching nuns to resign. He also suggested that experiments with secular dress had resulted in serious abuses and some scandal in the diocese. One of the women who resigned, Sister Grace, responded: "We're sorry to be leaving. If things work out, we would like to come back. But only if the bishop changes his mind or we get a new bishop."[35]

The decision of many women religious to wear "civilian clothes" was driven by their profound desire to be part of the communities they serve.[36] This unveiling allowed the sisters to develop a closer connection with the women, children, and men they serve. They had never embraced the medieval concept of a religious life separate from the world, so these changes enabled the women to live out their charisms (gifts freely and graciously given by God) in full.

Adopting modern clothing demystified the often mysterious presence, allowing outsiders to see the actual woman behind the habit, thus allowing for more personal interaction whereby a sister could express and experience the wholeness of her humanity. In her book, *Guests in Their Own House: The Women of Vatican II,* Carmel McEnroy, who was present at the Vatican II sessions, underscored this point.

> A challenge was to get past the idea of a "good sister" who looked like an adult doll in the dress of another age. It was difficult to discover the real person of the individual sister and take her seriously when she was seen in the mass-produced habit that suggested she was a carbon copy of all her other dressalikes, leaving her little personal identity beyond "one of the sisters."[37]

The syncretic events—Vatican II, the second wave of feminism, and the civil rights movement—offered hope to many Catholics and non-Catholics alike. Vatican II empowered women religious to share the power and authority innate within the spiritual life. For most women religious, the struggle is lifelong: the hidebound patriarchy within the Church continues to manifest through systems of male-domination. When asked why she didn't leave the Roman Catholic Church for a more progressive church, Sister Mary Swain replied, "Because it's my church too."[38] Post Vatican II, there has been a proliferation of Roman Catholic feminist scholars: Rosemary Radford Ruether, Elizabeth Schussler Fioernza, Mary Luke Tobin, Elizabeth Johnson, and Sandra Schneiders, to name a few. Many women religious are actively involved in the peace, feminist, and civil rights movements.

Nevertheless, not all women religious were pleased with the Vatican

II attempts to modernize. A number of congregations felt betrayed by the actions of the council. For them, "the veil as a source of identity points to the very heart of religious life."[39] Even women who are already nuns have been known to change orders and move across the country in order to join a convent that adheres more strictly to traditions and the wearing of habits.[40]

The Council of Major Superiors of Women Religious describes the habit as a symbol, which "reminds the consecrated religious of their 'habit of being,' their mystery and mission. It proclaims to people: 'I am set apart, I am here for you.' When they see us, they should see Christ." The council explains, "The habit and veil witness to the world that we know ourselves at once both to have been chosen by the One and that we have chosen the One—that Jesus Christ is truly our spouse and that we know we are not alone in this consecration."[41] The directives of Vatican II did not do away with the habit; it simply asked the religious to be actively mindful and prayerful regarding the style of habit. Women who take the veil do so as an intentional act of devotion and commitment to Christ.

Currently, there are an increasing number of women joining orders in full habit. While the national numbers show a decrease in religious vocations, Mother Regina Pacis, provincial superior of the Sisters of St. Francis of the Martyr St. George, reports that orders "such as the Dominican Sisters of St. Cecilia of Nashville, the Sisters of Life, the Sisters of Mary Mother of the Eucharist, the Missionaries of Charity, and the Carmelite Sisters of the Most Sacred Heart of Los Angeles (among many others) have been experiencing tremendous growth in their communities."[42]

Sister Mary Emily, vocation director of the Dominicans of Nashville, said her order has nearly doubled in the last ten years, seeing more than one hundred new vocations in that period. Not only that, but there are currently an additional eighty women in formation, with an average of fifteen entering each year. Her community's median age is now thirty-six and the average age of those women entering is twenty-four.[43] Conservative orders where old traditions are emphasized are the only ones seeing real growth in membership and a decline in the average age of members.

Parallel trends in Protestant churches have brought a significant number of women and men flocking to the conservative megachurches,[44] which also have a strong sense of conformity and commitment to a specific set of ideals. According to the most recent report of the National Council of Churches for 2004, mainline Protestant denominations continue to experience a decline in membership.[45] Clearly, both the Roman Catholic Church and Protestant denominations are reflecting similar trends based on the shared culture within the United States.

But in the years following Vatican II, women removed the veil and refused to be defined according to tradition, clothing, and the institution. With the fresh air of Vatican II, they could now be "known as nuns by the way they talked and acted."[46]

NOTES

1. I use "unveiled" to distinguish those women religious who choose to dress in "civilian" clothing from those who continue to wear the traditional habit. Sr. Vicky (a pseudonym) and I were participants in the summer Clinical Pastoral Education program in a Catholic Hospital in 1986. She was exploring her call as a hospital chaplain.

2. Mary Luke Tobin, SL, *Hope Is an Open Door* (Nashville: Abingdon, 1981), 17.

3. Pope John XXIII's opening address to the council, October 11, 1962, www .churchdocs.org/vaticanII/j23open.html (accessed November 3, 2006). Pope John XXIII died June 3, 1963.

4. Quoted in Tobin, *Hope*,18.

5. "A Mind of Its Own," *Time*, November 3, 1964, www.time.com/time/mag zine/article/0,9171,830822,00.html.

6. Tobin, *Hope*, 28.

7. Michael Novak, *The New Nuns* (New York: New American Library, 1967), 18.

8. Joan D. Chittister, "No Time for Tying Cats," in *Midwives of the Future* (Kansas City: Leaven Press, 1985), 6.

9. "Decree on the Adaptation and Renewal of Religious Life" (Perfectae Caritatis), proclaimed by Pope Paul VI on October 28, 1965, sec. 17 www.vatican.va/archive/hist_councils/ii_vatican_council/documents/vat ii_decree _19651028_perfectae-caritatis_en.html (accessed November 3, 2006).

10. Elizabeth Kuhns, *The Habit: A History of the Clothing of Catholic Nuns* (New York: Doubleday, 2003), 151.

11. In the work of Carl Jung and Joseph Campbell, the power and role of symbols within religious expression are discussed extensively.

12. "Decree on the Adaptation," sec. 1.

13. 1 Corinthians 11:2–10 (NRSV). Paul probably wrote 1 Corinthians on his third missionary journey between 54 and 58 C.E. Bruce Metzger, *The New Testament* (Nashville: Abingdon Press, 1965), 180.

14. Galatians 3:28–29. "There is no longer Jew or Greek, there is no longer slave or free, there is no longer male and female; for all of you are one in Christ Jesus. And if you belong to Christ, then you are Abraham's offspring, heirs according to the promise." Paul probably wrote Galatians on his second missionary journey between 49 and 53 C.E. Metzger, *New Testament*, 180.

15. Karen Jo Torjesen, *When Women Were Priests* ([San Francisco]: HarperSanFrancisco, 1993), 45.

16. Tertullian, chap. 16, "Having Shown His Defence to be Consistent with Nature, and Discipline, Appeals to the virgins themselves," *On the Veiling of Virgins*, www.newadvent.org/fathers/0403 (accessed November 10, 2006).

17. Rule of Benedict, chap. 55, "On the Clothes and Shoes of the Brethren," www.osb.org/rb/text/rbeaad1.html#55 (accessed November 10, 2006).

18. Evangeline Thomas, ed., *Women Religious History Sources: A Guide to Repositories in the United States* (New York: R. R. Bowker, 1983), xxv.

19. J. Waterworth, ed. and trans., *The Canons and Decrees of the Sacred and Ecumenical Council of Trent* (London: Dolman, 1848), 25th session, http://history.hanover.edu/texts/trent/ct25.html (accessed November 4, 2006).

20. Kuhns, *The Habit*, 106.

21. Kuhns, *The Habit*, 110, 125.

22. Kuhns, *The Habit*, 127, 128.

23. Canon 1262, sec. 2: "Men should attend Mass, either in church or outside church, with bare heads, unless approved local custom or special circumstances suggest otherwise; women, however, should have their heads veiled and should be modestly dressed, especially when they approach the table of the Lord"; sec. 1: "It is desirable that, in harmony with ancient Church order, the women in church be separated from the men." The Code of Canon Law, 1917, www.womenpriests.org/traditio/cod_1917.asp#veiled (accessed November 10, 2006).

24. Canon 1342, sec. 2: "All lay people are forbidden to preach in church, even if they belong to religious congregations."

25. Tobin, *Hope*, 27.

26. Jeanne Reidy, "Nuns in Ordinary Clothes," in *The New Nuns* (New York: New American Library, 1967), 58.

27. Reidy, "Nuns," 5.

28. Reidy, "Nuns."

29. Kuhns, *The Habit*, 156.

30. Kenneth Briggs, *Double Crossed: Uncovering the Catholic Church's Betrayal of American Nuns* (New York: Doubleday, 2006), 93.

31. Originally founded in 1956 as the Conference of Major Superiors of Women (CMSW), the organization received canonical status in 1959. The organization changed its name to the Leadership Conference of Women Religious in 1971. Members of LCWR are Catholic women religious who are leaders of their orders in the United States. The conference has approximately 1,000 members, who represent about 95 percent of the 71,000 women religious in the United States (LCWR Web site).

    With the name Consortium Perfectae Caritatis, a splinter group of CMSW formed as a result of its concerns that the newly named LCWR deviated from "authentic" church teaching about the essentials of religious life. This group eventually began the present-day Council of Major Superiors of Women Religious (CMSWR), a canonically approved organization. Its statutes were definitively approved by the Vatican Congregation for Institutes of Consecrated Life and Societies of Apostolic Life on October 26, 1995 (CMSWR Web site).

32. Steven Roberts, "Coast Nuns Plan a Secular Order," *New York Times*, February 2, 1970.

33. Dorothy Vidulich, "'Radical' IHMs pioneered Religious Community," *National Catholic Reporter*, June 6, 1995.

34. Vidulich, "Radical."

35. "'Carolina bishop challenged by nuns,' Ban on Secular Clothing Provokes Resignations," *New York Times*, September 5, 1971.

36. Personal conversations with Mary Fran Lottes, SL, and Mary Swain, SL, 1998–2006.

37. Kuhns, *The Habit*, 143.

38. Personal conversation at the Loretto motherhouse, Kentucky, June 2003.

39. "Reflections on Habit and Veil by the Sisters of St. Francis of the Immaculate Heart of Mary," Council of Major Superiors of Women Religious, www.cmswr.org/habit_and_veil/cmswr_habit_and_veil.htm.

40. Cheryl Reed, *Unveiled: The Hidden Lives of Nuns* (New York: Berkley Publishing Press, 2004), 98.

41. "Reflections on Habit and Veil."

42. "Solution to reported 'nun' crisis not just financial but also spiritual," *Catholic News Agency*, July 28, 2006.

43. "Solution."

44. "In 1970, there were just ten such churches," says John Vaughn, founder of Church Growth Today, which tracks megachurches. "In 2003, there are 740. The average number of worshippers is 3,646, up 4% from last year." Luis Kroll, "Megachurches, Megabusinesses," *Forbes*, September 17, 2003, www.forbes.com/2003/09/17/cz_lk_0917megachurch.html.

45.   "Evangelical Lutheran Church in America, down 1.05%, Presbyterian Church (USA) down 4.87%, American Baptist Churches (USA) down 3.45% and the United Church of Christ, down 2.85%, for a total decline of 7.4%." National Council of Churches report, 2004, www.usatoday.com/news/religion/ 2006–10–31-protestant-cover_x.htm (accessed October 31, 2006).

46.   Reidy, "Nuns," 57.

REFERENCES

Borromeo, Sr. Charles, ed. *The New Nuns.* New York: New American Library, 1967.

Briggs, Kenneth. *Double Crossed: Uncovering the Catholic Church's Betrayal of American Nuns,* New York: Doubleday, 2006.

Coburn, Carol K., and Martha Smith. *Spirited Lives: How Nuns Shaped Catholic Culture and American Life, 1836–1920.* Chapel Hill: University of North Carolina Press, 1999.

Ebaugh, Helen Rose Fuchs. *Women in the Vanishing Cloister: Organizational Decline in the Catholic Religious Orders in the United States.* New Brunswick, NJ: Rutgers University Press, 1993.

Kuhns, Elizabeth. *The Habit: A History of the Clothing of Catholic Nuns.* New York: Doubleday, 2003.

McNamara, Jo Ann Kay. *Sisters in Arms: Catholic Nuns through Two Millennia.* Cambridge, MA: Harvard University Press, 1996.

Metzger, Bruce. *The New Testament.* Nashville: Abingdon Press, 1965.

Reed, Cheryl. *Unveiled: The Hidden Lives of Nuns.* New York: Berkley Publishing Press, 2004.

Thomas, Sr. Evangeline, ed. *Women Religious History Sources: A Guide to Repositories in the United States.* New York: R. R. Bowker, 1983.

Tobin, Sr. Mary Luke. *Hope Is an Open Door.* Nashville: Abingdon, 1981.

Torjesen, Karen Jo. *When Women Were Priests.* [San Francisco]: HarperSan Francisco, 1993.

Ware, Ann Patrick, ed. *Midwives of the Future: American Sisters Tell Their Story.* Kansas City: Leaven Press, 1985.

———. *Naming Our Truth: Stories of Loretto Women.* Inverness, CA: Chardon Press, 1995.

Weaver, Mary Jo. *New Catholic Women.* Bloomington: Indiana University Press, 1995.

5   The Amish Veil

Symbol of Separation and Community

JANA M. HAWLEY

In June 1991, I packed a U-Haul truck with my personal belongings and my ten- and eleven-year-old boys and moved to Jamesport, Missouri, to do a year of participant observation research living among the Old Order Amish. It was perhaps the most peaceful, reflective, and revealing year of our lives and resulted in lifelong friendships with several Amish friends with whom I remain in contact to this day.

When we live with a group of people outside our own culture for an extended period of time, we learn all kinds of things about that group. Although my research question had to do with business practices, I learned and have since written about many other aspects of Amish life.

In order to facilitate acceptance with the Amish, I adjusted my normal appearance, foregoing makeup and jeans, and adopting plain skirts and blouses. Because I grew up on a Kansas farm, I was given a measure of legitimacy that gained me quicker access. Shortly after I arrived, I found myself helping my new Amish friends make bread in a wood-burning oven, wash clothes in a diesel-powered washing machine, make candy on a kerosene stove and cider on an oak handpress, feed horses, work in an Amish-owned store, and quilt with women on several quilting projects. I drove thousands of miles (55,000 in one year!) as a "taxi" driver for the Amish who hired me to take them places—including Christmas shopping in Kansas City.

By the end of the year, I had attended Amish birthday parties, church services, auctions, weddings, "singings," volleyball games, work bees, quilt frolics, hospital visits, barn raisings, and a multitude of more routine daily chores. I gained a great respect for the Amish, a remarkable degree of acceptance, and a profound understanding of their worldview, social structure, and level of technology.

The Amish are a large Christian-based group whose core values focus on separateness from the world and commitment to tradition, family, and community. These values have set them apart from the rest of the world, making them a curiosity for many Americans, and this curiosity has caused the media to make them the subject of movies, news stories, and even reality TV.

The Amish are a permutation of the sixteenth-century Swiss Anabaptist movement that was part of the Protestant Reformation in Switzerland, Germany, and France. They believe that church and state should be separate and that the final authority for Christianity is the scripture. They were often violently persecuted in Europe and escaped to North America in the late 1600s to settle in William Penn's religious freedom area near Lancaster, Pennsylvania. Since then, they have migrated to other rural areas throughout the continent, primarily Ohio, Indiana, Missouri, and Iowa. The Amish migrate for two primary reasons: schisms among the members regarding orthodoxy/progressiveness; and the search for viable farmland away from congested urban encroachment so that agrarian integrity can be maintained. Today many of the midwestern Amish have little social or ideological connection with the Pennsylvania Amish and as a result, distinct differences have evolved.

Despite predictions, the Amish have not assimilated into the dominant American culture, nor has their population become smaller over the years. Instead, their large family sizes and relatively small attrition has resulted in a population growth that has gone from more or less 6,000 in 1900 to approximately 200,000 today.

Amish often refer to themselves as *plain*. Their primary tenets of faith include rejection of violence, submission of the individual members to the authority of the Amish community, development of self-sustaining agricultural lifestyle in a commitment of stewardship of the land, refusal of infant baptism, and independence of the Amish church from the authority of the state.[1]

The Old Order Amish are located in rural communities throughout North and Central America. Each Amish community is unique with its own set of rules called the *Ordnung* (pronounced ott-ning). Outsiders have difficulty understanding why Amish from some communities might use a tractor engine mounted on a flatbed wagon to power the farm equipment and facilitate the workload, while another Amish community strictly enforces the use of only horse-drawn power. Yet another Amish community might allow a transistor radio in the barn while other communities strictly forbid any radios. These variances reflect community-specific rules of the Ordnung and result in a continuum of orthodox Amish (Old Order) on one end and progressive Amish (Beechy Amish) on the other. The Amish often compare their own districts to others as "higher" or "lower." It is these varying rules that also explain variations in Amish dress (figure 5.1).

Regardless of community-specific details of the Ordnung, the values that rule daily life of the Amish include modesty and stewardship toward personal property and self; sharing of wealth through an intricate system of mutual aid; a dedicated work ethic that focuses on farm life; and a commitment to thrift.[2] Through dress, lifestyle, horse and buggy culture, language, appearance, and technological simplicity, the Amish have established a determined boundary that keeps them separate from the world so that they can more carefully manage their social control and therefore their existence.

For most Amish, clothing represents several dimensions of their cultural values, including nonconformity to the broader culture, humility, modesty,

Figure 5.1. Drawing of Amish prayer coverings. Whether the caps are tied at the chin or allowed to fall loose depends upon levels of orthodoxy: *left,* a woman from a lower (more orthodox) church community; *right,* someone from a higher (more progressive) community. Drawing by Megan Brusca.

utility, and group conformity. Although the relative orthodoxy of Amish dress varies from one community to another and results in what outsiders see as a confusing breadth of acceptance for Amish dress, Amish clothing has remained relatively unchanged for nearly a century. For men in the Old Order Amish, clothing consists of broadfall pants with suspenders, high shoes, and no zippers. The male hat is a shallow-crowned straw for the summer and for work, and felt for the winter and for Sundays. Vests and Sunday apparel use hooks and eyes and no buttons because buttons are seen as prideful. Dress for Old Order women consists of a white prayer cap made of organza, a black bonnet, a shawl, cape, apron, black stockings, and a dress. The long dress, apron, and shawl are intended to conceal the body, and the bonnet to follow the biblical notion of "shamefacedness."

Across time, some changes in dress have occurred, but very few. Over the past century, shoes, eyeglasses, and head scarves have been introduced for workdays. Amish clothing has evolved as outsiders interact with them and as members of other Amish communities visit from other states. Just as in mainstream America, change usually occurs from those who are leaders, or in the case of the Amish, "on the edge." For the Amish, change often comes through the young people during *rumspringa,* an institutionalized period of experimentation during adolescence, or by marginalized Amish who are often found breaking the rules.

Similar to technological differences within communities, Amish dress also varies by community and is based on the Ordnung rules. For example, some Amish communities require that Amish women use straight pins to close their dresses while other Amish communities use snaps for dress closures. When I lived in Jamesport, a young girl was visiting from an Amish community in Indiana where snaps were used to close the dresses. In Jamesport, straight pins were used. Concern from the elders immediately was raised because young Jamesport girls were seen trying to "get by" sewing snaps onto their dresses. A special meeting was held and the girl from Indiana was told that if she did not remove all the snaps from her dresses and start using straight pins like the other girls in Jamesport, she would have to return to Indiana. This is one example of how social control is exerted. While she was in Jamesport, the Indiana girl removed the snaps from her dresses, but she stayed on only a few months because she decided Jamesport was too strict.

In some Amish communities, women are required to wear black shoes. In other communities sneakers are allowed except on Sundays. Some Amish men are permitted a $3\frac{1}{2}$-inch brim on their hats while for others, hat brims are only $2\frac{3}{4}$ inches wide. These subtle but community-specific rules are controlled by the Ordnung and parallel the rest of the community's relative level of progressiveness.

Amish dress serves as both a separator and identifier. As a primary tenet, the Amish strive to be separate from the world and believe that appearance serves as a constant reminder of their beliefs. They also believe that the Church, rather than fashion designers and business owners, should control identity. Furthermore, the fashion system's notion of planned obsolescence contributes to waste rather than thrift, another tenet of the Amish belief system.

Amish dress acts as a form of boundary maintenance and contributes to notions of community and belonging. Members of the same community are easily recognizable from within the group, though outsiders may not notice the subtle differences of one Amish group from another. During my research year, I attended a horse auction with some of my Amish friends. In the center of the arena was a young Amish boy and I asked my friend whether he was from Jamesport. My friend said, "No, can't you tell by his hat? The brim is much smaller!" To me, the hat looked the same, but to my Amish friend, an insider, there was an obvious difference.

Once, I drove some Amish friends to a wedding in Iowa, and when everyone went indoors for dinner, all the men took off their straw hats and threw them under the same tree. There must have been at least a hundred straw hats under that tree. How will they ever know which hat belongs to whom when they come out? I thought. To me, they all looked alike. Yet after dinner, each man easily found his own hat from under the tree as if each were a different color!

These stories illustrate how outsiders lack the understanding of the subtle differences in community identifiers, while insiders fully comprehend who belongs to which community by simply *reading* the dress cues.

Amish, both men and women, cling to head coverings as part of their Amish convictions. And while it is true that Amish clothing customs are steeped in religious leanings and traditions from the Bible, after a year of living among the Amish I am convinced that for many Amish, several of their customs derive more from deep-seeded convictions of what it means to be culturally Amish than from religious conviction. I believe that if you asked most Amish women why they wear prayer caps, they would say that it is because, "that's what Amish do" rather than cite some religious principle.

The Amish belief system is Christian-based and as such, their head coverings stem from 1 Corinthians 11, which dictates that men should have their heads uncovered for prayer, but that women should cover their heads at all times even when they are not praying. There are primarily two reasons for this belief: submission to God and to man; and because the Bible says women are to "pray without ceasing." Hair is also discussed in this passage, which makes clear that men's hair should be short and women's should be long.

Head covering is usually worn across the range of Anabaptist groups

(Amish, Baptists, Brethren, Hutterites, Mennonites, Bruderhof Communities, and Quakers). For Amish women, the prayer cap is made of white Swiss organza and must always be worn in public. The style of the prayer cap and how it is worn depends on the orthodoxy of the Amish community. In low churches, the prayer cap strings are tied tighter under the chin and have less starch and therefore form. In progressive or high communities, the cap strings are not tied at all (or are nonexistent), and the cap is highly formed with heavy starch.

In Jamesport, the level of orthodoxy fell somewhere in the middle but tilted slightly toward the higher end of the continuum. The women's prayer caps had a medium starch and the strings for the married women were joined in a bow tied low away from the chin. For the teenage girls, the strings were not tied at all and they often used the strings as a tool to toss when flirting with the boys. The amount of starch used to keep the shape in Jamesport was *medium*.

I once took a family to a wedding in Iowa. On the way home, the teenage daughter pouted to her mother in the car because she wanted a cap shaped like her Iowan cousin's cap. Her mother argued, "a cap like that, with all that starch, shows way too much pride. The church elders would have a fit." But the daughter rebutted that the Iowa caps were so much more modern and stylish and that it wasn't fair that she couldn't have one too! "I think I'll just move to Iowa," she said.

Amish women are not supposed to cut their hair, but during rumspringa the young girls will often cut bangs so that when they are wearing their non-Amish clothes they appear more "stylish." When they revert to Amish clothes, they pull their bangs back with bobby pins hidden under their prayer caps and hope the church elders don't see them. One group of girls was admonished by their mothers to tuck their bobby pins in better because they were showing and surely the bishop would see them at the gathering that was about to take place! There are constant checks and balances to control appearances: young Amish girls were not supposed to cut their hair, but because they had, mothers stepped in to help control the situation as best they could.

In the Jamesport dry goods stores, stacks of bandana squares in a plethora of colors are merchandised to match the fabrics used in women's dresses. Amish women, particularly unmarried girls and younger women, use the bandanas as head coverings when they are working. Usually they match or color coordinate with their dresses, which explains the wide range of colors available in the stores. I overheard one group of young Amish girls talking—in tones as ordinary as any teenager in a mall—about the need to shop in order to buy head scarves to match the new work dresses that they had made.

In years past, most Amish women made their own prayer coverings and bonnets, but today each community has a seamstress who makes her living sewing head coverings for the women of the community. In addition, there are several Web sites that feature a wide variety of religious head coverings for all Anabaptist groups. Although the Internet might seem an odd medium for marketing to a culture that does not use electricity, in Jamesport the Amish have access to computers through their non-Amish friends in the downtown business community or at the local library. They do not often use the computer, but they are aware of sites such as the one that sells prayer caps and it would not be uncommon for them to order through their local library. The Amish learn of these Web sites by word of mouth and through the two nationally distributed Amish newspapers, *Die Botschaft* and *The Budget*.

Children are acculturated to the wearing of the veil from a very young age. At about four, they begin dressing just like their adult counterparts, including the head covering. From fourteen until marriage, however, girls wear a black prayer cap during Sunday service. This indicates that the teenagers are in their cohort rumspringa years and also that they are available for courtship.

Amish tenets expect Amish women to have their heads covered in public at all times. But there exists a public/private notion of place when it comes to covering the head. Once a very close level of friendship is established, an Amish woman may allow herself to be seen by a non-Amish female friend without her head covering when in a private place. This happened on several occasions between me and a couple of women who became my close friends in Jamesport. But it is rare and occurred only after a certain degree of trust had been established.

Married Amish women are supposed to wear the black bonnet over the prayer cap when in public, but they often do not. The bonnets are hot and cumbersome. Occasionally church hierarchy puts its foot down and decides to enforce the rules. During this social enforcement period, the women will be seen wearing their bonnets more often—or at least carrying them, so that if they spot a church elder they can quickly revert.

Both regional differences and levels of orthodoxy occur in the prayer cap and the bonnet. Not only does it depend on how high or low the community is, but also on whether the community is Midwest Amish or Pennsylvania or Ohio Amish. Unique differences abound for each region.

The history of Amish clothing is hard to establish. Some of it goes back to European peasantry, some to early American colonial times. Some can be traced to rural America and some embraces cultural canons of separatism, humility, and avoidance of fashion. Over the years little has evolved, but change undoubtedly *does* occur.

Amish continue to draw appeal from outsiders in part because of their amazing resistance to modernization as they maintain their cultural traditions. For those of us who belong to a lifestyle that seems too busy, too laden with e-mails and annoying cell phone tones, their nostalgic lifestyle has appeal. My year among the Amish in Jamesport was one of the most peaceful and enjoyable of my life. I teach fashion merchandising at a major university and to know me, and my "fashionable" lifestyle, you would not think that I could escape to a year of plain living. Among other things, I now understand that for the Amish, dress is an index of their commitment. They succeed when their dress communicates that they are loyal, humble, conforming, thrifty, and faithful. Ironically, both the Amish and I use dress as a way to integrate with and separate from our environments.

NOTES

1. John A. Hostetler, *Amish Society* (Baltimore: Johns Hopkins University Press, 1993).
2. Jana M. Hawley, "The Commercialization of Old Order Amish Quilts: Enduring and Changing Cultural Meaning," *Clothing and Textiles Research Journal* 23, no. 2 (2005): 102–14.

6 "What is subordinated, dominates"

Mourning, Magic, Masks, and Male Veiling

JENNIFER HEATH

For Nita Hill and Susan Edwards

In February, just before Lent, we drive from La Paz to Oruro. Uncle Luis switches on the embassy car siren to startle the crowds walking along the steep roads to carnaval. Their goods and babies are carried in vibrant woven cloths strapped across their backs. The women sport brown derbies or white top hats and layers of immense, brightly colored skirts that spin like tops. Daddy bawls Luis out, but the Quechua, Aymara, and Uru folk trudge on, laughing and waving, toasting us with bottles of beer and chicha. *Everyone's got the spirit . . . and the spirits.*

In Bolivia, there are many fiestas throughout the year and we attend them all. Even our street is called Seis de Agosto, after the day when the Virgin of Snows is honored with a dance heralding the sowing of potatoes. But of all Bolivia's dancing celebrations the one in Oruro is the most famous. Oruro is the home of the Diablada (figure 6.1).

The dancers leap and whirl to the vibrating, high-pitched tunes of Altiplano flutes, strings, and drums. The devils' gargantuan plaster heads are painted searing scarlet, emerald, and gold, ears fanned like flames, rippled noses with cav-

Figure 6.1.   A devil dancer in Oruro, Bolivia, ca. 1943.
Photographed by the author's late mother. Courtesy
of Jennifer Heath.

*ernous nostrils on puckered, evilly wrinkled faces. Their eyes bulge. Their glassy
fangs are razor sharp. The monsters wear crowns of grinning reptiles riding between their horns. These are not strictly Christian* diablos. *They originate with
Wari, a giant Andean god of the Urus, who lived, before the coming of the con-
quistadors, with lizards, serpents, and toads inside the mountains of Uru-Uru.
The memory of Wari mingles with the spirit of Supay, a malevolent trickster, who
frequented mines and caves and liked to baffle the people by distracting them from
their proper worship of Pachamama, mother earth.*

(I long to dress up as China Supay, his female counterpart, and prance like the big girls in pretty skirts, some wearing beautiful gringa masks, peach and pale.)

Across colonial time, Supay and Wari have morphed into Tío, protector of llamas, cows, donkeys, and long-exploited miners. Earlier today, the miners decorated the seated figure of Tío, who guards the excavation with his giant erection. They offered him liquor and sacrificed a llama.

Now diablos, China Supays, and a hundred Seven Deadly Sins swirl through the plaza. Flirting, menacing, and laughing, they are only yards from the church door when angels burst onto the scene, led by the Archangel Michael himself. They fight ferociously, with swords and fancy footwork, for this is a battle between darkness and light, good and evil, past and present.

Kusillus, *clowns with red cloth faces, part monkey, part imp, grab my mother, then me, from the crowd. Now we are part of a masquerade that infiltrates a history veiled by falsities—the European victor's version of the tale. It is "a celebration of rebellion. Time stops. The community abandons the alien logic of daily events and lives at its own rhythm: the eternal mythic present where past heroic ages converge with a utopian future. . . . What is subordinated, dominates."*[1]

Workers parade with picks and shovels, emblems of their unions. The Ch'utas— *Indians from La Paz—turn up wearing masks of wire screen with pink cotton linings, beards of silk tassels, eyebrows made of rickrack and button ornaments. (Years later, in the 1980s, I will be reminded of the Ch'utas when I visit Nicaragua during the Sandinista triumph. Students by day, the rebels donned wire masks much like these to take up arms at night against the Somoza dynasty and the upholders of banana republicanism.)*[2]

Round one goes to Lucifer. The dancing battle continues toward the church door. In Oruro at carnaval, the indios *reel through the thin haze of Christianity back to their ancient gods and places.*

Round two belongs to Archangel Michael. The frenetic mystery play ends. The dancers, still dressed in costume, and the onlookers, still dazed by the journey, pile into Mass. Lucifer, his minions, the Chinas, the angels, my mother and father, and Uncle Luis all kneel.

The priest unveils the sacred vessel that contains the Host.

My mother had a vast mask collection. They were shaped from every imaginable material and bore every imaginable facial expression. They ranged from debonair types with twiddly mustaches—like Uncle Luis—to Japanese Noh drama characters. There were tigers, jaguars, frogs, and monkeys. Some masks were funny, some teasing, some sinister. Some were frightening with streaming, matted goat hair or mocking tongues and bulbous bloodshot eyes. There were cloth masks too, and folded into a carved Chinese trunk with an assortment of ethnic clothing and headgear were a variety of veils: among them an Afghan *chadri,* a Saudi *abaya,* an Omani *batula,* a Palestinian *kufiyya.*

I was a solitary child, wrenched from pillar to post by diplomatic life, with only my imagination to keep me steady company. The masks were my dear friends and companions. I talked to them, sang to them, and occasionally, I was allowed to take one from the shelf, hold it to my face, and look in the mirror.

To see myself transformed was thrilling and scary. Young as I was, I understood—dimly—that masks are lenses for peering into the spiritual unknown and that one of their jobs is to unlock the door that separates the daily from the divine. In all human societies, masks play an essential part in rites of passage and renewal, as decoys or disguises, for blessings and fertility, in drama, and more. They perform in the borders between so-called reality—*this* world—and the supernatural—*that* world. As scholars have long noted, masks are instruments for metamorphosis or hierophany.

Now and again, I was also allowed to try on the veils. It seemed their function and effect frequently overlapped with that of the masks.

Simulacrum and concealment, protection and belligerence, nature and antinature, lament and celebration, men and women—these and other alliances of symbol and actuality constitute a complex labyrinth of the meanings of masks and veils. There is a dizzying array of mask-and-veil practices and associated lore to consider. To write briefly about where they intersect and collide is a little like driving bumper cars on the Los Angeles freeway.

The uses of masks and veils are diverse and impossible to generalize.[3] Their actions—and the *re*actions to them—differ widely, yet there are some basic shared tendencies we can perceive repeatedly. "In order for masking to have meaning and relevance, it needs an audience, a minimum of one observer."[4] The veil, in contrast, can be about imperceptibility and can be used to render the wearer, or the audience, invisible. Nevertheless, the veil—as modern geopolitics shows—is also its own theater.

Both ideas originate in nature. Surely our first inklings of veiling emerged from observing the fog, the snow, the cloud-obscured moon, eclipses, reflections in water, and half-visible elements that conceal spirits more powerful than our helpless human selves. And nature's enigmas must have deepened, for instance, with the birth of a child veiled by the caul (occasionally, though rarely, called a mask), a portion of the membrane that remains over the face of a fetus. From time immemorial it's been thought that the caul bearer is exceptional. In the West, she is considered not only fortunate and destined for greatness but has powers of divination, "the sight."

Masking, too, may have been learned by observing nature. "Frogs and reptiles [are] major players in traditional mythology and they strongly convey the masking aspect of nature" as they transform from tadpoles or shed their skins. Things in nature frequently seem to be other than they are. "Early humans might have seen an animal's changing exterior to be masking some invisible mystery of regeneration within."[5]

In some cases, masking is employed to reintegrate us with nature, and in others it is a method of guarding against the terrifying unknown wilderness beyond our control. "When we compare a shaman's mask and an astronaut's helmet, we find they are not so dissimilar if we understand them both as protective armor."[6] The same has been true of the veil when it is worn as a shield against the unknown, whether tangible—as during colonialist aggression—or mystical—as before the divine presence.

Veils are commonly associated with women and assumed to be made of cloth (often romantically sheer), whereas masks—wearing and dancing in them—are largely a male occupation (even when the masks represent women) and are generally representations of beings, typically decorated with pigment and/or objects thought to be sacred (and that become collectible art objects when removed from their native environments). Masks and veils are not necessarily restricted to facial coverings but may encase the entire body.

The patriarchal view holds that men are envoys of "culture," while women are closer to "nature." The Greeks considered female genitals to be mysterious and hidden and therefore women were destined, *designed*, for internal activities requiring they be removed from public gaze. With some exceptions (such as the Bolivian China Supay maskers), "men have dominated masking practices . . . drumming, masking, and sacrifice. . . . Underlying this monopoly is the apparent male need to symbolically and culturally control fertility for the group and society."[7] Among the Ebira in Nigeria, "contemporary opinion has it that 'God made things double: masquerading for men and witchcraft for women.'"[8] Witchcraft is an often secretive art, practiced in the shadows.

In studies today about veiling among women—usually limited to Islam and discussions about oppression—male veiling is overlooked. "Men's veiling, an ethnographic fact, becomes an anomaly, particularly against the common misunderstanding that only women veil."[9] Masking can be a form of male veiling. In men's secret societies, the mask hides and protects the mysteries, with much the same effect as the veil, which segregates women from men in numerous cultures. The chadri or *burqa* with only crocheted eyeholes worn by Afghan women and the exquisite Omani batulas (also called *burgu*) of burnished indigo that resemble ancient Greek helmets might be masks. Conversely, the satin hoods, usually referred to as masks, worn by Spanish male penitents, might be veils. Depending on how they are employed, masks and veils are instruments of separation (e.g., during funerals or secret rites) or incorporation (e.g., during weddings or fertility rites).[10]

The first masks, if not mud or suet smeared on the face, were likely to have been cloths. A Samoyed shaman covers his face in order to aid concentration. "Among the Tadibei Samoyed, the shaman blindfolds his eyes [with a kerchief] so that he can enter the spirit world by his own inner light." What's more, the head must always be wrapped in cloth, "otherwise it is impossible to shamanize."[11]

Ancient Greek and Roman men did not regularly sport headgear, but in the act of sacrifice they veiled with the borders of their *palla* (cloaks) or togas.[12] The official headgear of a Roman *flamen* (priest) looked like an aviator's cap with a chin strap, called *apex*.[13] Without it, the duties of priesthood could not be conducted, nor would these men be recognized as members of the priestly—and patrician—class.

At Delphi in ancient Greece, the masked oracle, the Pythia, sat in a cave veiled by gases rising from a cleft in the ground. The message itself was cloaked in riddles. "The truth occurred in the listener listening. When people were 'misled,' it was not by the falsity of the oracle, but by the poorness of their own listening."[14]

The Greek mathematician Pythagoras (ca. 580 to 507 B.C.E.) spoke of two grades of initiates: those-who-listen and those-who-learn. Listeners were made to sit behind a veil. Throughout history, countless traditions have dictated that students and/or worshipers situate themselves behind a curtain to better absorb the message. "'With reference to the veil,' Plutarch inquired, 'why do people veil their heads when worshipping the gods?' The answer is simple: to separate themselves from the profane and to live only in the sacred world, for seeing is itself a form of contact."[15]

This is illustrated in Nathaniel Hawthorne's 1836 story, "The Minister's Black Veil," in which Mr. Hooper, an ordinary New England parson, appears one Sunday before his scandalized congregation wearing a cloth over his face. "While he prayed, the veil lay heavily on his uplifted countenance. Did he seek to hide it from the dread Being whom he was addressing?" Hooper refuses to remove the veil and confronts fear wherever he goes. But no amount of loathing or pleading can persuade him to remove it. Even the woman he loves is denied:

> This veil . . . is a type and symbol, and I am bound to wear it ever, both in light and darkness, in solitude and before the gaze of multitudes, and as with strangers, so with my familiar friends. No mortal eye will see it withdrawn. This dismal shade must separate me from the world: even you, Elizabeth, can never come behind it.

Hooper is not withholding a secret sin. Rather his motives are to separate himself from the profane. Indeed, "the black veil had one desirable effect, of making its wearer a very efficient clergyman. By aid of his mysterious emblem—for there was no other apparent cause—he became a man of awful power over souls that were in agony for sin." Even on his deathbed, the old preacher declines to remove the veil.

> "Why do you tremble at me alone," cried he, turning his veiled face round the circle of pale spectators. "Tremble also at each other! Have men avoided me, and women shown no pity, and children screamed and fled, only for my black veil? What, but the mystery which it obscurely typifies, has made this piece of crape so awful? When the friend shows his inmost heart to his friend; the lover to his best beloved; when man does not vainly shrink from the eye of his Creator, loathsomely treasuring up the secret of his sin; then deem me a monster, for the symbol beneath which I have lived, and die! I look around me, and, lo, on every visage a Black Veil."[16]

The parish buries Hooper in his veil, the vehicle with which he moved into the sacred, a process that must take place through separation. Yet the congregation can never resign itself to the purity of Hooper's intention, nor do any of the parishioners understand his calling but persist in believing it is somehow a masquerade or subterfuge.

The New England parishioners' revulsion to the veil is not surprising: Christian men customarily do not veil, unless momentarily or for celebrations such as Semana Santa (holy week)—Palm Sunday to Easter Sunday—when cities and towns in heavily Catholic countries overflow with processions. Among my mother's collection, preserved in a small cedar box, stored in the Chinese trunk, was the *capirote* (conical cap) of a Spanish *Nazareño*. These penitents parade behind effigies of Christ, bearing life-size crosses or transporting large religious images. The *confradías* (brotherhoods) are traditionally male-only, although this is gradually changing. Their tunics vary in color, depending on their professions and places of origin. The tall capirotes point to heaven, to salvation. The face coverings are entirely blank with only eyeholes (not unlike the burqa) and are meant to mark the silence of Christ's suffering. The stillness evoked by this complete envelopment (with fabric) implies veiling. The presentation within the context of spiritual celebration and ritual performance implies masquerade.

The notorious first letter from Paul to the Corinthians lays down the

Christian traditions: "For a man ought not to have his head veiled, since he is the image and reflection of God; but woman is the reflection of man. . . . For this reason a woman ought to have a veil on her head, because of the angels."[17] Roman Catholic women have been required to cover their heads at worship and women religious "take the veil"—once literally, but for many today, in the post–Vatican II era, symbolically. The monk's cowl, an emblem of the Catholic holy man, however, seems merely to be a holdover from medieval lay garments—a device to keep the head warm. The tonsure—a shaved spot on the head, which resembles the Jewish *yarmulke* or skullcap—apparently began in the Eastern church, but by the sixth century had become a distinguishing feature of priests and monks in the Western church.[18] To Jewish men the yarmulke is a reminder that God is always above them, regardless of their stature. By contrast, "Male monastics received the tonsure to open the mind to receive God—[whereas] women had to cover their heads in humility and deference as ordered by Paul."[19]

A humeral veil, a cloth or shawl covering the shoulders and hands, is worn by Roman Catholic subdeacons when handling sacred vessels, and at certain times during the Mass in the elevation of the Host to prevent its contamination by the fingers of the officiating priest.

The Zoroastrian veil—variously called *padân, paiti-dâna,* or *panûm*—also serves as an antipollutant. Priests, who are always male, tie a double-layered white cotton rectangle across their mouths and noses to prevent saliva from defiling the sacred fire or other holy offerings. The priest also wears the mouth veil to avoid contamination of those whom he purifies. Occasionally, a veil is placed on the face of a corpse. Zoroastrianism is one of the world's oldest continuing religious traditions, and the mouth veil is said to resemble that of the ancient Roman *flamines,* who used them during their fire rituals.[20]

Jainism—an ascetic religion of India, founded in the sixth century B.C.E.—emphasizes *ahimsa,* noninjury to all living things. Monks and nuns sometimes wear muslin cloths, *muhapatti,* over their mouths and noses to avoid killing flying insects with the hot air of their breath and to prevent saliva from falling on sacred texts or revered images.

Masks and veils (and particularly hats and other headgear, such as crowns) are universal signals of rank and social status. "The head is the dwelling place of the spirit. . . . (Celts hung heads of slain enemies from house rafters to gain protection from the dead person's spirits, and Greeks, Jews, Semites, and Norsemen kept human heads so that they might serve as oracles.) Kali wore a garland of skulls, and so on and on around the world."[21]

Aside from the mouth veils worn by priests during religious ceremonies, Zoroastrianism—though patriarchal—does not restrict women or men to the veil, nor are today's Parsi (South Asian Zoroastrian) women sequestered.[22] Whether veiling and seclusion were commonplace in pre-Islamic Iran, when Zoroastrianism was prominent, is arguable. However, during the Sassanid dynasty (226 C.E.–651 C.E.)—the last great empire before the Islamic invasion—men, as well as women from imperial households veiled themselves from public view. "Sassanian kings also wore veils that draped [over their faces] from their crowns so as to separate them from, and denote their superiority over, commons."[23]

Growing up outside the United States, surrounded by plenty of other atrocities, I was ignorant for years of the Knights of the Ku Klux Klan. My first response was disgust at their murderous actions; my second was shock that their outfits were replicas of the Spanish *penitentes'* capirotes and robes. I've been told that the Klan borrowed its costuming from the Nazareños, but I've never found proof. Yet what an irony! In addition to African Americans and Jews, Roman Catholics are the prey of choice for men and women of the Klan. Although they gather in the name of Christianity, the KKK is horrifically far from being a brotherhood veiled in devout silence and suffering. Their groupthink, mass energy, and unidentifiability supply them with a perverse form of courage. They are among the most continuously active and egregious terrorist groups in modern history, exploiting anonymity for the sake of violence and social control.

"Anonymity de-individualizes."[24] It "converts the figure to a cipher that stands for something other than itself (the embodied and personified nation state, or an 'inward looking' polity)."[25] Where preparation for war involves masking and body painting—or donning a uniform—brutality toward the enemy is found to be considerably higher than in straightforward, uncamouflaged combat. A study in the 1980s of fifteen societies where warriors changed their appearances showed that "twelve were high on the index of 'killing, torturing, or mutilating the enemy,' while only one of the eight with unchanged appearance was so aggressive."[26] It would seem that as a masculine device, in too many instances, the mask has been a weapon and a facilitator of penetration, which breaches the veil sheltering the sacred from the sacrilegious, the delicate tissue between peace and war.

Masking or veiling to exhibit power where it is otherwise lacking is often seen in conflicts of struggle against the state. Veiled or not, the guerrilla chronically teeters on the edge of impotence against military might. Face-covered street fighters—for example, Mexico's Zapatistas, or fighters in the Palestinian intifada, or the Basque separatist group ETA[27]—can evince militancy and strength even as they are outnumbered and outgunned. In these cases, "anonymity is critical for survival but anonymity also enables a metonymic expansion of meaning that is dislocated and replaced within a larger landscape of modern forms of state terror and resistance."[28]

The male domestic workers who labored for my family during our postings in Central and South Asia displayed another form of veiling within the protocols and powerlessness of servitude. "Material aspects of veiling that mute the body, which have been so well documented for women, are highly communicative modes to establish men's identity as workers in households."[29] They did not wear actual veils, their faces were uncovered, but unless they were actively conducting their duties within the house or garden, our domestic workers, like others in those societies, were secluded in the kitchen and the servants' quarters, places neither my mother nor I ever saw, although my younger brother—being a male child without authority—had the run of both areas. The workers sometimes dressed in colonial garb and had bare feet or used soft-soled slippers. They spoke quietly, eyes lowered. It is the purdah of poverty and subservience.

To mask or veil is to erase other roles and/or create new ones—to be someone or something else.

The men of the Tuareg, Berber-speaking people who inhabit western and central Sahara, are perhaps the most renowned of male veilers (figure 6.2).

Figure 6.2.   A Tuareg couple in Timbuktu, Mali, 2005.
Among the Tuareg, the men veil. Tuareg women do not
wear face veils, though they will sometimes hold their
head scarves over their faces to show reserve or modesty.
Photo by Alida Jay Boye.

In the Air Tuareg dialect [the male veil] is called *tegelmoust.* . . .

The veil is worn continually by men—at home, traveling, during the
evening or day, eating or smoking, sleeping and even, according to some
sources, during sexual intercourse. . . . A noble . . . does not expose his
mouth. . . . The veil is a mark of maturity. Only as a youth approaches maturity, at about the age of seventeen, does he wear a veil. Unveiled youths and
slaves do much of the menial work and the herding. Tuareg women are not
face-veiled at all, but they do pull their shawls across the lower parts of the
faces when expressing reserve.[30]

Tuareg men recognize one another through their eyes and a wide range of identifying characteristics other than the face. The veil itself becomes the mode of communication, worn more loosely among strangers than among familiars. Gestures—pulling the veil high and tight or letting it go slack—are signs of status and influence. "By concealing the primary communication zone of the mouth . . . the Tuareg decreases his vulnerability to others by *symbolically* removing himself from the interaction."[31] To show his mouth among his people is considered shameful.

While Tuareg male veiling is notable, it is a "crucial, neglected, and overlooked fact . . . that men in Arab society veil. . . . For at least several centuries before Islam, evidence"—found in numerous sources from poetry and song to the Hadith[32]—"shows that Arab men veiled."[33] Faces were covered in various situations, such as public celebrations, for reasons including modesty, as well as protection against the evil eye, especially if the man was particularly handsome.[34] "Even less known are reported incidents that the Prophet Muhammad himself face-veiled on certain occasions." Images showing Islam's messenger with a veiled face may be accurate reflections of this male veiling tradition and not necessarily a mere artistic device to avoid violating religious injunctions against portraying his facial features (and thus idolizing him).[35]

Masks affirm the existence and truth of myths in daily life. The myths lead us into the otherworld, where, dressed appropriately, wearing the appropriate persona, we may gain entrance. Worldwide, people wear masks and enact masquerades to mourn, confront, or mock death, as during Mexico's *Día de los Muertos*—Day of the Dead—festivities. Death masks, like those found on Egyptian mummies or on the remains of Mayan kings, offer the deceased passage into the spiritual world and everlasting life. Like abstract portrait masks of the dead in primal cultures, realistic death masks molded from plaster casts placed on the face as soon as the person expires—a continuing Western practice[36] thought to have begun in the Middle Ages among royalty—are vessels in which the spirit is stored so that the living may call upon them in times of need.

Worldwide, the living wrap themselves in mourning weeds and veils to lay bare their sorrow and display their anguish. "At least as far back as the ancient Greeks, female mourners were distinguished by their head coverings."[37] The dead, too, are shrouded and swaddled for the journey into the afterlife.

> Socrates covered himself with a veil after drinking the hemlock, thereby separating himself from the world of the living to be incorporated in the world of the dead and of the gods; but having asked Crito to sacrifice a cock to Aesculapius—that is, wishing once again to act like a living man, he uncovered his face and covered it again immediately afterward.

It is said that Julius Caesar veiled his face at the moment of death, and when "the Romans 'dedicated' to the gods, they intended, by veiling the designated victim, to separate them from this world in order to incorporate them into the other, the divine and sacred."[38]

The dead chief of the Kanak people of New Caledonia is put to rest sitting up, his face veiled in a fishnet, believed to catch the spirits who reside in the same world as the fish. Masks and veils are essential props for resolving and accepting death. Through them, we move "from the biological stage of being betwixt and between to something culturally concrete."[39]

The bereaved everywhere set themselves apart from the community by altering their dress or physical appearances, wearing sackcloth or coating themselves in ashes, or today by simply pinning a black ribbon on a lapel or around a sleeve. Hair also plays a part. In some societies, hair is the spiritual and/or sexual and/or political equivalent of the veil. In certain areas of Nigeria and India, a woman's hair is cut or shaved when she is widowed, while women and men "in dozens of North American tribes, express sorrow by cutting the hair. . . . Cutting the hair has a double significance. Immediately it points to vulnerability, misery, a lack of care about one's appearance. But eventually it is a reminder of regrowth."[40]

In the Irish tale "The Romance of Mis and Dubh Ruis," a young girl loses her father and, having performed no *caoineadth*—the wailing lament that is an essential rite of separation—becomes hirsute and bestial, feral, roaming fields and forests, killing livestock and deer with her long nails and teeth, eating the meat uncooked. It is not until the musician Dubh Ruis accepts the challenge of his chieftain to kill or tame her that Mis is freed from her trap on the threshold between life and death, a sort of psychic veil. The long hair covering her body falls away, she keens and lets go of her grief, bringing body and soul together. At last, she returns, whole and human, to daily life.[41]

Victorian male and female mourning garb could be as elaborate as any full-on ceremonial regalia worn by a Siberian shaman, as ornamented as the mourning garments of the Tahitians recorded by Captain James Cook during his eighteenth-century Pacific Ocean voyages. European elite once wore costumes so ornate that the veils, hats, coats, and shoes, the crepe, chamois, silk, and lace, the ribbons, bows, and feathers—along with meticulously prescribed behavior—were indeed masquerade for a post-industrial rite of passage.

In 1963, first lady Jacqueline Kennedy must have been well aware of the effect on Americans as she stood draped from crown to waist in black mourning for her fallen husband, President John F. Kennedy. The image helped ensure the nation would never forget. And perhaps for her, per-sonally, the act of wearing that extraordinary veil provided necessary soli-tude, insulation, and consolation.

In the 1972 edition of *Amy Vanderbilt's Etiquette,* the author dismissed the wearing of veils and, almost as an aside, even the wearing of hats at funerals. . . .

Mourning clothes provided a marker and thus a kind of insulation for those who wore them—rare luxuries now that we have nothing that alerts the community to the presence of a mourner.[42]

The ancient Celts spoke of the "thin," where the spiritual and material rub against each other. This veil between the worlds falls away during three days beginning on October 31, at the Celtic new year of Samhain, when the graves were opened and the dead walked abroad. Día de los Muertos, observed on the same days, is a pre-Columbian tradition retained and slightly recostumed when the Catholic Church conquered Mexico. The sa-cred, darkening hours, as the calendar approaches the winter solstice, were adopted by Christianity as All Saints Day, All Souls Day, and All Hallow's Eve. But primordial roots can never be completely buried. In secular life, Samhain became Halloween, whose masked festivities are celebrated in

North America and the United Kingdom by people of all ethnicities. Even in our skeptical times, we require contact with the spirits of the dead.

> The crisis posed by [life] transitions generates the energy required to stage rites of passage. During dangerous and precarious times the world of spirits is as unsettled as the world of humans. Rites of passage provide a way to deal with the biological changes by placing them within a cultural context. Culture is called upon to frame these traditions, to provide meaning where there may be none. This cultural response is frequently offered through the agency of the masquerade.[43]

Masks and veils permeate our lives so thickly, so variously, that they inevitably feed as well as are fed by barefaced realities.

My mother is dead. The house fire took her and everything she treasured, including the masks and veils stored in the Chinese trunk. Even after the business of death is done—the wake, the Mass, the paperwork—and I have returned home to my joyful, comforting children, my mother's spirit inhabits me, stabbing my chest like a knife day and night for months.

I have a small mask collection of my own. One night, alone in the house, I arrange them around a mirror on a table and surround them with candles. One by one I lift the masks to my face, as I did when I was a child, peer at my altered and distorted reflection, and invoke whatever magic might be lurking in my living room to exorcise me of my sorrow.

When I have tried on all the masks, I wrap my shoulders in the black veil my mother wore at my father's funeral. I blast the music she loved: Chopin, The Chieftains, Marvin Gaye, Beethoven, the flutes and strings and drums of the Altiplano.

Then I dance. I dance like the diablos, Chinas, and Ch'utas until I collapse to the floor. I cover my face with my mother's black veil. I weep softly as the pain lifts and leaves me.

NOTES

1. Fernando Montes, "To Cover in Order to Uncover," in *Máscaras de los Andes Bolivianos*, ed. Peter McFarren (La Paz, Bolivia: Editorial Quipus, 1993), 24.
2. The wire screen masks of the Sandinista guerrillas were simple, with painted faces, recalling the "John Canoe" masks of nearby Belize.

3. This essay does not presume to be a comprehensive study of masks, merely a personal meditation on the relationships between masks and veils.

4. John W. Nunley, introduction to *Masks: Faces of Culture*, ed. John W. Nunley and Cara McCarty (New York: Harry N. Abrams, 1999), 15.

5. John W. Nunley, "Prehistory and Origins," in *Masks*, 31.

6. Nunley, introduction, 17. In the preindustrial world, nature represented desire, awe, and the fearsome unknown. Today masked comic-book and movie characters spend most of their time avenging the harm created by humans against humans and/or confronting the technology that threatens us. We have been—or so we believe—victorious over nature. It's rare, if not impossible, among all these masked upholders of justice and goodness to find an Eco-Hero, champion of Nature!

7. Nunley, introduction, 16; and "Prehistory and Origins," 37.

8. John Mack, *Masks and the Art of Expression* (New York: Harry N. Abrams, 1994), 41.

9. Fadwa El Guindi, *Veil: Modesty, Privacy and Resistance* (New York: Berg, 1999), 117–18.

10. As Pernet notes in *Ritual Masks: Deceptions and Revelations* (Columbia: University of South Carolina Press, 1992), 136–57, women breaking prohibitions surrounding masks can lead to fatal punishments. This is not unlike what might befall a strange man who trespasses in women's quarters therefore violating the veiled sanctuary. Indeed, Pernet cites an example of Mende belief that "if a man stepped on . . . a strand [of fallen raffia from a woman's] sacred costume he would contract genital elephantiasis." And in *The Rites of Passage*, trans. Monika B. Visedom and Gabrielle L. Caffee (Chicago: University of Chicago Press, 1960), 10–11, Arnold van Gennep defines rites of passage as "a special category, which . . . can be further analyzed and subdivided into rites of separation, tradition rites and rites of incorporation. These three subcategories are not developed equally by all peoples or in every ceremonial pattern: rites of separation are prominent in funeral ceremonies, rites of incorporation at marriages. Transition rites are prominent in marriage, pregnancy, betrothal and initiation, both magico-religious and secular." This brings to mind the notion that today's young Muslim women, who are avidly embracing the veil, may be doing so as a gesture of incorporation to signal solidarity with Islam as it is being attacked from the outside.

11. Mircea Eliade, *Shamanism: Archaic Techniques of Ecstasy* (Princeton: Princeton University Press, 1974), 167, 148, 146.

12. Janet Mayo, *A History of Ecclesiastical Dress* (New York: Holmes and Meier, 1984), 22.

13. The *flamines* were an ancient pontifical college made up of priests who served the cults of Jupiter (ruler of the gods), Mars (god of war), and Quirinus (a

deity presiding over Roman social life, related to the peaceful aspect of Mars). A fourth cult was formed in 44 B.C.E. devoted to Julius Caesar.

14. Personal correspondence with Nita Hill.

15. van Gennep, *Rites,* 168.

16. Nathaniel Hawthorne, "The Minister's Black Veil," in *Tales and Sketches* (New York: Library of America, 1982), 373, 378, 381, 383–84.

17. 1 Corinthians 11:1–10 (NRSV).

18. Mayo, *Ecclesiastical Dress,* 22.

19. Rebecca Sullivan, "Breaking Habits," in *Consuming Habits: Adorning the Transnational Body,* ed. Anne Brydon and Sandra Niessen (Oxford: Berg, 1998), 117.

20. Jivanji Jamshedji Modi, *The Religious Ceremonies and Customs of the Parsees* (Bombay: British Indian Press, 1922), 56.

21. Gary Edson, *Masks and Masking: Faces of Tradition and Belief Worldwide* (Jefferson, NC: McFarland, 2005), 19.

22. In India, Zoroastrians, who emigrated from Iran in the tenth century, are called Parsi. Today there are only about 150,000 Zoroastrians worldwide, 25,000 of them still in Iran, where the women are required to veil. A *Guardian* article dated 04 October 2006, "Ancient Religions Clash in Modern Iran," by Robert Tait, offers a fascinating, if brief, look at ways in which Zoroastrians are treated in Iran today.

23. Jamsheed K. Choksy, "Women in Sassanian and Early Islamic Times," in *Women in Iran: From the Rise of Islam to 1800,* ed. Guity Nashat and Lois Beck (Urbana: University of Illinois Press, 2003), 50.

24. Cara McCarty, "Offense/Defense" in *Masks,* 290.

25. Radhika Chopra, "Invisible Men: Masculinity, Sexuality, and Male Domestic Labor," *Men and Masculinities* 9, no. 2 (October 2006): 152.

26. Philip Zimbardo and Richard Gerring, *Psychology and Life,* 11th ed. (Glenview, IL: Scott Foresman, 1985), 615, 617.

27. The group's name stands for *Euskadi Ta Askatasuna,* which in Basque means "Basque homeland and freedom."

28. Chopra, "Invisible Men," 155.

29. Chopra, Invisible Men," 159. The author adds, "The idea of the body as a surface of signs that suggests an interior body in consonance with its visible displays is constantly interrogated by the regulatory practices directed toward the servant body by the employer 'other.'"

30. El Guindi, *Veil,* 123–24.

31. Robert Murphy, "Social Distance and the Veil, part 1," *American Anthropologist* 66, no. 6 (1964): 1264.

32. Reports of the words and deeds of the Prophet Muhammad—sometimes referred to as the sayings of the Prophet—considered an authoritative source of revelation, second only to the Qur'an.

33. El Guindi, *Veil*, 117.
34. Ernest Crawley, *Dress, Drink and Drums: Further Studies of Savages and Sex*, ed. Theodore Besterman (London: Methuen, 1930), 76.
35. El Guindi, *Veil*, 117, 119.
36. A fascinating Web site, http://thanatos.net, displays death masks from Dante to Shakespeare to Chopin to James Joyce to Alfred Hitchcock and Bruce Lee.
37. Katherine Ashenburg, *The Mourner's Dance: What We Do When People Die* (New York: North Point Press, 2003), 203.
38. van Gennep, *Rites*, 168.
39. John W. Nunley, "Rites of Passage," in *Masks*, 82–83.
40. Ashenburg, *Mourner's Dance*, 189.
41. Jennifer Heath, "The Romance of Mis and Dubh Ruis," in *On the Edge of Dream: Women in Celtic Myth and Legend* (New York: Penguin / Putnam, 1998), 157–67.
42. Ashenburg, *Mourner's Dance*, 203, 206.
43. Nunley, "Rites of Passage," 66.

REFERENCES

Ashenburg, Katherine. *The Mourner's Dance: What We Do When People Die.* New York: North Point Press, 2003.

Beane, Wendell C., and William G. Doty, eds. *Myths, Rites and Symbols*, vol. 1, *A Mircea Eliade Reader.* New York: Harper and Row, 1976.

Brydon, Anne, and Sandra Niessen, eds. *Consuming Habits: Adorning the Transnational Body.* Oxford: Berg, 1998.

Crawley, Ernest. *Dress, Drink and Drums: Further Studies of Savages and Sex.* Edited by Theodore Besterman. London: Methuen, 1930.

Edson, Gary. *Masks and Masking: Faces of Tradition and Belief Worldwide.* Jefferson, NC: McFarland, 2005.

Eliade, Mircea. *Shamanism: Archaic Techniques of Ecstasy.* Princeton: Princeton University Press, 1974.

El Guindi, Fadwa. *Veil: Modesty, Privacy and Resistance.* Oxford: Berg, 1999.

Hawthorne, Nathaniel. *Tales and Sketches.* New York: Library of America, 1982.

Heath, Jennifer. *On The Edge of Dream: The Women of Celtic Myth and Legend.* New York: Penguin / Putnam, 1998.

Mack, John, ed. *Masks and the Art of Expression.* New York: Harry N. Abrams, 1994.

Mayo, Janet. *A History of Ecclesiastical Dress.* New York: Holmes and Meier, 1984.

McFarren, Peter, ed. *Máscaras de los Andes Bolivianos* [Masks of the Bolivian Andes]. La Paz, Bolivia: Editorial Quipus, 1993.

Modi, Jivanji Jamshedji. *The Religious Ceremonies and Customs of the Parsees.* Bombay: British Indian Press, 1922.

Murphy, Robert. "Social Distance and the Veil." *American Anthropologist* 6, no. 6 (1964).
Nashat, Guity, and Lois Beck, eds. *Women in Iran: From the Rise of Islam to 1800.* Urbana: University of Illinois Press, 2003.
Nunley, John W., and Cara McCarty, eds. *Masks: Faces of Culture.* New York: Harry N. Abrams, 1999.
Pernet, Henry. *Ritual Masks: Deceptions and Revelations.* Translated by Laura Grillo. Columbia: University of South Carolina Press, 1992.
Stausberg, Michael, ed. *Zoroastrian Rituals in Context.* Leiden: Brill, 2004.
van Gennep, Arnold. *The Rites of Passage.* Translated by Monika B. Visedom and Gabrielle L. Caffee. Chicago: University of Chicago Press, 1960.

7 I Just Want to Be Me

Issues in Identity for One American Muslim Woman

PAMELA K. TAYLOR

I will never forget the time I was hissed by an audience simply for being who I am. I was giving a lecture about women in Islam at Harvard University. The moderator had introduced me as a graduate student at the Harvard Divinity School and an active member of the Harvard Islamic Society. When I took the podium, I smiled at the people who had come to hear me speak and told them I was also a full-time mom to a delightful one-year-old. At that point, a hiss sprang from the crowd like a snake striking its prey.

I was astounded and appalled. What, I wondered, had I said or done to deserve such a rebuff? Wasn't I living the feminist dream? Didn't I have it all—a career and a family? Wasn't I pursuing higher education—a master's degree—while raising my child with the help of my supportive husband? Did the mere fact that I chose to wear a head scarf, to follow a religion that many believe is oppressive to women, negate all that? Was it okay for your average American woman to value family and children but not a Muslim one? (Figure 7.1)

Figure 7.1 Veiled women
in Kolkata, India, 2006.
Photo by Sheryl B. Shapiro.

My second reaction was anger. What right had these people to judge me based upon a scrap of cloth and a preconceived notion of who I was and what they thought I stood for? I had not even begun to express my thoughts, my opinions, my true self, and already they had pigeonholed me, inaccurately, as an oppressed, downtrodden woman who had no independence, no intellectual life, indeed no life at all outside family, despite the fact that such assumptions were patently false.

I started wearing *hijab* (the Muslim head scarf) some twenty years ago, soon after my conversion to Islam, as a clear statement that I did not want to be judged by my body, my beauty, or the lack thereof, but as an individual, for my personality, my character, and my accomplishments. It was, for me, an unambiguous rejection of the objectification of women by men, by advertisers, by the beauty and fashion industries and Hollywood. I abhor the horrific toll such objectification takes upon the self-esteem of

women, the devastating diseases of anorexia and bulimia that are sweeping our young people and the oversexualization of our society and our
youth that is encouraged by the mass media. My choice to wear a head
scarf was, essentially, the most dramatic, proactive, feminist statement that
I could make in my personal life, an in-your-face rebellion against the feminine mystique. I was, at the time, immensely gratified by my decision. I
had no idea of the battles it would engender—battles that would echo my
fight against the objectification of women—on the one hand a struggle to
be seen for myself, rather than as a symbol of women's oppression, and
on the other, a struggle against being seen as a symbol of idealized faith
or, conversely, self-righteous piety. Although I remain committed to and
satisfied with my decision on a personal level, I cannot help but feel the
bitter irony of having swapped one form of objectification for another.
Paradoxically, the struggle to be viewed as an individual with a unique
personality and character has not only been with mainstream American
feminists, but within the Islamic community as well.

Non-Muslim Americans in general, like my audience at Harvard, are
often quick to judge Muslim women who wear the head scarf—and we are
surprisingly numerous—as oppressed, in need of liberation and empowerment. We are often viewed with pity or condescending sympathy. Equally
often, it is assumed that we are uneducated and that we do not have or have
been barred by male relatives from interests outside the house and family.

Even worse, since 9/11 and the 2003 U.S. invasion of Iraq, we are increasingly seen as proponents of militant political Islam, or even terrorism. As the media bombard us with images of angry women wearing head
scarves, and news of violent acts committed by Muslims, the hijab has become more and more associated with extremist Islam. In comparison, the
trickle of news about hijabed women—conservative, moderate or liberal
in faith—engaged in interfaith dialogue, in peace activism, in social work
or sports, in medicine, education, engineering or any other "normal" pursuit cannot compete. Thus hijab is, more and more, being associated with
violence and intolerance.

Muslims in general also have a variety of reactions. Some assume hijabed women, especially converts, are highly pious, exemplars of Muslim
womanhood. We are often celebrated as true Muslims and chosen to rep-

resent the community to the news media, to student groups who visit the mosque, and at interfaith events. This is especially true of those of us with higher education or other accomplishments, who are used by the community to challenge stereotypes about Muslim women.

Others think we are holier-than-thou extremists, with a hypocritical piety marked by intolerance and judgment of those who chose not to wear a scarf. This set of Muslims often scorns women who wear the hijab as symbols of all that is wrong with the worldwide Muslim community, and as proponents of a totalitarian vision where people are forced to adhere to religious practices whether or not they believe in them.

The reality is, of course, that there are women who fall into each of these categories, and there are just as many who do not fit in any of them. Lumping all hijabed women into a single group is just as meaningless and harmful as lumping all Muslims, or all Jews, or all blacks, into a uniform, stereotyped unity.

As a feminist, as a humanist, I reject these forms of stereotyping as emphatically as I reject the objectification of women's bodies. And, for the most part, I relish the challenge and the opportunity they present to shatter people's preconceived notions of what it means to be a Muslim woman. There is a great satisfaction in seeing people, Muslim and non-Muslim alike, reevaluate their notions of what it means to be a woman, a feminist, a Muslim, and accept that there can be such a thing as an American Muslim feminist, or, perhaps, an American feminist Muslim.

At the same time, there are days when I wish people would simply accept my choice of clothing and move on. It is, after all, a scrap of cloth, and there are a multitude of problems that Muslim women around the world face, ranging from oppressive political regimes to domestic abuse, from limited access to education and work opportunities to warfare and the problems associated with living in a war zone or being a refugee, from honor killings to female genital mutilation, from laws that baldly discriminate against women in marriage, divorce, and custody to tribal punishments that are a complete perversion of justice. These are real issues, grave problems, which affect the daily lives of women in horrific ways and should be the focus of feminists, whether they're Muslim or not. Clothing is, in comparison, a trivial issue. That it has become the battleground of choice between Islamists and secularists, between the East and the West, is a source of great frustration to me. Our energies would be so much better spent confronting truly serious problems.

I suppose it is not surprising that the hijab has become a defining symbol. It makes for effortless imagery, defining and delineating its wearer at a single glance in a way that the news media simply cannot pass up. As we saw in Afghanistan, it is easily used by Western diplomats and feminists to symbolize all the ills of a misogynist society, even though it is not in and of itself misogynist. For Muslims, it is the single most obvious marker of faith—even more unambiguous than a beard or a turban—thus a woman who wears hijab is often the first choice of spokesperson when a community wants to say, "We are serious Muslims," while making a point about human rights, terrorism, or any other unrelated argument. This is true both at the local level, and the national one where it appears mandatory to have at least one hijabed woman on the forefront of communications—for example, Ingrid Mattson, vice president of the Islamic Society of North America; Edina Lekovic, communications director of the Muslim Public Affairs Council; or Sheema Khan, honorary chair of the Canadian Council on American-Islamic Relations.

And yet, I lament that so much energy has been tied up into worry about what women wear. Isn't this exactly why I donned the scarf: to get beyond what women look like, what their clothes imply?

There are days when I am tired of the battles, when I feel demoralized to the point of wanting to abandon the scarf so that I might be invisible again, not a symbol or a pawn. Worse, there are days when I feel that I cannot continue to wear it, because so many—Muslim and non-Muslim alike—may assume that I support militant political Islam. I can cope with people thinking I am oppressed, or ignorant. (It only takes someone about two minutes talking to me to figure out that's not the case.) I can deal with those who think I am far more pious or judgmental than I am. (Again, it takes only a short conversation to put those misapprehensions to rest.) But I am so opposed to the positions of the militant Islamist movement—their goal of implementing and enforcing *shari'ah* (the Islamic code of law as devised by classical scholars) as civic law, their understanding of what Islam is: a set of rules to be obeyed; and of who God is: a fierce and retaliatory judge; and the type of society God enjoins: one in which morality is enforced from without, rather than nurtured from within, and in which Muslims and non-Muslims are inevitably divided and in confrontation with one another, their willingness to resort to unthinkable violence as a means to their ends: suicide bombings, kidnapping, and beheadings—that to be associated with them, even wrongly, is unbearable.

Ironically, among the objectionable opinions of political Islam (there are many; and I would love to discuss them all, but they are beyond the scope of this essay) is the opinion that hijab is all about modesty, not about rejecting the objectification of women or about her demanding to be viewed on the basis of character, but rather about controlling sexuality, primarily alleviating men's sexual appetites. This belief posits that men's sexuality is wild, nearly uncontrollable, that a woman who is not properly robed will create desire beyond proportion, and that therefore, the solution is to cover women, and keep them away from men. What a bitter pill! These Muslims are using the hijab, not as a liberation from objectification, but merely as a substitute for its other forms. The very beauty I saw in the hijab has been nullified, abandoned, supplanted by a reductionism akin to the one I tried to leave behind.

In American society, women are exploited for their beauty—used to sell cars, music, and movies. In Islamist societies, such as Saudi Arabia, Iran, or Taliban Afghanistan, they are controlled, their lives constricted— their entire selves shut up within clothing with requirements they wear *abayas*, face veils, or *burqas*; shut up within segregated stores, restaurants, banks, and parks; shut up by laws requiring them to stay in their houses unless accompanied by male relatives. Either way, women are reduced to their bodies, their sexuality. American exploitation and Islamist modesty are flip sides of the same coin—one that damages women's self-esteem, endangers their health, and limits their choices in life.

In this manner, I have to admit, hijab does intersect with the more pressing issues facing Muslim women. For Islamists, the supposed uncontrollable nature of men's sexuality is used to justify segregation in the mosque, in education and society at large, reducing the sphere of women's work to arenas where they will come in contact only with other women (such as women's banks, women's universities, etc.) and the confinement of women within their homes. For them, wearing hijab—which is supposed to eliminate the sexualization of women and facilitate interactions that are based upon capabilities and character—is not enough; practices with serious repercussions to the quality of women's lives are seen as necessary to go hand in hand with the hijab.

As a Muslim, as a woman, as a feminist, I find it increasingly difficult to wear the hijab, which I have found so gratifying in my personal life, in face of this political Islam that is gaining in popularity and is more and more being seen by non-Muslims as the "true" face of Islam. I donned the hijab to reject the exploitation of women for their sexuality; I wonder if someday I will take it off again in order to reject the suppression of women for their sexuality.

Wearing it, I feel conflicted. I cannot justify giving any moral support to Islamists I might come in contact with, and I cannot bear the thought that non-Muslims might think I agree with Islamist positions. And yet, I also feel conflicted about not wearing it. I believe that hijab should mean only what it means to the individual wearing it, just as I believe that a woman should never have to fear rape, no matter what she is wearing. Why should I give up something that has served me in ways I chose and wanted and benefited from, simply because other people think it means something to me that it does not?

A further complication in the matter is that the growing effort required to fight for hijab to mean only what it means to the individual wearing it seems less and less justifiable. All those issues confronting Muslim women in Muslim-majority societies are not going away. And any effort put into defending hijab, in explaining what it means to me, and stating that I don't subscribe to legalistic, totalitarian Islam, takes away from efforts to counter traditions and distortions of shari'ah, which threaten women's lives and happiness daily.

And then again, at the same time, I am well aware that my wearing hijab gives me clout in the struggle to rid Muslim societies of these harmful practices and interpretations. A non-hijabed women, especially a convert, is easily dismissed as not serious about her faith, as "corrupted" by feminism and the West. A hijabed woman has passed a litmus test and is not so readily rejected by other members of the community. While I dis-

dain this judgmentalism—there are many, many Muslim women who do
not wear hijab but who are very serious about their faith and living a life
of virtue and good works—I recognize that my wearing hijab gives me
an opportunity that those who chose not to wear it will have to fight for.
I can argue for women's right not to wear the hijab without it appearing
self-serving; I can argue for reform of Muslim societies, without anyone
questioning the sincerity of my faith. Indeed, it is clear that my arguments
stem not from a wavering faith, but rather from my deep commitment to
what I see as truly Islamic.

It feels like a perversion, this reason to wear hijab, since it plays to a
stereotyping I reject. But at times I think the ends justify the means. If, as
a hijabed woman, I can more effectively support a woman's right not to
wear hijab, or more important, her right to live without fear of violence
for personal choices, her right to vote and serve in the government, to travel
and work as she chooses, to conduct her personal relationships as she sees
fit, then that is one more reason for me to continue wearing the hijab.
Indeed, there are times I wonder if I have a right not to wear it, if by wearing it I can be more effective in fighting for women's civil and human rights.

Is this a Machiavellian use of hijab? Perhaps. Do I wish I could return
to the carefree days when I wore hijab only because it fit my personal view
of the world? Absolutely. But at the same time, I am willing to use a tool
when I have it. The benefit—safety and better lives for women all over
the world—seems worth the loss of purity.

It is my belief that the problems facing Muslim women around the globe
must be tackled on many fronts: from a secular, humanist perspective, from
a human rights standpoint, and from within the religion of Islam itself.
Indeed, I believe that religious arguments have the most power to effect
widespread social change at this time.

Many of the problems, which ironically give Islam and Muslims a bad
name, are not only totally unsanctioned by the Qur'an (Islam's revealed holy
book) and by the Hadith (stories of Prophet Muhammad's life, his teachings, the things he did) but are actively in contradiction to the principles
of Islam, the methodology of Islamic jurisprudence, and the letter of Islamic
law. Just as terrorism has no place in the Qur'anic view of the world, neither do oppressive governments, spousal abuse and honor killings, the vir-

tual imprisonment of women in their houses, punitive punishments, or any of the other horrors many Muslim women have to cope with.

The Qur'an and Prophet Muhammad condemned these sorts of practices. They recognize the equality of all human beings, regardless of race, class, ethnicity, or gender.[1] Men and women are described as being created of like nature, with the same rights.[2] Their spiritual duties are identical.[3] Marital decisions are described as being based upon mutual consultation, and husbands and wives are depicted as protective garments for one another.[4] A woman's wealth is hers to do with as she sees fit; her right to earn money, to own property, and to inherit wealth, all of which remain hers if she marries, is explicitly guaranteed in the Qur'an.[5] Her right to marry whom she chooses and to divorce if she pleases has also been established in the Qur'an and the teachings of the Prophet.[6] Bearing and raising children is presented as a right, not a requirement.[7] Housework is not a duty, but a contribution.[8] Amazingly, some 1,400 years ago, Prophet Muhammad did his share around the house, helping with mending, cooking, childcare, and cleaning. He never raised a hand against his wife, or his children.[9] The women amongst his companions were merchants, soldiers, teachers, judges, doctors, scholars, and farmers, as well as mothers.[10]

While there are a few troubling verses that need to be dealt with,[11] the Qur'an and the teachings of the Prophet provide a powerful tool to challenge the currents within modern and traditional Islam that are prejudicial against women. They provide resources for Muslims to seriously reevaluate traditional rulings, particularly with reflection on the inherent biases of the men who formulated the shari'ah and how many of their opinions regarding women are simply unacceptable now that we know much more about what it is to be human, male or female. Many of their legal rulings are not only invalid but even contradictory to the spirit and the letter of the Qur'an. The Qur'an itself can be, and is, used to challenge those rulings.[12]

Hand in hand with this is a much-needed challenge to modern Islamist formulations that have little or no place in the Islamic worldview— totalitarian forms of Islamic rule, punishments that penalize the victim rather than the aggressor, the ever narrowing definition of what is permissible, and views on the role of men and women that are limiting and harmful to both genders but have a particularly negative impact on women.

Religion is often used—or abused—to justify discriminatory or misogynist practices. The Qur'an and the teachings of the Prophet are powerful tools in the struggle to eliminate domestic violence, clitoridectomies, laws requiring or forbidding certain clothing, and laws limiting women's participation in any arena, be it political, economic, social, or spiritual. Although I find it sad and discomfiting that wearing hijab is politically expedient, I cannot deny that continuing to wear hijab allows me to speak to an Islamist, conservative, or traditionalist audience with more authority than I would if I chose to abandon it. It makes me a more effective advocate for Muslim women than I would be without it. As a person who speaks to Islamic groups on campuses and in conferences, who is active in my local mosque, in various national organizations, and in interfaith groups, I come in contact on a daily basis with the more conservative elements of our community; thus, the impact of my wearing or not wearing hijab is significant, not something that makes a difference only once in a while but has implications for women's welfare on a regular basis.

At times, that alone seems good enough reason to wear the scarf. At times, I feel I should never give up the fight for women to be free to wear whatever we want to wear without being stereotyped or having to suffer harmful consequences. At times, when I'm flipping through *Cosmo* at the doctor's office, I feel again that surge of pure delight that I've managed to find the single most effective figurative flip-off to the beauty industry.

But mostly, I don't think about hijab. I worry about war, about women living in the shadow of oppressive regimes, about poverty and hunger, about unfair laws and wasted lives. And that, it seems to me, is the way it ought to be—all things in proportion. The hijab is, after all, just a scrap of cloth—a politically and emotionally charged scrap of cloth, but an article of clothing nonetheless. My energies are better spent making this world a kinder, safer, and more just place for all people.

NOTES

1. For instance, see Qur'an, 49:13, which rejects any superiority of one person over another except on the basis of righteousness: "Oh Mankind! Verily We have created you male and female, and made you into tribes and nations that

you might learn. Verily, the most honored of you in God's eyes are the most pious. God is all knowing, all aware." Or the following, which equate male and female believers in absolutely equal terms, both in the spiritual and the mundane worlds:

- 9:71. The believers, men and women, are protecting friends of one another.
- 4:32. To men is the benefit of what they earn, and to women is the benefit of what they earn.
- 4:7. Men shall have a share in what parents and kinsfolk leave behind, and women shall have a share in what parents and kinsfolk leave behind.
- 33:35. For men and women who are devoted to God—believing men and believing women, obedient men and obedient women, truthful men and truthful women, steadfast men and steadfast women, humble men and humble women, men who give in charity and women who give in charity, men who fast and women who fast, men and women who remember God often—God has prepared forgiveness and a rich reward.
- 3:195. I shall not lose sight of the labor of any of you who labors in My way, be it man or woman; each of you is equal to the other.

2. See 4:1. "O mankind! Be conscious of your Sustainer, who has created you out of one a single soul, and out of it created its mate, and out of the two spread abroad a multitude of men and women. And remain conscious of God, in whose name you demand your rights from one another, and of these ties of kinship. Verily, God is ever watchful over you!" Ironically, in this account of creation, because the word for soul—*ruh*—is feminine, a literal translation would read "who has created you out of a single soul, and created from her, her mate, and from the two spread a multitude of men and women."

3. See again 33:35, quoted in full in note 1.

4. For instance, in 2:233, the Qur'an talks about how child-rearing decisions should be made within the family: "If, by mutual consent and consultation, they decide to wean the child, it is no sin for them." And in 2:187, "they are raiment for you, and you are a raiment for them."

5. Again, see 4:7 and 4:32, quoted in full in note 1. The first verse specifies that both men and women inherit from their kinfolk, and the second assigns the wages/earnings of an individual, male or female, to that individual, not to the spouse or their parents. See also 4:19, "And do not treat [your wives] with harshness, that you might take away part of the dowry you gave them"; and 4:20, "But if you decide to take one wife in place of another, even if you had given the latter a whole treasure for dowry, take not the least bit of it back."

Here we see that the dowry is the woman's and hers alone, not something that her husband has control over, or a right to.

6. As for marriage, see Bukhari vol. 7, bk. 42, no. 67. "Narrated Abu Huraira: 'The Prophet said, "Do not marry a widow or divorcee except with her agreement; and do not marry a virgin until you have sought her permission." The people asked, "O Allah's Apostle! If she is shy, how can we know her permission?" He said, "Her silence indicates permission."'" As for divorce, there are numerous hadith to establish that women freely divorced their husbands if they so chose. Bukhari vol. 7, bk. 43, no. 69, narrates that a matron was given a divorce because her father did not get her consent; Bukhari vol., 7, bk. 43, no. 197 tells the story of a woman who simply did not want to live with her husband any longer, and the Prophet consented to her divorce; Bukhari vol. 7, bks. 43, nos. 204–8 discuss the case of Barira who divorced her husband and remained divorced from him despite his following her in the street with tears streaming down his face. The Qur'an addresses wife-initiated divorce in 4:128–30. "And if a woman has reason to fear maltreatment or abandonment by her husband, it shall not be wrong for the two to set things peacefully to rights between themselves: for peace is best. . . . But if they separate, Allah will compensate each out of His abundance. Allah is ever All Embracing, All Knowing."

7. This understanding is derived from different sources; the first set establishes the woman's right to raise her children, and the second establishes that she is not required to do so herself. Typical of the first set of sources is a hadith in which the Prophet says that the woman has more right to the children than the man in the case of divorce, which establishes that it is her right to raise her children. The second set includes the last part of Qur'anic verse 2:233. "If you decide to give your children out to a foster-mother, there is no blame on you, provided you pay what you offered, on equitable terms." This is borne out by the fact that Prophet Muhammad's own son was fostered by a blacksmith and his wife. (See Muslim book 30, hadith 5733 and 5734.) Thus the woman is not required to do the work of childcare but may hire someone to do it for her.

8. This ruling has been derived from the fact that the Qur'an never mentions women having any duties in the home, referring to good wives as ones who are pious and uphold God's laws (see 4:34, 66:5). In 30:21, God's purpose in creating mates for humankind is described: "And among His Signs is this, that He created for you mates from among yourselves, that you may dwell in tranquility with them, and He has put love and mercy between you: verily in that are Signs for those who reflect." Note, the purpose is not so they may ease a husband's burdens and work in his home.

This is further confirmed by the fact that the Prophet was in the habit of doing housework (see Bukhari vol. 7, bk. 64, no. 276), and by the following statement attributed to the second caliph, Umar al-Khattab: "Is it not true that she prepares food for me, washes clothes for me and suckles my children, thus saving me the expense of employing a cook, a washerman and a nurse, though she is not legally obliged in any way to do any of these things?"

9. Muslim bk. 30, no. 5756. "A'isha reported that Allah's Messenger (may peace be upon him) never beat anyone with his hand, neither a woman nor a servant."

10. There are too many references to be included even in this note, however several interesting books have been written about the wives and female companions of the Prophet, such as *The Scimitar and the Veil,* by Jennifer Heath (Mahwah, NJ: Hidden Spring, 2004), which profiles a variety of Muslim women including many from the time of the Prophet; *The Blessed Women of Islam,* by Muhammad Saeed Siddiqi (Lahore, Pakistan: Kazi Publications, 1982), which chronicles the lives of 62 early Muslim women; or *Muslim Women: A Biographical Dictionary,* by Aisha Bewley (London: Ta-Ha, 2004), an exhaustive compilation with short entries about hundreds and hundreds of Muslim women.

11. For instance, 4:34. "Men are the supporters of women, with that which Allah has bestowed upon some more than others, and with that which they spend of their wealth. Righteous women are piously devout, guarding in their absence that which Allah has guarded. As for those women on whose part you fear ill treatment, admonish them, then leave their beds, and then strike them; if they heed you, do not seek a way to harm them. Surely Allah is Most High, Most Great."

This rendition is one of the more benign; others state that men are the managers of women's affairs, that women are supposed to be devoutly obedient to men rather than to God, and that men should beat women in the case of disobedience, reflecting popular interpretations of the verse. Attempts are being made by modern thinkers, especially feminist thinkers such as Amina Wadud, to reinterpret or return to the true meanings many of the key words in this verse:

- *Qawamun,* which literally means "he who stands up" implying that men are to stand up for women, has nonetheless been interpreted by classical scholars to mean men are in control of women, managers of their affairs. In the context of the verse, *qawamun* clearly refers to financial support
- *Bi ma faddala Allahu Badahum ala badin,* literally, "with that which Allah blessed some of them over others." This verse, which has been inter-

preted to mean that men are in charge of women, "because Allah gave men more than he gave women"—*bi ma* being taken as "because" rather than the more literal "with that which." Read literally, the phrase is a comment that God has made some men richer than other men and they support women from whatever wealth God has given them; taken as the more conservative elements in modern Islam would have us take it, it presents Allah as favoring men over women, a notion that stands in direct conflict with other, extremely egalitarian verses and that, according to liberal and progressives must thus be rejected as the actual meaning.

· *Qanitat*, pious or devoutly obedient, used eight other times in the Qur'an to mean obedient to God, has been interpreted by some to suggest women should be obedient to their husbands' slightest whims as though they were God Himself. Again, modern Muslims from both conservative and liberal bents have made attempts to reclaim the original meaning of this word and deny that it gives men godlike authority over women.

· *Hafizun lil ghaibi bi ma hafiza Allahu.* This phrase is extremely vague, to say the least. Literally it means, "guarding that which cannot be perceived with that which God has guarded." Most commentators have understood this phrase to mean that a righteous wife guards her chastity while her husband is not around, i.e., she guards that which he cannot perceive because he is gone, that which Allah would have guarded: her faithfulness. While this interpretation is certainly acceptable, it may mean something entirely different, such as that she guards her faith (that which lies unseen in her heart), which Allah also guards.

· *Nushuz.* This word has been interpreted as everything from ill will to open rebellion. People who are more intent on suggesting that women should be obedient to men tend to take a wider understanding of *nushuz*, sometimes reading it as including even minor acts of negligence, while those who want to limit the scope of this verse tend to understand *nushuz* as a serious breach of marital relations or a violation of the marital contract. What is perhaps most interesting about this term, is that a few verses later (4:128–130), the Qur'an tells women what to do in case they fear *nushuz* from their husbands, telling them that reconciliation is allowed but also that if they separate and divorce, this too is permitted, and in the latter case, God promises to provide for both the husband and the wife. Of course, *nushuz* is often interpreted to mean desertion or cruelty in the latter context, rather than open rebellion or disobedience. Nonetheless, a strong case can be made for the equality of men and women in the marital relationship based upon the fact that both are counseled about what to do in the case of *nushuz*—the Qur'an, it is worth noting, uses identical wording, even if translators and interpreters choose to understand the meaning differently in different contexts; further, we can assume that women might well follow the same steps for reconciliation that have been recommended to men a few verses earlier.

· *Daraba.* This is perhaps the most problematical word in the Surah. It has a wide variety of meanings—everything from hitting, to striking a parable, to the mating of camels. Classical scholars universally understood it to mean hitting and went to great lengths to stipulate that it must be done in such as way as to avoid hurting or leaving a mark upon the woman, that it must not be done upon the face and should be symbolic, involving a small stick used for brushing teeth or even a folded piece of cloth. Some modern interpreters have tried to read *daraba* as striking a blow to the marriage—i.e., divorce. Others have suggested that it means the husband should return from his separation and make love to his wife in an attempt to revive the marriage. While these alternative readings are possible, they are not probable, and they stand in contradiction to various hadith that clearly indicate that the Prophet understood *daraba* to mean that the man was permitted to hit his wife, a thing he detested and did not practice—at one point he did separate from his wives for a month, but he skipped the step of hitting them and instead offered them the choice to remain with him without repeating the tricks that had created the initial problem, or to divorce him. Some feminists have suggested that if the Prophet could skip the step of hitting his spouse, then so too can ordinary Muslims.

For feminist Muslims, however, no matter what progressive readings can offer by way of palliation, this verse remains problematic, because it is so open to abuse and readings that are terribly detrimental to women and their daily lives.

Another instance of troubling verses is 4:7–19, which present the rules of inheritance and, for the most part, give males a greater share of inheritance than females of the same relation. Traditionalists are quick to point out that women have a right in the inheritance of their male relatives—that is, men are required to support women, thus they have a right to share in their husband's inheritance, or in case they are single, their fathers, or brothers, or uncles, and so on—thus what seems to be unequal is actually the only fair solution. Progressives, liberals, and feminist Muslims tend to think that this right doesn't balance out the equation and that, further, in modern society where brothers or uncles can no longer be counted upon to support their sisters and nieces, where divorce and single motherhood is rampant, the only sensible division is one that considers the economic needs of each individual.

The third Qur'anic verse worth noting is the first half of 2:282. "Oh you who have attained to faith! Whenever you give or take credit for a stated term, set it down in writing. And let a scribe write it down equitably between you; and no scribe shall refuse to write as God has taught him: thus shall he write. And let him who contracts the debt dictate; and let him be conscious of God, his Sustainer, and not diminish it by even a little. And if he who contracts the debt is weak of mind or body, or, is not able to dictate himself, then let him who watches over his interests dictate equitably. And call upon two of your men to act as witnesses; and if two men are not available, then a man and two women from among such as are acceptable to you as witnesses, so that if one of them should make a mistake, the other could remind her." This verse has been cited as a determination that women's testimony carries half the weight of a man's, and that her intellect is deficient when compared with male intellect. For obvious reasons, many modern Muslims have a hard time accepting this notion and point to numerous hadith in which a single woman's testimony was sufficient for the Prophet to act. (For instance, Tirmidhi, hadith no. 1270, relates the story of a woman who was raped: her testimony alone resulted in the man being punished while she was held blameless. Or Bukhari vol. 1, bk. 3, no. 88, which reports that two of the Prophet's companions were married, and a woman came and testified that she had nursed both of them, which would make them *mahrem*, unable to marry. Though the families had no knowledge of that, the Prophet required them to divorce because of the nursing.) Given these examples, many modern scholars have opined that women's witness is worth as much as men's, and that this verse is merely a recognition of the fact that in the day and age of the Prophet women might not have had as much knowledge about economic affairs as men, and thus it is no longer applicable, particularly in the case of a woman who is involved in business or who has training in economics. Another explanation that has been offered is the idea that in the case of a disagreement, the witnesses would have to be secluded together to confer privately about the contract, and it is preferable that a man and a woman not be secluded together, thus two women are needed to consult together; this clearly does not address why, then, the man is needed at all. While it might be nice to ignore this verse as many modern scholars suggest, it remains a fact that conservative and/or fundamentalist Muslims use it to justify all sorts of prejudicial judgments and treatment of women—everything from maintaining that women really shouldn't work outside the home since their intellect is flawed to invalidating their witness in all other cases, since it wasn't specifically mentioned in those cases that women could be witnesses as it was in this verse. As with the first two verses, sufficient effort can render the verses harmless, but such exercises are largely ignored by those who favor patriarchal family and social structures.

12.   For instance, shari'ah rulings on divorce are being challenged in countries such as India and Pakistan, where Muslim men have near unilateral right to divorce with neither registration nor maintenance requirements, while women are required to seek approval from a judge, prove just cause, and return their dowries. Scholars quote both the Qur'an and the Hadith to support the contention that women have equal rights to divorce, that they do not need cause, and that they are entitled to maintenance after divorce.

Also, various groups of Muslims have been exerting pressure on Nigeria, Saudi Arabia, and Iran to rescind laws that provide for the stoning of men and women convicted of adultery, citing the fact that stoning does not appear in the Qur'an. Along with this effort is a push to outlaw convictions based upon the pregnancy of unmarried women, and the double threat created by laws that result in women who report a rape being charged with adultery if they cannot produce four witnesses to the crime. Pregnancy has been deemed insufficient proof of adultery, as the sexual contact could have been nonconsensual. And the Prophet's example (cited in note 11) is in direct contradiction with the second case.

REFERENCES

The Qur'an—The translations cited throughout this work are original translations I made in consultation with various existent translations—Muhammad Asad, Muhammad Marmaduke Picktall, Yusuf Ali, and M. A. S. Abdel Haleem. For the non-Arabic speaker, my preferred translation is the one by M. A. S. Abdel Haleem, published by Oxford University Press in 2004.

Hadith—The hadith cited in this work come from Sahih Bukhari and Sahih Muslim.

- I use the eight-volume translation of Bukhari by Muhsin Khan. Bukhari divided his work into books, with each hadith numbered. Each of Khan's volumes comprises several of Bukhari's original books. Citations of Bukhari commonly list Khan's volume, with Bukhari's book and number.

- I use the four-volume translation of Muslim. Citations of Muslim commonly list book and hadith number, without reference to the volume number.
- The Muslims Students Association of the University of Southern California Hadith Database is a valuable resource allowing users to search both Bukhari and Muslim (www.usc.edu/dept/MSA/reference/searchhadith.html).

TWO

The veil of illusion has been cut away,
And I shall not go out wandering any more.

—*Sri Guru Grath Sahib*

8   "She freed and floated on the air"

Salome and Her Dance of the Seven Veils

SHIREEN MALIK

Was she the chaste young daughter of a manipulative mother? An evil temptress responsible for a holy man's death? A Judean princess living a traditional royal life?

She endures in popular imagination as a seductive oriental dancer, spinning wildly as layers of transparent veils slip from her body, until the seventh and final one is removed, revealing her brazen nakedness.[1] Through the ages, Salome has been created and recreated by countless male scribes, translators, authors, and artists, and by the women who portray her (figure 8.1).

Salome's story began almost two thousand years ago in the first century C.E. She was a young princess during the reign of Tiberius Caesar, when Pontius Pilate was governor of Judea. Her stepfather, Herod Antipas, was the Rome-appointed tetrarch of Galilee and Perea. The first written references to her are in the New Testament Gospels of Mark and Matthew, where she appears as a nameless culprit in the death of John

139

Figure 8.1.   Gustave Moreau, *L'Apparition* (The Apparition), 1874—detail. This painting is among the most celebrated portrayals of Salome. Harvard University Art Museums, Fogg Art Museum. Bequest of Grenville L. Winthrop, 1943.268. Photo by Katya Kallsen. © President and Fellows of Harvard College.

the Baptist, referred to simply as "the daughter of Herodias" or as "damsel."[2]

History records that Herodias deeply resented John the Baptist for his public condemnation of her marriage to Herod Antipas. "Herodias took upon her to confound the laws of our country, and divorced herself from her husband while he was alive, and was married to Herod [Antipas], her husband's brother by the father's side, he was tetrarch of Galilee."[3]

Scriptures recount the occasion of Herod's birthday:

> [He gave a banquet for] his lords, high captains, and chief estates of Galilee. And when the daughter of the said Herodias came in, and danced, and pleased Herod and them that sat with him, the king said unto the damsel, Ask of me whatsoever thou wilt, and I will give it thee. And he sware unto her, Whatsoever thou shalt ask of me, I will give it thee, unto the half of my kingdom. And she went forth, and said unto her mother, What shall I ask? And she said, The head of John the Baptist.[4]

Compelled by the oath he made before his guests, Herod reluctantly ordered the Baptist's execution and the display of his head on a platter. The obedient young girl then passed the grisly trophy to her vindicated mother.

Authorship and sources of information for the gospels are speculative; they were written decades after the events they describe. It cannot be said with certainty whether they relate accurate historical occurrences or evolved from previous tales and traditions transmitted orally through the ages, with inevitable variances in interpretation and bias.

The story of Herod's banquet and its aftermath is reminiscent of an episode that occurred in the Roman realm several centuries earlier. According to the writings of Plutarch, Cicero, Seneca, and others, in 184 B.C.E., Lucius Flamininus was expelled from the Roman Senate for ordering a man beheaded during a banquet, while he was consul of Gaul, simply to satisfy the whim of a paramour who wanted to see someone killed. Details of the incident vary, but Cato the Elder, official censor, whose task it was to scrutinize the lives and manners of the Roman patricians, determined that Flamininus's action was highly immoral, and an abuse of power that dishonored the government.[5] This well-known incident was often cited by Roman rhetoric teachers to discuss themes of cruelty and eroticism.

The name "Salome," identifying the daughter of Herodias, does not appear in writing until the end of the first century in the works of historian Flavius Josephus. "Herodias was married to Herod [Philip], the son of Herod the Great by Mariamme the daughter of Simon the high priest. They had a daughter Salome."[6]

Josephus goes on to tell us that as a young woman, Salome was married to her great-uncle, Herod Philip, who died a few years later. Her second husband, Aristobule (who was also her cousin), eventually became king of Armenia, giving her the title "queen of Chalcis and Armenia Minor." With him she bore three sons. Considering the course of her life and customs in the world of Salome's youth, it is highly improbable that a Judean princess of classical antiquity would have danced publicly before guests at a banquet. That was the role of entertainers. The historian makes no mention of a feast, a dance, or a head on a platter.

Josephus writes that Herod Antipas was concerned about John's influence on the people of the area and, fearing a possible rebellion, had him imprisoned and eventually executed in the fortress of Macherous.[7]

Early versions of Salome's story portray her as an innocent pawn of her mother's vengefulness. In the original Greek of the New Testament, Salome is called a *korasion*, meaning maiden or young girl,[8] but from the fourth century onward, her character transforms. As reverence grew for John the Baptist, she was perceived as increasingly immoral, and her image solidified as a dancing temptress and perpetrator of evil. Salome's tale provided inspiration for stories, mystery plays, oratorios, and a plethora of topics for moralizing sermons and cautionary tales.

Homily 48 on the Gospel of Matthew refers to John's execution as "a murder by way of a favor . . . a murder in the midst of a banquet," and adds, "For where dancing is, there is the evil one. For neither did God give us feet for this end, but that we may walk orderly: not that we may behave ourselves unseemly, not that we may jump like camels (for even they too are disagreeable when dancing, much more women)."[9]

A favorite subject for the flourishing iconographic arts, Salome, depicted in contemporary clothing, appeared in medieval paintings and murals, on windows, illuminated manuscripts, tapestries, and sculpture. The Salome theme inspired many of the world's most renowned artists, who typically represented her with the head of John the Baptist on a platter or dancing at the banquet.

Medieval Salome was often portrayed standing on her hands with legs bent toward her head, nearly touching the floor, in the manner of entertainers who performed throughout Europe. She was described as "vaulting and tumbling" before Herod.[10] Salome may not have been "bumping and grinding" or removing any veils, but jumping around on her hands with legs dangling in the air would not have been princesslike behavior. In the minds of many early church leaders, dancing, no matter what its form, was equated with sin. And Salome personified that sin.

One of the most popular myths in medieval Europe was that of the Wild Hunt—a cavalcade of apparitions whose earthly transgressions allowed them no final rest, evildoers who roamed the ravines, raced over the countryside, or dashed across the night sky. Herodias was often among this group of unruly spirits, along with other varied opponents of Christianity. (In that era, the name Herodias referred to both mother and daughter, or a composite of the two.)

Herodias is featured in *Atta Troll*, the 1841 lyric poem by German writer Heinrich Heine, whose French translation influenced many later authors. Heine's protagonist carries the severed head on her lively ride, lovingly kissing it and playfully tossing it in the air like a bouncy ball. Heine is credited with introducing the motive of unrequited love to account for the Baptist's demise,

Would a woman crave the head
Of a man she did not love?[11]

But nineteenth-century folklorist Jacob Grimm found similar themes even earlier in medieval Herodias lore: "She was inflamed by love for John which he did not return; when his head is brought in on a charger, she would fain have covered it with tears and kisses."[12]

Interest in the Herodias/Salome theme declined after the sixteenth century but was renewed with the publication of Heine's poem. Salome's popularity soared in the nineteenth century, especially in France, coinciding with the spread of colonialism and Europe's growing fascination with the East. Stereotyped notions of the other abounded—exotic, mysterious, sensual, debauched, violent, cruel, or as writer Rana Kabbani puts it: "The dance became invested with an exhibitionism that fascinated the onlooker: he saw it as a metaphor for the whole East."[13] The biblical tale of Salome's dance, well known throughout the Western world, provided a ready-made theme for artists of all genres. With infinite artistic license, they created their own versions of the Orient while altering, embellishing, or ignoring both the original gospel story and an accurate portrayal of people from Eastern lands.

With the "fashionable mode of fake historical orientalism," Salome became "the true centrepiece of male masochistic fantasies."[14] She provided a controversial literary character and offered her name to portraits of seminude artist models in pseudo-oriental garb. With the addition of a platter (with or without a head), a painting could readily be identified as "Salome." Museums are full of such images. "The Salome/Herodias figure was almost as popular among nineteenth-century artists as the Virgin Mary was among medieval artists."[15]

By the mid 1800s, a journey to the alluring East was a popular adventure for young men from England and the Continent, and the "dancing girls" were of particular interest. Since contact with local women was typically limited to public entertainers, often prostitutes, the travelers' tales presented a circumscribed portrayal of the women they encountered. Those travelogues, memoirs, ethnographic studies with Western biases, and early photographs of posed subjects added to the illusory depictions of Eastern women, fueling the imagination of ever-more writers, artists, and the general public.

Salome's heavy Renaissance garments began coming off, replaced by jeweled gowns, flimsy veils, or nothing at all. She was transforming from youthful maiden to a dancing destroyer of men.

Théophile Gautier, considered the founder of "exotic aestheticism,"[16] influenced a succession of orientalist writers with his 1847 poem, *Une Nuit de Cléopâtre* (One of Cleopatra's Nights). The dancing Cleopatra inspired many Salomes that appear in later writings.

Cleopatra herself arose from her throne, threw aside her royal mantle, replaced her starry diadem with a garland of flowers, attached golden *crotali* [finger cymbals] to her alabaster hands, and began to dance. . . . Poised on the pink tips of her little feet, she approached swiftly to graze the forehead of Meiamounn with a kiss; then she recommenced her wondrous art, and flitted around him, now backward-leaning, with head reversed, eyes half closed, arms lifelessly relaxed, locks uncurled and loose-hanging.[17]

In 1862, the chaste priestess Salambo emerged from the pen of Gustave Flaubert, dancing a private ritual of purification. "Salambo unfastened her ear pendants, her necklace, her bracelets, and her long white gown. . . . Salambo, her whole body swaying, chanted her prayers, and her clothes, one after another, fell round her."[18]

Arthur O'Shaughnessy's lengthy poem, "The Daughter of Herodias" (1870), is particularly significant, for veils have been added to the dancer's vestments.

> She freed and floated on the air her arms
> Above dim veils that hid her bosom's charms. . . .
>
> The veils fell round her like thin coiling mists
> Shot through by topaz suns, and amethysts,
>   And rubies she had on;
> And out of them her jewelled body came. . . .
>
> "Is there not wrought a madness in thy brain
> Each time my thin veils part and close again—
>   Each time their flying ring
> Is seen a moment's space encircling me
> With filmy changes—each time, rapidly
> Rolled down, their cloud-like gauzes billowing
>   About my limbs they fling?"[19]

The veils that fell around O'Shaughnessy's dancer are suggestive of Salammbo's clothes falling around her one by one, and of Salome's veils being cast off in later writings. The dancer's "jewelled body" reappears a few years later in works by French symbolist painter Gustave Moreau.

Images created on canvas were seen by thousands of people passing through art exhibitions in Paris, as artists "cranked out their obligatory . . . Salomes for the salons,"[20] generating ever more public interest in the oriental femme fatale. Displayed first in 1876, two celebrated works by Moreau were among the most popular. *Salomé dansant devant Hérode* (Salome Dancing before Herod) and *L'Apparition* (The Apparition) both portray a fantasized, bejeweled, seminude Salome.

Flaubert's florid prose introduces Herodias in the 1872 short story from *Trois Contes* (Three Tales).

> Under a bluish veil which concealed her head and breasts, one could just make out the arch of her eyes, the chalcedonies in her ears, and the whiteness of her skin. A square of dove-coloured silk covered her shoulders and was fastened to her loins by a jewelled girdle. Her black trousers were spangled with mandrakes, and she moved with indolent ease, her little slippers of humming-birds' down tapping on the floor.
>
> Going up on to the dais, she removed her veil. . . . Then she began to dance. . . . With her eyes half-closed, she twisted her body backwards and forwards, making her belly rise and fall and her breasts quiver while her face remained expressionless and her feet never stopped moving. . . . Without bending her knees, she opened her legs and leant over so low that her chin touched the floor. . . . She threw herself on her hands with her heels in the air, and in that position ran round the dais like a great beetle. Then she stopped abruptly.
>
> Her neck and her spine were at right angles. The coloured sheaths about her legs hung down over her shoulders and on either side of her face to within a cubit of the ground.[21]

The author's racy narratives of his experiences with dancers in Egypt, about which he wrote extensively, doubtless color his descriptions. Edward Said writes, "Flaubert's encounter with an Egyptian courtesan produced a widely influential model of the Oriental woman; she never spoke of herself, she never represented her emotions, presence, or history. *He* spoke for her and represented her."[22]

Unlike the nineteenth-century Egyptian dancers Flaubert would have been familiar with, his protagonist Herodias culminates her impassioned dance by throwing herself upside down and dashing around like a frenzied insect. She recalls the inverted figure of an acrobatic Salome from the biblical banquet scene on a tympanum of the cathedral of Rouen, the town of Flaubert's childhood home.

An important link in Salome's literary chain comes from Joris-Karl Huysmans in his 1884 novel *A Rebours* (Against the Grain). The hero, des Esseintes, is obsessed with the Salomé of Moreau's paintings. He considers her "the symbolic incarnation of old-world vice: "She is almost naked; in the ardour of the dance the veils have unwound themselves, the brocaded draperies of her robes have slipped away; she is clad now only in goldsmith's artistries and translucent gems."[23]

Amid lavish, erotic descriptions of her adornments, veils are unwinding and robes are slipping away—the oriental woman in all her splendor is stripping for the voyeuristic observer. Salome approaches the twentieth century as the seemingly irrational, decadent young woman of Oscar Wilde's controversial drama.

The best known of all Salome literature, Wilde's play has been analyzed and interpreted in countless ways. Herodias/Salome's passion for John, his rejection of her, and kissing the head are all elements from medieval tales that Wilde utilized. Blame for the biblical beheading had by this time shifted from mother to daughter.

In Wilde's version, the blasé girl snaps out of her ennui upon hearing Iokannon (John the Baptist) shouting from his prison in the cistern. Insisting that he be brought out so she can look upon him, she feels her virginal passions ignite when he stands before her. She lavishly praises his physical beauty (evocative of the Old Testament Song of Songs), but he bitterly rebukes her. Her adoration quickly devolves to revulsion. When the Baptist is back in his subterranean hold, she agrees to comply with Herod's persistent pleas, "By my life, by my crown, by my gods. Whatsoever you desire I will give it you, even to the half of my kingdom, if you will but dance for me. O Salome, Salome, dance for me!" She says, "I am waiting until my slaves bring perfumes to me and the seven veils."[24]

When the dance is ended, she adamantly insists on the Baptist's head as her reward. Herod, fearful of misfortune if he harms the man who may indeed be a holy messenger, desperately tries to convince her to accept something different from a long list of magnificent treasures. She is unrelenting. Herod finally complies and orders the execution. Salome receives the gruesome head on a silver shield and delivers to it a lengthy soliloquy, triumphantly kissing the dead lips. Her depravity so outrages the tetrarch, he commands that she be immediately killed.

Criticized for obvious stylistic and linguistic borrowings from numerous earlier writers, Wilde responded with his oft-quoted reply, "Of course I plagiarise. It is the privilege of the appreciative man."[25]

Wilde's *Salome,* originally written in French in 1891, was intended for production on the British stage the next year with Europe's leading actress, Sarah Bernhardt, in the title role. After several weeks of rehearsals, preparations came to an abrupt halt when the licensor of plays, citing an old law forbidding the portrayal of biblical characters on stage, refused to grant a permit. The Lord Chamberlain's office was unrelenting in its treatment of *Salome,* and the ban was not lifted until 1931, almost forty years later.[26] Occasionally the play was presented at small-scale venues to private audiences, thereby escaping the censorship imposed on public programs.

Salome was published in French in 1893 and in English the following year. Aubrey Beardsley's hermaphroditic illustrations, accompanying the English version, caused as much sensation as the text itself.

It is in Wilde's drama that Salome's seven veils are first introduced to the public. A simple stage direction, "Salome dances the dance of the seven veils," is all that is offered, with no further explanation. The author originally considered having *Salome* dance on her hands[27]—presumably without veils!

The quest to uncover Wilde's trail of inspiration leads more to speculation than explanation. An inscription to Aubrey Beardsley reads, "For Aubrey: for the only artist who, besides myself, knows what the dance of the seven veils is, and can see that invisible dance."[28]

Perhaps Wilde was influenced by the ancient Mesopotamian myth of Ishtar/Inanna. A well-read student, he would likely have known of the tale when it was deciphered from cuneiform tablets and printed in the *London Daily Telegraph,* 1872. The newspaper article relates that among a collection of mythological stories was "the cuneiform account of the descent of the goddess Ishtar into Hades. In her downward journey into the infernal regions she passes through seven gates, and parts with some ornament or article of attire at each gate."[29]

Symbolism abounds in reference to the number seven. It was ascribed mystical qualities in most early belief systems, and considered a perfect number—a combination of three and four together (the triangle and square). Esoteric exploration was rife in Oscar Wilde's nineteenth-century society. He was received into a freemasonry lodge while attending Oxford University in 1875; and would have been aware of diverse rituals and symbols. According to an encyclopedia of freemasonry, "the symbolic seven is to be found diffused in a hundred ways over the whole Masonic system."[30]

Although Wilde does not describe Salome's dance or suggest that she remove any veils, her dance is invariably assumed to be one of unveiling, thus revealing herself. In the opinion of one critic, "Unveiling was an appropriate image for the activity which Wilde regarded as the artist's primary duty: self-expression and self-revelation. In performing the dance of the seven veils, Salome is then perhaps offering not just a view of the naked body but of the soul or innermost being."[31]

Wilde's *Salome* was brought to the Paris stage in 1896, after much preperformance difficulty. One setback occurred on the final night of dress rehearsal. John the Baptist's head, on loan from the wax museum, slipped off the platter, smashed, "and the separate pieces of the prophet had to be glued back together for the performance."[32]

Wilde never saw his work presented. He was serving a prison term on charges of "gross indecency" for homosexual practices. Two years after his death in 1900, *Salome* was produced to great success in Berlin, where it was seen by the composer Richard Strauss.

Using an abridged version of the play's German translation for his libretto, Strauss set the text to music, premiering his opera *Salome,* with its dance of the seven veils, in Dresden in 1905. Choreography for *Salome* productions generally came from local ballet masters, inevitably differing from theater to theater, and often ending with a partially, completely, or seemingly naked dancer. The title role in Strauss's debut production was performed by the robust soprano Marie Wittich, who refused to perform the dance, protesting, "I won't do it, I'm a decent woman."[33] A member of the ballet corps switched roles with the diva for the dance scene, no doubt giving the impression of Salome shrinking in size, then plumping up when the singing resumed!

Salome's name and fame spread widely, immortalizing her dance of the seven veils, and confirming her image as a seductive, perilous woman. She appealed not only to the male voyeur, but also to women desiring to "escape bourgeois domesticity's constraints."[34]

The stage was set for an American premiere at the Metropolitan Opera House on January 22, 1907. Anticipation ran high. *Salome* was sung by a hefty Olive Fremstad, who, after removing the first of the seven veils, was replaced in the dance by the lithe ballerina Bianca Froelich who continued with "posturings and shiverings and serpentine movements."[35]

Along with enthusiastic praise for the opera's debut came ardent criticism. A letter published in the *New York Times* two days after the first performance objected in particular to the final kiss on the lips of the disembodied holy head and complained that "'Salome' is a detailed and explicit exposition of the most horrible, disgusting, revolting, and unmentionable features of degeneracy."[36] The Met's financiers—including J. P. Morgan and W. K. Vanderbilt—decided, at the behest of Morgan's daughter Anne, that the program's controversial content might damage the reputation of the prestigious opera house. The show was closed after opening night, and *Salome* was banned from the Met until 1934, greatly increasing her notoriety.

Florenz Ziegfeld's 1907 *Follies* featured a Salome dance performed by Mlle Dazie, who, capitalizing on the "Salomania" craze, opened a school for aspiring performers in the theater's roof garden. By the following year, scores of Salomes were swirling veils and kissing papier-mâché heads in music halls and on vaudeville stages across the country. An entertainment lineup would hardly be complete without a Salome act, and audiences could count on seeing some flesh. In Strauss's opinion, "the capers cut in later performances by exotic variety stars indulging in snakelike movements and waving Jochanaan's head about in the air went beyond all bounds of decency and good taste."[37]

Before Salome became commonplace, music and dance from the Middle East could be experienced at world's fairs in major international cities. Chicago's 1893 World's Columbian Exhibition gave nearly thirty million visitors the opportunity to view mock villages and theaters of Algeria, Persia, and Turkey, along with a Moorish Palace and the exciting Street in

Cairo. The public saw native people in traditional attire demonstrating aspects of their daily lives. At the popular theaters, crowds poured in to watch dancing girls perform the infamous "belly dance," so labeled by a fair promoter. The fair provided a multicultural experience, beyond the images of Eastern temptresses and harem beauties featured in orientalist paintings or French colonialist postcards. Female performers were costumed in multiple layers of clothing, wearing shoes, stockings, and various kinds of head coverings, with not a belly or breast to be seen. Nevertheless, many among the puritanical public were shocked by the loose movements of uncorseted bodies, hips swaying to strange, unfamiliar music. Moral outrage, of course, increased attraction to the shows and promoters' profits.[38]

After the exposition, countless American women reinvented themselves as exotic dancers. Pseudo-oriental "hootchy-kootchy" dancers sprang up across the country in dime museums, variety shows, burlesque houses, and on vaudeville circuits, in concert saloons, carnivals, and circuses.

As the Victorian era passed into the Edwardian, social change was under way throughout the Western world. Suffragists campaigned for women's voting rights, the physical culture movement was gaining acceptance, and dress reformers advocated loosening the laces of breath-constricting corsets. The status of theatrical dancing, which was typically held in lower repute than the other performing arts, started to shift in the early twentieth century, along with a growing demand for commercial entertainment. A new type of solo female performer began emerging, laying the foundation for what became the modern dance movement.

The first such dancer of renown was American-born Loie Fuller (Marie Louise Fuller), whose career was launched in Paris in 1892. Expanding on the skirt-dancing tradition of the 1890s, she enthralled audiences with her skillful manipulation of masses of voluminous silk upon which colored lights were projected. Like many performers who followed her—Ruth St. Denis (Ruth Emma Dennis), Maud Allan (Ulah Maud Allan Durrant), Mata Hari (Margaretha Geertruida Zelle), Ida Rubenstein, and countless others—*la Loïe* expanded her repertoire by creating Salome pieces during her career.

Serge Diaghilev's Ballets Russes of Paris premiered *La Tragédie de Sa-*

Figure 8.2.   Maud Allan in
A Vision of Salome, 1918.

lomé in 1913, featuring Tamara Karsavina, widening the scope of Salome's appeal still further. Lavish theatrical productions of an imaginary Orient contributed to the burgeoning public passion for exotica in entertainment, personal fashions, and home furnishing.

In the decade preceding World War I, Salome's popularity was at its height. The theme provided "an inspiration and a challenge for choreographers, a stepping stone to fame for a number of dancers, an affront to self-appointed protectors of the public morality, a bonanza for publicity agents and reporters, and an unparalleled drawing-card for the public."[39]

Maud Allan, Canadian-born and San Francisco–bred, took London by storm in 1908 with her *Vision of Salome,* performing for eighteen months at the Palace Theatre of Varieties. Though she also presented "classic" dances similar to her contemporary, Isadora Duncan, it was her dance pantomime of Salome (and no doubt the revealing costume) that garnered her fame (figure 8.2). Allan was admired for her grace and charm—feminine ideals of her society. She was praised for artistically abstracting "the vulgar reality and physicality of authentic Eastern dance."[40] According to a critic of her time, "her dancing as Salome, though Eastern in spirit through and through, is absolutely without the slightest suggestion of the vulgarities familiar to the tourists in Cairo or Tangier."[41] Appropriating a stereotyped image of the exotic female other, Allan represented the supposed essence of the East, but her very "Westernness" is what made her dancing acceptable to Edwardian audiences. Like most performers who achieve celebrity, Allan's dance pantomime and costume were widely copied.

Oscar Hammerstein sent the popular vaudevillian mimic Gertrude Hoffman to London to observe Allan's *Vision of Salome*, study it, and reproduce the dance in New York, which she did to much acclaim. She took the show on the road, and so did her own imitators, spreading Salome's allure to an ever-expanding audience. By the time Maud Allan was contracted to present her *Salome* in America, it was no longer a novelty.

Salome made her first known film appearance in 1908—a one-reeler for Vitagraph—*Salome; or, The Dance of the Seven Veils*, followed by several other short films. In 1918 Theda Bara (Theodosia Goodman), the archetypal Hollywood vamp, was featured in a long-lost silent film—*Salome*. The iconography of the vamp, rooted in the 1890s, was "drawn from stereotypical representations of the oriental temptress, grafted on to the Victorian female vampire."[42]

In 1922 Alla Nazimova, with springy baubles sticking out of her dark curly wig, starred as a petulant, Wildean Salome in the earliest film still available for viewing. We watch her disappear behind four attendants, then reemerge on the scene wearing a short white playsuit and blonde wig. Enveloped in a huge diaphanous veil, she spins around and around before Herod, her mother, and the court.

The glittery, fantasized costume of Maud Allan and others before her, with beaded halter top and gossamer skirt (unlike anything worn at the time in the Middle East), is familiar attire for today's stereotyped belly dancer, in both East and West. Popularized in venues ranging from carnival sideshows to ballet spectaculars, the two-piece costume eventually made its way to Cairo. Cross-acculturation between the film capital of the Middle East and Hollywood influenced depictions of oriental dancers everywhere.

Movie starlet Rita Hayworth portrays a good-girl Salome in the 1953 adaptation—a Hollywood favorite that is frequently aired on television. Dancing, jumping, crawling toward a lustful Herod, she purposefully removes a succession of multicolored veils, in a vain attempt to save the Baptist's life.

Key elements of Wilde's drama and Strauss's opera—eroticism, perversion, obsession, seduction, death, set in a morally charged religious context—suggest why the story still has prurient appeal. Since her inception as a barely mentioned biblical character, the legendary Salome continues to be recreated and redefined. The dance of the seven veils, whether for public entertainment or as a new-age metaphor for personal transformation, endures into the twenty-first century.

NOTES

1. The term "oriental dance," from the Arabic *raks sharqi* (dance of the East/ Orient), is used to designate a style that is typically, but not exclusively, an improvisational solo dance. It originated in North Africa and the Middle East (an Anglo designation for a vast geographic area with diverse traditions). It is referred to by different names in local languages and known in English also as Middle Eastern dance (regional folkloric dances) and belly dance.

2. Mark 6:22–24, Matthew 14:1–12 (AV).

3. Flavius Josephus, *The Works of Flavius Josephus: Comprising the Antiquities of the Jews; A History of the Jewish Wars; and Life of Flavius Josephus, Written by Himself,* trans. William Whiston (Philadelphia: Leary and Getz, 1855), 554.

4. Mark 6:22–24.

5. Marcus Tullius Cicero, *On Old Age and On Friendship,* trans. Harry G. Edinger (New York: Bobbs-Merrill, 1967), 21; Plutarch, *The Lives of the Noble Grecians and Romans,* trans. John Dryden (New York: Modern Library, 1932), 423–24; Lucius Annaeus Seneca, *The Elder Seneca Declamations,* trans. M. Winterbottom, Controversiae bks. 7–10 (Cambridge, MA: Harvard University Press. 1974), 235–43. Some accounts add that Seneca, in relating how the story was pre-

sented by his teacher, said the paramour first *danced* for Flamininus, seducing him into granting her request for the head of a man who offended her. However, there is no apparent reference to a dance in Seneca's writings; his version relates that Flamininus and his lover were dining. Other accounts vary as to whether the paramour was male or female.

6. Josephus, *Works*, 554. "Salome" was also the name of Herodias's maternal grandmother, sister of Herod the Great.

7. Josephus, *Works*, 116–19.

8. James Strong, *The Exhaustive Concordance of the Bible . . . also Brief Dictionaries of the Hebrew and Greek Words of the Original with References to the English Words* (New York: Methodist Book Concern, 1890), 43.

9. Philip Schaff, ed., *A Select Library of the Nicene and post-Nicene Fathers of the Christian Church: Saint Chrysostom: Homilies on the Gospel of Saint Matthew* (Grand Rapids, MI: W. B. Eerdmans, 1956), 299.

10. Joseph Strutt, *The Sports and Pastimes of the People of England* (London: Thomas Tegg. 1838), 208.

11. Heinrich Heine, *Atta Troll*, trans. Herman Scheffauer (New York: B. W. Huebsch, 1914), 115.

12. Jacob Grimm, *Teutonic Mythology*, trans. James Steven Stallybrass (New York: Dover Publications, 1966), 285. Grimm asserts that during the Middle Ages, the biblical Herodias/Salome story was mixed up with "native heathen fables" and hence she was subjected to a variety of punishments for her evil deeds. In some tales she was blown into a perpetual whirlwind, in others she was condemned to ride in the ghostly Wild Hunt until Judgment Day. Herodias/Salome suffers a gory end in tales of her crossing a frozen river that cracks underfoot; as she falls through the crack, her head is severed by the sharp broken ice.

13. Rana Kabbani, *Imperial Fictions: Europe's Myths of Orient* (London: Pandor, 1986), 69.

14. Bram Dijkstra, *Idols of Perversity: Fantasies of Feminine Evil in Fin de Siècle Culture* (Oxford: Oxford University Press, 1986), 49, 37.

15. Patricia Kellogg-Dennis, "Oscar Wilde's Salome: Symbolist Princess," in *Rediscovering Oscar Wilde*, ed. C. George Sandulescu (Gerrards Cross, UK: C. Smythe, 1994), 224.

16. Mario Praz, *The Romantic Agony*, trans. Angus Davidson (London: Oxford University Press, 1970), 203.

17. Théophile Gautier, *One of Cleopatra's Nights and Other Fantastic Romances*, trans. Lafcadio Hearn (New York: Brentano's, 1899), 74.

18. Gustave Flaubert, *Salambo*, trans. E. Mathers (New York: Hart, 1976), 175–76.

19. Arthur W. E. O'Shaughnessy, "The Daughter of Herodias," in *An Epic of Women and Other Poems* (1870; New York: Garland, 1978), 118–28.

20. Dijkstra, *Idols,* 387.

21. Gustave Flaubert, "Herodias," in *Three Tales,* trans. Robert Baldick (New York: Penguin, 1961), 120–22.

22. Edward Said, *Orientalism* (New York: Vintage Books, 1978), 6.

23. J. K. Huysmans, *Against the Grain* [A Rebours] (New York: Dover, 1969), 120–22.

24. Oscar Wilde, "Salome," in *The Complete Illustrated Stories, Plays and Poems of Oscar Wilde,* trans. Lord Alfred Douglas (London: Chancellor Press, 1991), 50, 52.

25. Richard Ellman, *Oscar Wilde* (New York: Alfred A. Knopf, 1988), 376.

26. William Tydeman and Steven Price, *Wilde/Salome* (Cambridge: Cambridge University Press, 1996), 93.

27. Ellman, *Wilde,* 343.

28. Barbara Belford, *Oscar Wilde: A Certain Genius* (New York: Random House, 2000), 203.

29. "The Past": What May be Found in Assyria—Expected Results of Renewed Excavations," [from *London Daily Telegraph,* December 26, 1872], *New York Times,* January 12, 1873.

30. Albert G. Mackey, *An Encyclopedia of Freemasonry and Its Kindred Sciences* (Chicago: Masonic History, 1946), 930.

31. Katharine Worth, *Oscar Wilde* (New York: Grove Press, 1983), 66–67.

32. Tydeman and Price, *Wilde/Salome,* 28.

33. Richard Strauss, *Recollections and Reflections,* ed. Willi Schuh, trans. L. J. Lawrence (London: Boosey and Hawkes, 1953), 151. The appearance of nudity was achieved with the wearing of "fleshings"—flesh-colored tights or body stockings. Fleshings were popular in nineteenth-century displays of *tableaux vivants*—living pictures or statuary. Motionless, costumed models posed to recreate works of art or literary characters.

34. Gaylyn Studlar, "Out-Salomeing Salome" in *Visions of the East: Orientalism in Film,* ed. Matthew Bernstein and Gaylyn Studlar (New Brunswick, NJ: Rutgers University Press, 1997), 106.

35. "Strauss's 'Salome' The First Time Here," *New York Times,* January 23, 1907.

36. "Salome Condemned," *New York Times,* January 24, 1907.

37. Amy Koritz, "Oscar Wilde's Salome," in *Gendering Bodies/Performing Art: Dance and Literature in Early Twentieth-Century British Culture* (Ann Arbor: University of Michigan Press, 1995), 85.

38. For information and photos of the fair see Hubert Howe Bancroft, *The Book of the Fair: An Historical and Descriptive Presentation of the World's Science, Art, and Industry, as Viewed Through the Columbian Exposition in Chicago in 1893* (Chicago: Bancroft, 1893); and James W. Shepp and Daniel B. Shepp, *World's Fair Photographed* (Chicago: Globe Bible, 1893).

39. Richard Bizot, "The Turn-of-the-Century Salome Era: High-and Pop-Culture Variations on the Dance of the Seven Veils," *Choreography and Dance* 2, no. 3 (1992): 72.
40. Helen Davies, "A Model of Womanhood: Ideology as Style in the Work of Adeline Genee and Maud Allan" (master's thesis, Simon Fraser University, Vancouver, BC, 1992), 59.
41. Amy Koritz,"Dancing the Orient for England: Maud Allan's 'The Vision of Salome, '" in *Meaning in Motion: New Cultural Studies of Dance,* ed. Jane C. Desmond (London: Duke University Press, 1997), 140.
42. Tydeman and Price, *Wilde/Salome,* 154–55.

REFERENCES

Bancroft, Hubert Howe. *The Book of the Fair: An Historical and Descriptive Presentation of the World's Science, Art, and Industry, as Viewed Through the Columbian Exposition in Chicago in 1893.* Chicago: Bancroft, 1893.
Belford, Barbara. *Oscar Wilde: A Certain Genius.* New York: Random House, 2000.
Bernstein, Matthew, and Gaylyn Studlar, eds. *Visions of the East: Orientalism in Film.* New Brunswick, NJ: Rutgers University Press. 1997.
Bizot, Richard. "The Turn-of-the-Century Salome Era: High-and Pop-Culture Variations on the Dance of the Seven Veils." *Choreography and Dance* 2, no. 3 (1992).
Cicero, Marcus Tullius. *On Old Age and On Friendship.* Translated by Harry G. Edinger. New York: Bobbs-Merrill, 1967.
Cherniavsky, Felix. *The Salome Dancer: The Life and Times of Maud Allan.* Toronto: McClelland and Stewart, 1991.
Current, Richard Nelson, and Marcia Ewing Current. *Loie Fuller: Goddess of Light.* Boston: Northeastern University Press, 1997.
Davies, Helen. "A Model of Womanhood: Ideology as Style in the Work of Adeline Genee and Maud Allan." Master's thesis. Simon Fraser University, Vancouver, BC, 1992.
Dijkstra, Bram. *Idols of Perversity: Fantasies of Feminine Evil in Fin de Siècle Culture.* Oxford: Oxford University Press, 1986.
Ellmann, Richard. *Oscar Wilde.* New York: Alfred A. Knopf, 1988.
Flaubert, Gustave. *Salambo.* Translated by E. Mathers. New York: Hart, 1976.
———. "Herodias." In *Three Tales,* translated by Robert Baldick. New York: Penguin, 1961.
Fuller, Loie. *Fifteen Years of a Dancer's Life, with Some Account of Her Distinguished Friends.* Boston: Small, Maynard, 1913.
Gautier, Théophile. *One of Cleopatra's Nights and Other Fantastic Romances.* Translated by Lafcadio Hearn. New York: Brentano's, 1899.

Glasscock, Jessica. *Striptease from Gaslight to Spotlight*. New York: Harry N. Abrams, 2003.

Grimm, Jacob. *Teutonic Mythology*. Translated by James Steven Stallybrass. New York: Dover, 1966.

Heine, Heinrich. *Atta Troll*. Translated by Herman Scheffauer. New York: B. W. Huebsch, 1914.

Huysmans, J. K. *Against the Grain* [A Rebours]. New York: Dover, 1969.

Josephus, Flavius. *The Works of Flavius Josephus: Comprising the Antiquities of the Jews; A History of the Jewish Wars; and Life of Flavius Josephus, Written by Himself*. Translated by William Whiston. Philadelphia: Leary and Getz, 1855.

Kabbani, Rana. *Imperial Fictions: Europe's Myths of Orient*. London: Pandor, 1986.

Kendall, Elizabeth. *Where She Danced*. New York: Alfred A. Knopf, 1979.

Koritz, Amy. "Dancing the Orient for England: Maud Allan's 'The Vision of Salome.'" In *Meaning in Motion: New Cultural Studies of Dance*, edited by Jane C. Desmond. London: Duke University Press, 1997.

———. "Oscar Wilde's Salome." In *Gendering Bodies/Performing Art: Dance and Literature in Early Twentieth-Century British Culture*. Ann Arbor: University of Michigan Press, 1995.

Laforgue, Jules. *Moral Tales*. Translated by William Jay Smith. New York: New Directions, 1985.

Macclintock, Samuel. *Herodias: or Cruelty and Revenge, the Effects of Unlawful Pleasure, Illustrated in a Sermon, on the Death of John the Baptist. Preached at Portsmouth, to the Rev'd Dr. Langdon's Congregation, on Lord's Day, June 14th, 1772*. Portsmouth, NH: D. and R. Fowle, 1772.

Mackey, Albert G. *An Encyclopedia of Freemasonry and Its Kindred Sciences*. Chicago: Masonic History, 1946.

Maeterlinck, Maurice. *The Plays of Maurice Maeterlinck*. Translated by Richard Hovey. New York: Duffield, 1906.

Mallarmé, Stéphane. *Herodias*. Translated by Clark Mills. New York: Voyages Press, 1957.

Manor, Giora. *The Gospel According to Dance: Choreography and the Bible: From Ballet to Modern*. New York: St. Martin's Press, 1980.

Michel, Artur. "Salome and Herodias, from the Bible to Martha Graham." *Dance Magazine*, February–March 1946.

O'Shaughnessy, Arthur W. E. *An Epic of Women and Other Poems*. 1870. New York: Garland, 1978.

Pearce, Joseph. *The Unmasking of Oscar Wilde*. San Francisco: Ignatius Press, 2004.

Plutarch. *The Lives of the Noble Grecians and Romans*. Translated by John Dryden. New York: Modern Library, 1932.

Said, Edward. *Orientalism*. New York: Vintage Books, 1978.

Saladin, Linda. *Fetishism and Fatal Women: Gender, Power, and Reflexive Discourse*. New York: P. Lang, 1993.

Sandulescu, C. George, ed. *Rediscovering Oscar Wilde*. Gerrards Cross, UK: C. Smythe, 1994.

Schaff, Philip, ed. *A Select Library of the Nicene and post-Nicene Fathers of the Christian Church: Saint Chrysostom: Homilies on the Gospel of Saint Matthew*. Grand Rapids, MI: W. B. Eerdmans, 1956.

Seneca, Lucius Annaeus. *The Elder Seneca Declamations*. Translated by M. Winterbottom. Controversiae, bks. 7–10. Cambridge, MA: Harvard University Press, 1974.

Shelton, Suzanne. *Divine Dancer: A Biography of Ruth St. Denis*. New York: Doubleday, 1981.

Shepp, James W., and Daniel B. Shepp. *World's Fair Photographed*. Chicago: Globe Bible, 1893.

Steegmuller, Francis. *Flaubert in Egypt: A Sensibility on Tour*. London: Bodley Head, 1972.

Stowe, Harriet Beecher. *Woman in Sacred History: A Series of Sketches Drawn from Scriptural, Historical, and Legendary Sources*. New York: J. B. Ford, 1873.

Strauss, Richard. *Recollections and Reflections*. Edited by Willi Schuh, translated by L. J. Lawrence. London: Boosey and Hawkes,, 1953.

Strong, James. *The Exhaustive Concordance of the Bible . . . also Brief Dictionaries of the Hebrew and Greek Words of the Original with References to the English Words*. New York: Methodist Book Concern, 1890.

Strutt, Joseph. *The Sports and Pastimes of the People of England*. London: Thomas Tegg, 1838.

Tydeman, William, and Steven Price. *Wilde/Salome*. Cambridge: Cambridge University Press, 1996.

White, John S. *The Salome Motive*. New York: New York City Opera,1947.

Wilde, Oscar. "Salome." In *The Complete Illustrated Stories, Plays and Poems of Oscar Wilde*, translated by Lord Alfred Douglas. London: Chancellor Press, 1991.

———. *Salome: A Tragedy in One Act*. Translated by Lord Alfred Douglas. New York: Dover Publications, 1967.

Wolkstein, Diane, and Samuel Noah Kramer. *Inanna, Queen of Heaven and Earth: Her Stories and Hymns from Sumer*. New York: Harper and Row, 1983.

Worth, Katharine. *Oscar Wilde*. New York: Grove Press, 1983.

Zagona, Helen Grace. *The Legend of Salome and the Principle of Art for Art's Sake*. Geneve: Droz, 1960.

9 "He hath couerd my soule inwarde"
Veiling in Medieval Europe and the Early Church

DÉSIRÉE G. KOSLIN

The Western custom of covering married women's hair was firmly established in the medieval and early modern period. Its origins go back, at least, to Syro-Mesopotamian, archaic Mediterranean, and late antique contexts. In Greek black-figure vase painting of the sixth century B.C.E., Attic brides, goddesses of the hearth, as well as Helen—abducted and returned—are shown with the *himation,* an outer wrap, drawn over their heads. In the Babylonian Talmud, it was a serious transgression for a married woman to venture outside with uncovered head.[1] Women as potential objects of family shame through predatory male sexuality needed actual or figurative protective covers for their honor, and the veil provided one such barrier. Jerome Neyrey argues—by quoting sources from ca. 400 B.C.E., including Philo, Xenophon, and Hierocles—that Egyptians, Greeks, Jews, Persians, and Romans shared cultural gender expectations by keeping their women veiled. This practice metaphorically replicated the walls of the women's quarter where infants nursed, food was prepared, and clothing woven and produced.[2] Referring to this tradition, John Chrysostom (ca. 347–407 C.E.) stated,

> Many of the customs still in force in one way or another reveal the sobriety and severity of deportment of those earlier days. Among these is the convention regarding feminine attire which prescribes that women should be so arrayed that nobody can see any part of them, neither of the face nor of the rest of the body, and that they themselves may not see anything of the road.[3]

The Spanish church father Leander of Seville (ca. 540–ca. 600) elaborated on virtuous dress in a rule he composed for the monastery of his sister Florentine, admitting frankly that these dress requirements were necessary to counter temptations originating in male desire:

> Do not wear stunning clothes, anything having a pleat, for the eye is curious before and behind, and do not wear dresses that billow. Be careful of clothes carefully and diligently patterned and bought at a very high price, for that is the care of the flesh, that is the eager desire of the eyes . . . use garments that cover the body, that conceal a maidenly decorum, that keep out the rigors of cold; not those that produce the incentive and capacity to fleshly lust.[4]

In evaluating these and other injunctions of the church fathers for religious women in this period, Jo Ann McNamara has commented, "It was perhaps a mixed blessing that these same men invested so many of their own spiritual aspirations in the purity of women. In their writings they lament their own failures of chastity, while protesting that women became in some sense the vessels of their redemption."[5]

On her wedding day, a bride in republican or imperial Rome bound her hair with woolen bands, *vittae*, that she had woven herself. She would wear them henceforth under her head covering, first under the bridal, red *flammeum*, then below the matronly, white or colored *stola* or *palla*, and, as a widow, beneath the dark, *ricinium* veiling.[6] It is this late antique veiling practice and color symbolism that spread in early Europe as it adopted Christianity. As chaste women in the early centuries established houses for communal living, the veil of widowhood and mourning became the symbol for their status as brides of Christ. To "take the veil" still means to become a nun, and "the veil" is synonymous with a nun's life. In the words of Saint Agnes, John Alcock (1430–1500), bishop of Ely, addressed the nuns in his diocese:

> He hath couerd my soule inwarde and myn heed with a veyle that and if I
> wyll loue ony man better than hym [Christ] I shall goo to the colour of my
> veyle and that is euerlastynge deth.[7]

Here, Alcock called forth an early female saint to direct his nuns in interiorizing, self-corrective scrutiny of their innermost thoughts through the metaphor of the black veil. Nuns' somber veils had long traditions and were mentioned in patristic writings, such as the prose poem *De virginitate*, by Saint Aldhelm (d. 709), composed for the nuns of Barking, in which he describes unsuitable attire for the religious:

> This sort of glamorization consists in fine linen shirts, in scarlet or blue tu-
> nics, in necklines and sleeves embroidered with silk; their shoes are trimmed
> with red-dyes leather; the hair of their forelocks and the curls at their tem-
> ples are crimped with a curling iron; dark-grey veils for the head give way to
> bright and colored head dresses which are sewn with interlacings of ribbons
> and hang down as far as the ankles.[8]

For the next several centuries long veils continued to be regarded as signs of worldly luxury and an abuse among nuns. Tenxwind, abbess of the Augustinian Andernach convent, chastised her colleague Hildegard of Bingen (1098–1179) because she let her nuns appear in church in "loosened hair and white silk veils reaching the floor." By return letter Hildegard stated that her nuns were allowed to wear tiaras, crowns, and long veils on feast days only, and that they wore the black veil required by the rule at all other times.[9]

Before taking the veil and becoming professed as a nun, a novice received a white veil in a ceremony that constituted a first, symbolic act of renunciation. All her worldly clothes were cast off and replaced by simple, monastic garments. While secular women covered their hair under their veiling, novices and nuns were tonsured, perhaps the most radical step of divestment for a medieval woman. Clerical tonsure was required for (male) monastics from the sixth and seventh centuries, but tonsure for cloistered women is not mentioned in the rules until the thirteenth cen-

Figure 9.1. Lucy carried heavenward by angels—obituary illumination. Egerton rotulus 2849, British Library.

tury.[10] Some rules specify the frequency for maintaining a short haircut, to the ears, four to six times a year. Medieval artists have paid attention to the tonsuring of religious women, particularly the one that Saint Francis gave Clare on Palm Sunday in 1212.

After serving the novitiate, the nun-to-be would be professed by the local bishop. At this time, she received the new signs of her status as a bride of Christ, a ring, the black veil, and the order's other dress components, all specifically blessed.[11] The veil, given at profession by the officiating bishop, was kept for her burial. An extraordinary visualization of this practice is seen in a thirteenth-century English obituary roll where the soul of Abbess Lucy of Castle Hedingham in Essex (founded 1233), naked except for the black veil, is conveyed to heaven in an ascension cloth carried by two angels (figure 9.1).

The representations of medieval nuns' veils appear in a great diversity of color, styles, and manners of draping. In the texts of the period, there's

a similar state of ambiguity, in contrast to the great specificity in the post-
and Counter-Reformation orders.[12] In the comparatively few manuscript
illustrations depicting nuns before 1200, there is little agreement on the
color or length of this simple square or rectangle of a textile substance,
which consisted of two layers, a black fabric worn over a white fabric, the
latter usually showing under and around the black. The white underveil
was made of linen or possibly hemp, as was a shift worn under the woolen
tunics. Exceptionally, silk is mentioned in monastic records for this purpose, and at times, depictions seem to indicate the transparency and drape
of this fiber. The black veil fabric was made of fine wool, dyed linen, or
possibly silk. To prevent a veil from slipping off the head, tucks, ties, and
pins were used, anchored into the vittae or other invisible coif.

In a donor portrait in a rulebook of ca. 990, Abbess Uta of Niedermünster
and an accompanying nun are shown in veils of various light shades (Bam-
berg SB Ms.lit.142: 58 and 90v.) as they receive their rule from Caesarius
of Arles (ca. 470–542). His rule was quite specific on the topic of dress,
"Let them have all their clothing only in simple and respectable color, never
black, never bright white, but only natural or milky-white."[13]

To color fabric by dyeing was seen by many as frivolous and false. In
the late fourth century, Jerome compares virginity and vice in textile
metaphors, "once wool has been dyed purple, who can restore it to its
previous whiteness?"[14] In a manuscript illumination of ca. 1020, the all-
white veil of Abbess Hitda of Eichstätt, however, cascades in frills to the
small of her back as she presents her evangeliary to Saint Walburga (710–
79), depicted in secular dress (Darmstadt HLHB Ms.1640: 6). The artist
must have had a very specific vision of this extraordinary veil, in layers
of the finest textures of silk or linen. The frothy edges may well represent a headdress similar to the "interlacings of ribbons" that Aldhelm described above.

During the twelfth century, an accompaniment to the veil, the chest-
and throat-covering wimple, was introduced. Its evolution can be traced
in illustrations of secular and religious women, among them a twelfth-
century Spanish picture-Bible and saints' lives, one of the "Pamplona
Bibles" (Amiens BV Ms.108: 236v.), which shows Saint Euphemia of Chal-
cedon, venerated in Galicia, in a snugly draped veil covering both her chin

and head. This image may be taken as an example of the transition in female medieval headdress as the wimple becomes independent of the veil.
One of the early illuminated pontificals, manuals for bishops, is instruc-
tive in showing the manner of draping as the white underveil of the nun-
to-be is seen at the point of being covered by the black veil. Many
variations of this one-piece headdress certainly continued in use throughout the medieval period; secular and religious women are depicted in headdresses artfully draped from plain cloths of linen, often with frilled edges,
while the lay religious, *conversae*, employed simpler versions than the aris-
tocratic nuns.

The rich folds of the ca. 1238 depiction of Hildegard of Bingen in a
Cologne chronicle (Brussels BR 467; 64) shows the fully detached wimple, possibly anchored to a headband under the black veil. This medieval
accessory can be defined as a separate, relatively fine textile in linen or
silk, which covered the throat, chest, and often part of the chin. It is present
in depictions of nuns as well as those of many secular women from the
thirteenth century onward. Ideas for this style may have come from the
East and southern Europe during the Crusades and the intensified contacts with sophisticated cultures where veiling of all women was routinely
observed. It may also have depended on a related phenomenon: the arrival of the horizontal loom from the Middle East. It soon became established in Europe and allowed faster production of yardage.[15] Most silk
textiles, however, continued to arrive via the northern or Mediterranean
trade routes, although the nascent silk industries in Italian city-states such
as Lucca, and later Florence, were in rapid development. It has been noted
that the fabrics used in veils and wimples became finer from the thirteenth
century, although it is difficult to determine whether this is a change based
on observations of painterly conventions of the period or on actual proof
of new and finer fabric qualities being produced; what seems to be certain is that rates of fabric production increased vastly.[16]

In a late thirteenth-century miniature, two elegant abbesses are depicted,
one of whom has been identified as Gertrude of Nivelles. Their veils, revealing some hair underneath, have been drawn over supports built above
the ears, giving the fashionable "horned" silhouette; this ensemble appears
to have required two cloths, the lower wimple covering chest and throat

(Paris BNF n.a.fr.Ms.16251: 115v.). Wimple fashions appear to be incremental: at first the extra fabric fills the gap between tunic and throat; by the fourteenth century it envelops the chin; and by the fifteenth century crimped, pipe-pleated, or goffered examples seem to be de rigueur. These fluted wimples required exacting preparation before donning, and similar styles survive in various traditional collars and headdresses in folk traditions of Europe. Fine, bleached linen was first soaked in starch, then stretched flat and crimped or pleated while wet with the aid of a gauge. The pleats were then held in place with clamps until dry when the garment could be shaped to conform to head contours. Freshly pleated fabric was required for each wearing.[17]

Issues of class and social rank may also be observed in the veils of the secular and the religious. Veil qualities appear with a rhetorical edge in a fifteenth-century miniature (Paris BNF Ms.lat.9474:111v.) depicting the raising of Lazarus. His sainted sisters Martha of Bethany and Mary Magdalene are seen in laywoman's white and nun's black veiling respectively, referring to their distinctly different active and contemplative natures. Martha's simple white veil is edged in dark stripes, a style worn by humble lay penitents of Italy, often engaged in charitable or practical work. These veils were probably made of practical and hardwearing fustian, a linen and cotton fabric. Mary's black veil denotes her status as consecrated and cloistered. Both, however, wear elegant, transparent wimples of silk or finest linen, worn over starched, accordion-pleated collars complementing the haloes of the two saints.

In the Low Countries during 1349–51, Abbot Gilles le Muisit of St-Martin was lecturing women of different orders on their comportment. They included a group of Beguines, dressed in hooded mantles that covered their white head veils (Brussels BR Ms.IV.119:84). The utterly humble dress of the noncloistered Beguines is rarely depicted and described, as this group was at first loosely organized and did not have a rule. It seems that there was little uniformity in the color and cut of the women's dress, although all wore great veils of black or dark gray wool that enveloped them completely from head to heel.

All veils were not simply cloth rectangles, and in several late medieval manuscripts black fabric hoods are seen, made of a folded fabric stitched along one side. When placed on the head with the seam at the back, the hood's peak would fall forward, forming a small flap at the crown of the head, often seen in depictions of simple countrywomen. Very short, black veils also appear in depictions of late medieval German Benedictine nuns, indicating restraint and frugality.

Since the earliest centuries, nuns who embellished their veils with embroidery or precious materials were targets of much scorn from the supervising clergy and other critics. As we have seen, depictions in the early period record veil volume and length, while later artists take pains to render other status signifiers in explicit, didactic detail. Thus, a psalter made in Salisbury ca. 1250 depicts nuns in numerous historiated initials, with red or white pins in their veils clearly rendered, probably designating gold or silver ornaments. They appear to hold the nuns' black veils tacked in place to the white underveil as they also add a fashionable touch (London RCP Ms.409:176, 182). In thirteenth-century England, pins were imported from France and restrictions on their use by the religious were issued with regularity, attesting to their widespread popularity as well as to their cost.[18]

Distinguishing marks on the nuns' veils are seen in a number of manuscripts in the fourteenth century. A 1353 life of Saint Hedwig of Silesia, commissioned by the Cistercian nun Juliana of Trebnitz, seems intended to establish dynastic and propagandistic purposes, showing the saint with her local royal family along with images of the monastic inmates. Abbess Gertrude and her nuns, each of them named, appear in black veils with small, frontal crosses (Malibu JPG 83.MN.126, Ms. Ludwig XI :46). Similar crosses are seen in a pontifical of Roman use in which the bishop blesses three Cistercian virgins, dressed in light colors, upon consecration (Paris BNF Ms.lat.17336:47, 99v.). The Cistercian sermologium of the late fourteenth century (Oxford Bodleian Ms.Douce 185: throughout) shows the nuns wearing hatched veils, interpreted here as fine, transparent silk, over their white underveils marked with red crosses.

The most distinctive emblem seen in medieval nuns' headdresses is surely the crown of white linen bands adorned with five red cloth patches that the Birgittines placed over their black veil.[19] The compounding of symbolic elements is elaborate, signifying the cross and the five wounds that encircle the head of each Brigittine *Sponsa Christi* at all times, placed over the veil as the token of her mystical marriage (Stockholm KB A12:129v.; and Stockholm KB A 75:1v.).

In Italy, the art of developing edges of fabrics became a great specialty in the postmedieval centuries. At first such edgings appear as modestly dentellated and then in fully developed *punto in aria* (stitch in air) laces, creating an intermediary zone between object and nonobject. An incipient stage of this focus on the "unseen" is displayed in the nuns' veils in the miniatures of the manuscripts of the papal privilege given to the ascetic Augustinian hermits and nuns of Cremona in 1496. Here the nuns' white underveils are rendered as transparent in finest linen, while their purled edges form new, emphatic intermediaries between the black veil and the body (Bergamo BAM Cassaf.1.10; 14v.).

In metaphor and in actual usage, the idea of the veil resonates through many of the world's cultures with vernacular and spiritual meanings of illusion, protection, secrecy, and submission. In medieval Europe, it is associated with modesty and virtue while at the same time its color and type often denote status as well as stages in life. The supposedly insignificant dress styles of the female religious, and especially their headdresses, have been represented in this period with a great variety of intent and expression. This diversity points to a history of a dress accessory that is neither linear nor conformist in spite of repeated efforts by those who aspired to impose control. The veils of the medieval religious can therefore be said to feature several sets of binary opposites: submissiveness and independence, piety and waywardness, compliance and subversion.

NOTES

1. Babylonian Talmud, Ketuboth, 72b. Similar legislation appear throughout the period; in the late fourteenth-century legal code of Gotland, Sweden, the fine for pulling off a free woman's veil or headdress, in part or entirely, was as much as for exposing her entire lower body, see Tore Gannholm, *Guta Lagh* (Lund, Sweden, 1994), 63.
2. Jerome Neyrey, "What's Wrong With This Picture? John 4, Cultural Stereotypes of Women, and Public and Private Space," *Biblical Theory Bulletin* 24, no. 2 (1994): 77–91.

3. Ora.33.48–51, quoted in Neyrey, "What's Wrong," 80.

4. Leander's "Training of Nuns," in *Iberian Fathers*, vol. 1, *Martin of Braga, Paschius of Dumium, Leander of Seville*, trans. Claude W. Barlow (Washington, DC, 1969), 195. The Latin version is available in part on Migne, PL 72.873–894, and in its entirety in A. C. Vega, *El 'De Institutione virginum' de San Leandro de Seville* (Escorial, 1948).

5. Jo Ann McNamara, *Sisters in Arms: Catholic Nuns through Two Millennia* (Cambridge, MA.: Harvard University Press, 1996), 49.

6. Judith Lynn Sebasta, "Symbolism in the Costume of the Roman Woman," in *The World of Roman Costume*, ed. Judith Lynn Sebasta and Larissa Bonfante (Madison: University of Wisconsin Press, 1994), 48–50.

7. John Alcock, *Spousage of a Virgin to Christ: An Exhortacyon made to Relygyous Systers*, English Experience, no. 638 (Norwood, NJ: W. J. Johnson, 1974).

8. *Aldhelm: The Prose Works*, trans. Michael Lapidge and Michael Herren (Port Credit, Ontario: P. D. Meany, 1979), 127–28.

9. See translation by Hartmut Boockmann, "Gelöstes Haar und seidene Schleier: Zwei Äbtissinen im Dialog," in *Streifzüge durch das Mittelalter: Ein historisches Lesebuch* (Munich: Rainer Beck, 1995), 213.

10. Further primary source information on tonsure is noted in the rites of the pontifical of Durandus, see Michel Andrieu, *Le pontifical romain au Moyen-Âge* (The Vatican, 1938–41), 3:412.

11. See Désirée Koslin, "The Robe of Simplicity: Initiation, Robing, and Veiling of Nuns in the Middle Ages," in *Robes and Honor: The Medieval World of Investiture*, ed. Stewart Gordon (New York: Palgrave, 2001), 255–74.

12. For the case of England, Sally Thompson has thoroughly accounted for this diversity in *Women Religious: The Founding of English Nunneries after the Norman Conquest* (Oxford: Oxford University Press, 1991).

13. Emilie Amt, *Women's Lives in Medieval Europe: A Sourcebook* (New York: Routledge, 1993), 230.

14. In a letter to Paula's daughter-in-law, Laeta, Letter 107, translated and quoted by Joan M. Peterson, "Handmaids of the Lord: Contemporary Descriptions of Feminine Asceticism in the First Six Christian Centuries," *Journal of Early Christian Studies* 6, no. 3 (summer 1998): 258.

15. In terms of economic importance, introduction of the horizontal loom certainly ranks with, if not surpasses that of, for instance, movable type.

16. Françoise Piponnier and Perrine Mane, *Se vêtir au Moyen Âge* (Paris: A. Biro, 1995), 98; according to the authors (62), surviving representations are too few to allow developments and chronologies to be established. Finely woven textiles had a long history, however, and were always prestigious and exclusive. The technological improvements certainly made such goods more widely available. By the later Middle Ages, painters excelled in ways of ren-

dering such status fabrics as almost "invisible," well known from the painted panels by Jan van Eyck, Robert Campin, etc.

17. Goffering (or gauffering), indicating a hot iron (as in waffle making), is a term used for hot pleating, suitable for fibers like wool or silk. See Eric Kerridge, *Textile Manufactures in Early Modern England* (Dover, NH: Manchester University Press, 1985), 173.

18. The 1222 Council of Oxford stated, "nuns . . . shall not dare to carry silver or golden tiring-pins in their veil," quoted in Eileen Power, *Medieval English Nunneries, c. 1275–1535* (Cambridge: Biblio and Tannen, 1922), 585.

19. An identical crown emblem was previously used by the Premonstratensian and Cistercian female branches in Germany, see R. Norberg, "Den Heliga Birgitta och Codex Gisle i Osnabrück," *Fornvännen* 34 (1939): 226–39, a discussion continued by Renate Kroos, "Der Codex Gisle I. Forschungsbericht und Datierung," *Niederdeutsche Beiträge für Kunstgeschichte* 12 (1973). For a fuller account on this and related topics, see my dissertation, "The Dress of Monastic and Religious Women as Seen in Art from the Early Middle Ages to the Reformation" (1999, UMI Dissertation Services, www.umi.com).

SARAH C. BELL

It turns out that Di was like a lot of brides.  She was property, chattel, a royal bargaining chip, a brood mare.

And what happens if neither spouse likes the MERCHANDISE?

Maybe that's where the tradition of the SHEER VEIL came from.

After all, in the Bible, Jacob was tricked into marrying his beloved Rachel's sister Leah,  who was hidden under a full veil.

When we were little, we had no idea  how many different ways women have, and do, veil themselves for marriage.

Unmarried women often wear veils to show modesty.  At wedding ceremonies, the bride wears the veil as a sign of submissiveness to her groom.

But there are more reasons than that ...

Many cultures believed that a bride was vulnerable to EVIL SPIRITS

This was the belief in Ancient Rome, China, and the Far East.

Apparently, EVIL SPIRITS inhabit much of the planet  AND THEY ARE AFTER OUR WOMEN.

Ancient Chinese held a sacred umbrella over the bride... to protect her from these nasty BUGGERS.

In the Far East, the veil disguised the beauty of a bride,  that might attract the attentions of unwanted entities.

In Ancient Rome, they even fashioned the bride's hair into a LARGE SPIKE

to ward off horned demons and keep her pure for her husband.

In Japan, brides wore horned headdresses

to veil the "horns" of jealousy, ego and selfishness (demons for her husband)

Anglo-Saxon & Anglo-Norman brides wore their hair as a sort of veil,

flowing down their backs as an emblem of their virginity.

The wedding veil is still seen as a symbol of PURITY

It is worn throughout the ceremony and removed at the end to prove that the bride is PURE.

But after that veil comes off, boy, it's

NO HOLDS BARRED

Maybe the veil is a throwback from a time when

a potential groom tossed a blanket over the girl he liked and carried her away.

The veil even shows up in MYTHOLOGY

Ishtar, ancient Goddess of Love, came from the depths to her intended, vapors from the earth and sea, covering her like a veil.

Even the word "NUPTIAL" comes from the Latin word "NUBO," meaning,

i veil myself

So why is it that we "liberated" Western brides still wear the VEIL?

My friend recently got married. She wore a lovely veil, and her father "gave" her away.

My friend is a lawyer. And an almost militant feminist.

Maybe the veil, for us, is just a fashion choice. Or maybe we are

Sometimes sentimental about belonging to our daddies, or nostalgic about being currency.

There is a rich history behind veiling at weddings, and many reasons for it.

But I think it's really the EVIL SPIRITS...

11 After Eden

The Veil as a Conduit to the Internal

All of the honor of the king's daughter is internal.

During Eve's short life before eating from the tree, she recognized the body's purpose with a swift transparency.

When the soul wanted to pray, the body would rise.

In Eden, no chasm gaped between wishing to serve the soul and serving it; no delay between wanting and the thing wanted. Eve saw that matter and spirit were aligned, that all was part of a whole, that the body was meant to articulate the spiritual reality. Like all of nature's elements, the body was not an entity separate from holiness.

> God created man in his image; in the image of God he created him; male and female he created them.[1]

The Jewish idea that the body has a spiritual purpose comes from these words, and the sublime wording highlights the unique status of humans, where human creation is referred to three times.

Figure 11.1. Illustration by Maureen Selwood
with Megan Cotts, 2006.

The phrase "in his image" does not suggest that God has a physical
form. It really should be translated "*with* his image." The phrase refers to
the mold created for humans in order to make them. The Hebrew letter
bet, which means "with," appears immediately before "his image," telling
us that God created humans *with* an image or mold. Notably, *bet* is used
instead of *kaf* (which means "like"); if *kaf* had been used instead, the phrase
would have meant "*like* God's image," implying that humans have a physical likeness to God. But God has no form. The *bet* is there, thus the mold,
coin, or die; these are the metaphors of Rashi (Rabbi Shlomo Yitzhaqi),
the French medieval commentator who describes how God created the
first human through a kind of stamping procedure.

The twentieth-century Israeli Torah scholar Nehama Leibowitz explains
that "The duties, responsibilities, and glory of humans derive from this
verse."[2] In other words, human beings have ethical and spiritual obliga-
tions, and each physical part of man and woman corresponds to an invisible divine element.

Later, after Eve ate from the tree of knowledge of good and evil, it was as if a veil had descended upon nature, obscuring the spiritual realm. The physical now appeared to be the only reality.

Paradoxically, a "veil"—clothing and other coverings—became the conduit through which Eve would maintain a relationship with the internal kingdom, the soul, and the unseen. By deemphasizing the physical, Eve developed a spiritual life after Eden.

I go to Monsey (an area in Rockland County, New York, just outside New York City, where a large number of religious Jews live) for the first time. A friend invites me to spend Shabbos (the Jewish Sabbath begins Friday night at sundown and lasts twenty-five hours) with a religious family who lives there, a rabbi and his wife and their nine children. This family had become my friend's family in many ways, providing support, guidance, and a light, warm, buoyant atmosphere. The weekend passes through me, to paraphrase Emily Brontë, like wine through water.

Hungry for the spiritual life, I arrive in Monsey with an open heart and mind. The world of poetry—writing, reading, coordinating poetry events, teaching poetry, being mentored by poets—provides a certain amount of spiritual sustenance, but it's not enough. My writing comes out of an urgency and a joy in language, and poetry friends and mentors provide some sense of community, yet it isn't a *life*. So many of my poetry mentors have Christian backgrounds with Christian messages embedded in their work and teachings, and I am eager to embrace myself as a Jew; my Jewishness is slipping away from me. I am an overeducated poet and an uneducated Jew. I want to humble myself before my own religion.

During my stay in Monsey, I learn that the spiritual life emanates from the home and that it develops in the context of family life. It can be found in the kitchen and at the dining room table. *Shul* (synagogue) plays a role, but it's the home that integrates and filters religious feeling and ideas. While learning Torah and Talmud are paramount, it's how this learning funnels into relationships that creates the vibrancy and peace I witness around me. And the influence of women is strongly exercised in the home. The solid and animated family life moves me in the midst of memories of my own rocky childhood, and I notice a flexible balance between structure and wildness.

Each time I visit Monsey I come home to a dream. In my first dream, the rabbi says to me, "The food you are eating does not nourish you." I take this to mean that nonkosher food is not nourishing me spiritually. Also, the life I am leading in general is not providing for a part of myself that had long gone unfed.

For Eve, before eating from the tree, everything—her hand, bark, bird song, grass—was linked. The following lines from William Blake's poem "Auguries of Innocence" address the linkage between all elements, earthly and celestial:

> To see a World in a Grain of Sand
> And Heaven in a Wild Flower,
> Hold Infinity in the palm of your hand
> And Eternity in an hour.
> A Robin Redbreast in a Cage
> Puts all Heaven in a Rage.
> A dove house fill'd with doves & pigeons
> Shudders Hell thro' all its regions.
> A dog starv'd at his Master's Gate
> Predicts the ruin of the State. . . .
> If the Sun & Moon should doubt
> They'd immediately Go out.[3]

The poet Stanley Kunitz said about this poem: "I see all creation—and this stems in part from these couplets from Blake—as a single continuous web, all of whose single filaments are interconnected. If you touch the web at any point, certainly the whole web shudders. Everything that lives stands in connection with everything else on this planet. That is something Blake taught me."[4] Eve did not need poetry to teach her that heaven could be seen in a wild flower and that all the filaments of nature were interconnected; when she touched the web of creation at any point she could *feel* the whole web shudder.

I was raised by and among artists, writers, former hippies, and political activists. Progressive and liberal, my family lived on Manhattan's Upper West Side, and my world was intellectual and secular. Art and social justice were the primary values. Human rights and literature took the place of religion. My father had been a dedicated civil rights activist, and I was sent to a progressive elementary school based on the values of Dr. Martin Luther King Jr. I joined the Women's Issues Club in high school, and at Smith College I grew as a feminist. There was no other way to live, as far as I knew, yet I sensed a silent squelching of my own femininity and spirituality.

Judaism was a shock and a revelation. When I began to live inside of Judaism, I realized that I had stumbled upon an outlook that I had always believed in even though I had never been exposed to it before; I arrived at a place I had been waiting for, a place I had never imagined or knew existed, yet I felt as if I had been traveling toward it all along. The traditional gender roles in Monsey splashed over me like a fresh shower. I discovered a new kind of feminism embodied in these empowered women.

Later, the rabbi would tell me, "In the secular world, women have to decide what kind of object they want to be." The religious women I knew were stepping away from the game of objectification; they dressed modestly in public and focused primarily on internal work and spiritual development.

Observant Jewish men and women are careful to cover most of their bodies (according to *halakhoth*, Jewish law) when in public, even in summer; generally, the women I know dress elegantly but not provocatively. In her memoir, *Through the Unknown, Remembered Gate,* Emily Benedek writes about spending Shabbos in this same neighborhood in Monsey: "I look at a gorgeous dark-eyed woman with a baby in her arms and elegant clothes, silent, graceful. I see another woman, a blonde, with pale skin and fine features. She doesn't speak, but her body seems musical, her modesty like a song."[5] Benedek is noticing a specific approach that can be found among women in religious communities—care is taken to honor the gift of the body, and this care manifests itself by highlighting beauty modestly; a certain slant of light gleams through the reticence.

I think of the advice that Mary Oliver gave to poets: "Modesty will give you vigor. It keeps open the gates of prayer, through which the mystery of the poem streams on its search for form. Just occasionally, take something you have written, that you rather like, that you have felt an even immodest pleasure over, and throw it away."[6] Modesty in dress, as well as in poetry, can open up an untapped well. Paradoxically, throwing away a stunning line of poetry or covering the body can lead to creative or erotic power.

The body of the first human being was half man and half woman. When the female half was drawn and built from the being's side, "God endowed woman with more understanding than man."[7]

The Hebrew word for the type of understanding Eve excelled in is *binah* (according to the rabbis in the Talmud), which involves applied knowledge, a wisdom that arises in the midst of actual situations. It is a word derived from the Hebrew root *bein*, which means "between." Binah is the ability to distinguish between situations that on the surface seem similar but are really quite different. Perhaps our use of the contemporary phrase "a woman's intuition" has its roots in this ancient concept of binah. Eve's potential for contextual knowledge permitted a profound understanding of the relationship between the inner and the outer, the body and the soul, the emotions and the senses, human connection and physical contact.

After my next visit to Monsey I have another dream. It is summer. I am standing alone by a small private lake, and I am wearing a simple one-piece bathing suit, a towel thrown over my arm. Suddenly the rabbi turns the bend and is walking toward the lake in his bathing trunks. He looks up, sees me, and then immediately turns and walks away, knowing it was not appropriate to approach me there.

When Eve ate from the tree of knowledge, she almost completely lost her awareness of the explanations behind her body's functions. Remnants of that knowledge remained, and she had dim memories of the data regarding what her hand was for, her breast, her thigh, her earlobe, each strand of hair.

She now understood her body mostly in terms of its animal functions—each body part had its base purpose. Her thigh helped with walking, her hair protected her head from the sun, her breast could feed a baby, and her hand was useful in many practical ways. But what are the spiritual dimensions to these same body parts? She could not remember exactly. Ironically, she lost the knowledge of these dimensions when she ate from the tree of knowledge.

The Rebbe Menachem Schneerson, the last Lubavitcher rebbe, said, "If you are close when you should be distant, you will be distant when you should be close."[8]

I start to date men without touching them (*shomer nagea* it's called in Hebrew, "guarding the touch"), going by the traditional Jewish dating rule: you begin touching only after marriage. Dating is talking, getting to know each other's values, thoughts, and feelings, and sensing attraction. All without touching.

As feminists, long after the sexual revolution, my friends and I probably had never even heard of the concept of "waiting until marriage," except in the nineteenth-century novels we devoured. The sexual revolution created an environment that, ironically, did not allow choice for women. There was only one option: you became physically involved relatively quickly with a person you were attracted to and liked. You had no other choice.

I had watched myself and my friends fall like trees crashing in a storm, and I had a sense that the continual heartache I experienced was intensified by the physical contact I was having with boyfriends. When I began to remove that element when I dated men I experienced frustration, longing, and some loneliness but less despair and anguish. I also noticed that it was much easier to "screen men out" as the absence of touch produced a certain clarity. The person's nature could be more transparently viewed; the lack of touching made the dating experience less clouded. Touch summoned attachment whether the person was right for me or not. Shomer nagea let me gain a bit more insight in the midst of a difficult process. But I also learned that shomer nagea did not solve all dating problems. It was still a process rife with tremendous struggle.

I have a few dates with a gentle, intelligent, and attentive man. He is handsome, but there is something feminine about him. I call the rabbi's house and begin to tell his wife about the date.

"He is lovely and listening and thoughtful."

She says, "It sounds good."

But then I tell her, "He seems like an angel. Almost like he is not a man."

She replies, "I think you need to talk to my husband."

When he gets on the phone I tell him about the date. He says, "A twisted vision of men has been established in society. There is now a perverse notion of what it means to be a man. A real man is a giver." I take this in. A giver. It would take several years for me to absorb this new definition of a man. I wasn't ready yet.

The Rambam (Maimonides, or Moses ben Maimon, the renowned twelfth-century Sephardic rabbi, philosopher, and doctor) explains that when Eve ate from the tree of knowledge of good and evil, subjectivity was introduced to the world; before eating from the tree, Eve understood only *emet* and *sheker* (truth and falsehood). *Tov* and *rah* (good and evil) didn't interest her.

After Eden, Eve gained the "knowledge" of good and bad, and she no longer could remember accurately what was true. Now a chasm gaped between matter and spirit, and longing was introduced, often blurring the distinctions between truth and falsehood, which created inner confusion and chaos.

Before everything changed, Eve saw that truth (the spiritual world and how it manifested itself in the physical) was beautiful. John Keats intuited this perception regarding the relationship between beauty and truth in one of his letters where he wrote, "What the Imagination seizes as Beauty must be truth." And he ends his poem "Ode on a Grecian Urn" with the lines:

Beauty is truth, truth beauty,—that is all
Ye know on earth, and all ye need to know.[9]

Here Keats taps into what Eve knew in Eden: that beauty and truth are one. For instance, there was no question in Eve's mind about the beauty of her physical life with Adam. Their erotic life was beautiful because she could experience truth—or God—through it.

Misty Harper's poem "Door" evokes the connection between touch and the divine:

Your fingers brush mine and you
are wind in a convent where nuns
leave their windows open at night.

You touch and like a door I open,
until I lie in twenty narrow beds,
praying twenty different prayers.[10]

"Door" reveals the continual transformative quality of touch, religiously, imaginatively, and emotionally. Even the innocuous brushing of fingers can produce a kind of mystical revelation. The beloved becomes wind, which represents the divine force or breath. Wordsworth especially, and many poets before and since him, have invoked wind as a stand-in for the divine spirit. In Hebrew, the word for "wind," *ruach*, also means "divine spirit"; in addition, ruach is one of the words for the soul. Touch has the ability to open doors, to turn the beloved into the breath of a divine spirit, to trigger twenty different prayers.

I am dating a new person. Immediately the rabbi discerns that something is wrong. He says to me, "I am worried about you."

I tell the rabbi, "I love talking to him; we can walk blocks and blocks talking, and I never get bored. And he says he wants to carry my bags to the airport for me tomorrow."

The rabbi says, "Just because someone acts like a gentleman doesn't mean he is one." And then he says, "I want to know if he is good. Not what passes for good these days. I mean really good."

The rabbi suggests that I tell the man that I am dating for marriage and if that is what he wants then we can see each other. The man agrees. And we do not touch. Yet the connection—intellectual, physical, I can feel it all—is electric.

During my next visit in Monsey the rabbi says, "Can you find your own voice? Does he allow room for you? Some men think sharing means taking seven-eighths of the pie." He adds, "And this is reflected in the bedroom."

Later, when I tell the rabbi how the relationship fell apart, how the man had a dark past and a terrifying secret life, beyond what I could handle, a practically criminal situation with endless complications and dangers, the rabbi says, "The question is, why do you feel drawn to such a wild man? What attracts you to that wildness?"

I stare at him dumbly and say something like, "I probably want to work out my childhood in some way."

He says, "I think you want to be wild and don't know how to so you choose a wild man through which to experience your own wildness. For some reason you feel that you can only be wild through a man. You be the wild one, Eve."

How do I be wild? What is wild? I ask him, "How does one be wild?"

He says, "I don't know what you enjoy doing. Take dance lessons. Drumming. Something physical. Something wild. Do you know the Bee Gees?"

"Yes," I say and look at him wondering why is he asking me, and wondering how *he* knows the Bee Gees.

He then says, "Dance to 'Staying Alive.'"

For months I think about what it means to be wild. I ask people how to be wild. A friend buys me an enormous flower with a huge tall stalk, thick stem, a bursting orange tough blossom. A mentor tells me to write a novel in one week. Someone suggests that I travel somewhere exotic. I keep looking around me wondering what wild is. I buy the Bee Gees and listen to "Staying Alive" on my iPod and walk down the street and giggle to myself. When I go to Monsey I watch the women. Is she wild? What about her? These women with elegant clothing and that mysterious internal light. How is the rabbi's wife wild? I watch her open the refrigerator door, gather her grandchildren in her arms. Now she is about to teach a class at the school she runs. Now she is laughing. What is it? How is she wild?

Eating from the tree seemed like it would be rewarding; if Eve ate the fruit, perhaps she would achieve something even better than she already had. The serpent, jealous of Eve's sexual life with Adam, which connected them to God, seduced Eve into a place where the "I" dominates. Before they ate from the tree, temptation addressed Adam and Eve with "you." If they were in a situation when something tempting and forbidden came into sight such as the fruit from the tree, an inner voice said, "*You* would like this."

That "you" was relatively easy to ignore. It represented a theoretical desire. Eve would have a detached thought such as "Something in me thinks I might want this." It was not difficult to dismiss a thought like this.

Once desire begins to speak in the first person, it's a different situation. Then it's unequivocally "me." The serpent persuaded Eve to think, "There is no question about it. I want this."

Adam and Eve crossed over from hearing "you" to "I" when they ate from the tree. The snake was able to make Eve step into the gap, to cross over into a personal desire detached from God's desire, which created a haze that obscured the center. Now a sense of dread permeated existence. Marie Howe, in her poem "Part of Eve's Discussion," imagines Eve's first moment stepping into this new stage:

> It was like the moment when a bird decides not to eat from your hand, and flies, just before it flies, just before it flies, the moment the rivers seem to still and stop because a storm is coming, but there is no storm, as when a hundred starlings lift and bank together before they wheel and drop, very much like the moment, driving on bad ice, when it occurs to you your car could spin, just before it slowly begins to spin, like the moment just before you forgot what it was you were about to say, it was like that, and after that, it was still like that, only all the time.[11]

Bewilderment dominates human experience after Eden, which leads to doubt. In fact, kabbalistic sources refer to the tree of knowledge as the tree of doubt. Human consciousness shifted, and for the first time, there seemed to be a dichotomy between matter and spirit. This created a problem for the body, which could now be seen as having only animal or practical purposes, devoid of spiritual meaning. The man and woman immediately covered themselves with the tree's leaves, the very one from which they ate.

I meet a man for dinner at a Japanese restaurant. Originally from South Africa, he is tall, goofy, and warm. A little nervous and shy, absentminded and intellectual. There is something sensual around his mouth; he has a full head of blond hair and a short-cropped gray beard; he is nervous, fumbles with his coffee; we have a lot in common, and I sense goodness there, but I am not sure if I am attracted to him.

The rabbi listens to everything and then says to me, "It's too bad that he is not narcissistic or manipulative, because then you would be attracted to him." I take a moment to absorb this comment.

"But he is not manly!" I cry. "He doesn't have a certain manly quality that attracts me."

The rabbi says, "The erotic connection can be very powerful with a man like this."

The rabbi has shocked me out of my own foolishness, and I pray daily to break out of the grip of an old script of attractions and be open to a new kind of attraction. It works. But then, suddenly, the man has to travel to Australia for four weeks on a business trip.

The rabbi says, "Let him go to Australia. Let him go. A man respects a woman who has needs, not a needy woman. A woman is abundant. A woman assumes she is loved."

I would begin a new kind of inner work.

After Adam and Eve's crisis, God performs a great act of kindness. Like a parent with children, God clothes Adam and Eve: "And God made for Adam and his wife garments of skin and clothed them."[12] Covering their bodies allowed the two beings to view their bodies more accurately in the face of their new mind-set and the new world in which they found themselves. They had a sense that something nonanimal, linked to the divine, lay in the body's uses and functions; and not exposing their bodies allowed them to contemplate this mystery and to get closer to the spiritual reality they had lost. They saw that now, when the body is exposed in nonintimate settings, it is more difficult to remember the spiritual derivation of the body's holiest parts, and this forgetting produces shame.

The teachings of Judaism encourage people, especially women, to dress modestly because their inner worlds are considered to be so vivid and rich. In Psalm 45, the psalmist wrote: "All of the honor of the king's daughter is internal." (In the psalms "king" is a stand-in for God, and the "daughter" here refers to women). The Hebrew letters in the word "inside," *panim*, can also be found in the Hebrew word for "face." The fact that these two seemingly opposite meanings—inside and face—are made up of the same exact letters suggests that the outer and the inner are not opposites; rather, they are intimately connected and actually reveal each other.

Emily Dickinson explores this connection in a poem's first lines:

The Outer—from the Inner
Derives its Magnitude—

Not only does Dickinson suggest here that the outer draws its grandeur from what is inside (she goes on to write, "The Inner—paints the Outer—"), but she ends the poem with the idea that the mystery of the internal kingdom was not meant to be exposed:

The Star's Whole Secret—in the Lake—
Eyes were not meant to know.[13]

After Eden, it's difficult to discern the divine purpose of the outer world; the purpose is inside, "in the Lake." What is holiest is secret; we rush to hide what is most sacred to us; "what is hidden is blessed."[14] The Torah is carefully covered in shul. The tabernacle that the Jews carried in the desert, which represented the dwelling place of God on earth, required special coverings to deemphasize its sparkling exteriors; the coverings allowed the Jews to contemplate the awesome spiritual presence hovering below the surface. Hanna, the future mother of Samuel, prayed for a child by scarcely moving her lips.

The way the Torah itself was written reflects this concept of hiding the deepest truths. The *midrashim,* stories orally passed down at which the Torah's language hints, often offer the most nuanced textual interpretations. The contemporary literary and Torah scholar Avivah Gottlieb Zornberg describes *midrash* as the repressed unconscious of the Torah. "The midrash," Zornberg explains, "offers an answer to a repressed question."[15] In other words, midrashim emerge from what the Torah cannot say directly. Meaning lies in the white spaces between words. From the pregnant silences in the Torah comes the hidden midrash.

God is not seen but hidden in the world. In fact, the word for "world," *olam* in Hebrew, includes the same letters as the word "hidden." The world itself, the veil of nature, gives us the opportunity to find God. And "the veil"—or clothing we use to cover our bodies—allows us to experience our internal richness. Isaac Bashevis Singer ended a story with these lines: "There are certain lights that must remain hidden, or else human free will would come to an end. There are certain unions that have no need to couple. There are certain truths that are perceived less the more evident they become."[16] And, as Emily Dickinson suggests in the following poem, the truth blinds us when it's revealed:

Tell all the Truth but tell it slant—
Success in Circuit lies
Too bright for our infirm Delight
The Truth's superb surprise

As Lightning to the Children eased
With explanation kind
The Truth must dazzle gradually
Or every man be blind–[17]

I have always applied these lines to poetry, to the idea that when writing poetry, we must hide truth or emotion in order to provoke feeling in the reader, who cannot be dazzled unless truths are given over with ease, slanted gradually rather than directly. Now I see these lines can also apply to slanting the truths of the body gradually. A modest poem and a modest woman restrain themselves in order to evoke the wildness of the inner life. When women are attentive to modesty in dress, they are being reticent about a cherished reality. They are telling it slant.

Another dream: I am sitting in a room across from a therapist, a woman. She says to me, "Halakhoth provide the channel through which the spiritual life can flow."

After the dream, I write a poem that ends with this couplet:

The laws are a channel.
A space for God to descend.

I begin a poem with the line, "Does the head covering open the interior eye?"

The rabbi asked, "Does love flow from body or soul?

"The body is self-absorbed, the soul has a limitless quality and can merge with something greater than itself. The body is clay, it only absorbs, it's limited.

"We grow by our spiritual yearnings, not by our bodily yearnings. We are diminished by excessive material cravings. Spiritual yearnings expand a person.

"Overcome your will. Overcome your limited sense of who you are, of your identity. Let your soul expand, see beyond, believe in potential, yearn for more and expand. It's what you want but didn't know it.

"Soul knowledge is an internal event. Open will. Give up your want to get what you wanted. Open to what you sought without knowing it, to what you wanted all along."

NOTES

1. Genesis 1:27. *The Torah: With Rashi's Commentary*, ArtScroll Series, Sapirstein ed. (Brooklyn: Mesorah Publications, 2003). This work is the source for all scriptural verse not otherwise identified except for the chapter epigraph, Psalm 45:14, which comes from *The ArtScroll Tehillim* (Brooklyn: Mesorah Publications, 1988), 96.
2. Nehama Leibowitz, *New Studies in Bereshit (Genesis)*, trans. Aryeh Newman (Jerusalem: Maor Wallach Press, 1995), 13.
3. William Blake, *The Essential Blake* (New York: Ecco Press, 1987), 62.
4. Stanley Kunitz, "Interviews/Exchanges. The Productions of Time: Stanley Kunitz on William Blake. A Conversation with Jason Shinder," *Agni* 52 (2000), www.bu.edu/agni/interviews-exchanges/print/2000/52-kunitz-shinder.html.
5. Emily Benedek, *Through the Unknown, Remembered Gate* (New York: Schocken Books, 2001), 190.
6. Mary Oliver, *Rules for the Dance: A Handbook for Writing and Reading Metrical Verse* (Boston: Houghton Mifflin, 1998), 99.

7. Babylonian Talmud, Niddah 45b.
8. Simon Jacobson, *Toward a Meaningful Life: The Wisdom of the Rebbe Menachem Mendel Schneerson* (New York: William Morrow, 1995), 66.
9. John Keats, *Selected Poems and Letters* (Boston: Houghton Mifflin, 1959), 257, 207.
10. Misty Harper, *Guarding the Violins,* New American Poets Chapbook Series (New York: Poetry Society of America, 2005), 17.
11. Marie Howe, *The Good Thief* (New York: Persea Books, 1988), 3.
12. Genesis 3:20–21.
13. Emily Dickinson, *The Complete Poems of Emily Dickinson,* ed. Thomas H. Johnson (Boston: Little Brown, 1960), 216.
14. Babylonian Talmud, Brakhot 20a.
15. Avivah Gottlieb Zornberg, *The Particulars of Rapture: Reflections on Exodus* (New York: Doubleday, 2001), 10.
16. Isaac Bashevis Singer, "Androgynous," trans. Joseph Sherman, *New Yorker,* September 19, 2003, 100.
17. Dickinson, *Complete Poems,* 506.

REFERENCES

The ArtScroll Tehillim. Brooklyn: Mesorah Publications, 1988.
Benedek, Emily. *Through the Unknown, Remembered Gate.* New York: Schocken Books, 2001.
Blake, William. *The Essential Blake.* Edited by Stanley Kunitz. New York: Ecco Press, 1987.
Dickinson, Emily. *The Complete Poems of Emily Dickinson.* Edited by Thomas H. Johnson. Boston: Little Brown, 1960.
Harper, Misty. *Guarding the Violins.* New American Poets Chapbook Series. New York: Poetry Society of America, 2005.
Howe, Marie. *The Good Thief.* New York: Persea Books, 1988.
Jacobson, Simon. *Toward a Meaningful Life: The Wisdom of the Rebbe Menachem Mendel Schneerson.* New York: William Morrow, 1995.
Keats, John. *Selected Poems and Letters.* Boston: Houghton Mifflin, 1959.
Kunitz, Stanley."Interviews/Exchanges. The Productions of Time: Stanley Kunitz on William Blake. A Conversation with Jason Shinder." *Agni* 52 (2000), www.bu.edu/agni/interviews=exchanges/print/2000/52=kunitz=shinder.html.
Leibowitz, Nehama. *New Studies in Bereshit (Genesis).* Translated by Aryeh Newman. Jerusalem: Maor Wallach Press, 1995.
Oliver, Mary. *Rules for the Dance: A Handbook for Writing and Reading Metrical Verse.* Boston: Houghton Mifflin, 1998.
Singer, Isaac Bashevis. "Androgynous." Translated by Joseph Sherman. *New Yorker,* September 19, 2003.

The Torah: With Rashi's Commentary. Translated, annotated, and elucidated by Rabbi Yisrael Isser Zvi Herczeg et al. ArtScroll Series, Sapirstein ed. Brooklyn: Mesorah Publications, 2003.

Zornberg, Avivah Gottlieb. *The Particulars of Rapture: Reflections on Exodus*. New York: Doubleday, 2001.

12   Virtue and Sin

An Arab Christian Woman's Perspective

RITA STEPHAN

Is the veil a covering on a woman's head or is it the shield that guards and controls her? Growing up in Syria as a conservative Christian, I lived behind a veil without ever wearing a scarf. Yet, although I never wore the *hijab*, I was subject to the social veil that determined the lives of the virtuous and wicked, regardless of whether they were Christian or Muslim.

Most Christian women in Syria do not wear head scarves, but they live with various social restrictions that can function more or less like a veil. Growing up in Syria's capital, Damascus, I was taught that as a Christian living in a Muslim society, I was responsible for protecting myself by being at least as conservative as the Muslims. I never understood or internalized what this really meant until I began learning more about the complexities of Christian-Muslim social relations in the region.

Syria is among the few Arab countries with significant Christian minorities. Others include Egypt, Jordan, Iraq, Palestine, and Lebanon. Christians are estimated to be between 6.5 and 12 percent of Syria's total population. They are highly urbanized and live either in or around Damascus, Aleppo, Hamah, or Latakia. Most Christians have middle to high incomes and are educated beyond the primary level.[1] The earliest mention of Syria's Christians in the Bible is the conversion story of the apostle Paul of Tarsus on the road to Damascus in 36 C.E.[2] Even during periods of persecution in Europe, the early Christians were allowed to build churches and establish their communities in Syria under the protection of the various Islamic empires.

The Islamic expansions reached Greater Syria during the Rashidun caliphate (632–61) in the seventh century C.E. Since then, Christians have continued to practice their beliefs in exchange for paying *thima* taxes (a traditional poll tax, also called *jizyah,* paid by non-Muslim residents of a Muslim state). These special taxes guarantee them semiautonomous living status under the protection of the Muslim government. Today, Christians experience widespread religious tolerance in Syria and are represented in the government as well as in various professions.

Christians and Muslims are courteous toward each other's traditions and beliefs. Each symbolically celebrates the other's holidays and visits during special events. Some Muslim families in Damascus commemorate Christmas by decorating their houses with trees, exchanging gifts, and attending festivities. During the holy month of Ramadan, when Muslims around the world fast from dawn to dusk, my mother always cooked an elaborate *iftar* (breaking the fast) dinner on Thursday evenings for our Muslim neighbors. We children were not allowed one bite while our neighbors were still fasting.

This peaceful coexistence is best exemplified in the words of the late grand mufti of Syria, Sheikh Kuftaro, when a Canadian ambassador visited him and asked how many Christians there are in Syria. "Seventeen million," the grand mufti replied to the befuddlement of the diplomat. Perhaps there had been a mistranslation. Seventeen million is roughly the total number of people in Syria, and Christians are only a minority.

"There are seventeen million Christians in Syria," the grand mufti repeated, "and I am Christian," he said. "I have to be a genuine Christian, in order for me to be an accepted Muslim."[3]

As *ahl al-Kitab,* or people of the book (the Torah, the Bible, and the

Qur'an), Christians and Jews enjoy the respect and acceptance of Muslims while holding tight to their own faiths. The grand mufti's sentiments illustrate how coexistence has been fundamental for the three groups. Muslims are commanded to accept Christians and Jews, as fellows in the Abrahamic tradition, and are encouraged to consult them in instances where guidance is not provided in the Qur'an. Moreover, Muslims worldwide recognize Jesus as a prophet who had a miraculous birth. They also recognize Mary and Joseph as his mother and earthly father, and they respect Moses and many other prophets. Indeed, John the Baptist's burial site is located in the historic Ommayad Mosque in the heart of Damascus.

The majority of the Christian community in Syria belongs to various Eastern rites founded by early Christians—with a significant Roman Catholic presence and a small number of Protestants. The Eastern rites are still practiced as they were founded. In the Syrian Orthodox Church, women are not allowed to enter the temple under any circumstances, not even to clean it. Women are barred from attending Mass during their menstrual periods. At baptism, girls receive only godmothers, while boys are assigned a godfather and a godmother. A conservative dress code is expected inside the church, even during weddings and special celebrations. Spaghetti straps, short skirts, sleeveless blouses, and tight pants are forbidden. We once heard of a priest who refused to conduct a wedding ceremony unless the bride covered her bare shoulders with a shawl. Older women wear white or gray embroidered scarves during Mass, and when a husband dies, his wife is expected to cover her head for at least forty days.

For the last fifteen hundred years, while maintaining their own distinct characteristics, Christians and Muslims have shared many commonalities, including a strong sense of national identity. Many Christians share ideological pride with the Islamic-Arabic tradition and say, "We are Syrians first and Christians second."[4] Christians took part in founding the Arab nationalist movement and continue to support the current, secular Alawite government.[5]

While Christian minority status is guaranteed on the national and ideological levels, social relations with Muslims are more complex. Christians and Muslims are integrated but have many intergroup restrictions. These are tightly connected to family relations through which most socializing in both groups is done. The family's religious community dictates the individual's marriage choice, as well as how to live the married life and raise children. These social relations confined young Christians like me to a kind of social veil. We constantly guarded our reputations—that is, our virginities and our hymens—which differentiated honorable women from those who were sexually promiscuous. Our behavior reflected on our families and radiated into our communities, which were never to be disgraced. Blood on the sheets used to be shown to the family the morning after the wedding to ensure the bride was a virgin. Virginity was described as a match that could be lit only once. Only our husbands deserved the privilege of taking it, for they had earned it with the love, support, and respect they would give us the rest of our lives.

In order to guard my reputation, I was restricted to attending church-sponsored events and parties in private homes and only if I was chaperoned by my older brother. Muslims and Christians alike tell their children the same fable: "Love comes *after* marriage." Marriage is based on the logical conviction that the partner one chooses will be socially compatible and fit to build a healthy and happy family. Therefore, mixed marriages between Christians and Muslims are highly stigmatized by both religions. "He who marries outside his *melah* (social group)," my father said, "dies in his *elah* (ailment)." Hence—regardless of the couple's psychological and intellectual compatibility, love for each other, or even proximity in age—marriages based on social, economic, and religious compatibilities are the most desirable. Islam permits Muslim men to marry Christian women, but the reverse is punishable by law and religion. The state does not recognize the marriage as legitimate unless it is conducted according to the Islamic tradition. Therefore, a Christian man who wants to marry a Muslim woman must convert to Islam. As a minority population already experiencing attrition due to emigration, Christians are especially opposed to losing more members. When Muslim men elope with their "innocent" girls, the Christian family and the community are dishonored.

My aunt married a Muslim and thus her daughter, Mona, and three grandchildren are Muslims. My aunt's marriage violated a taboo that tainted her entire family in the early 1940s. To add to the problem, her husband divorced her and married two additional wives. My cousin Mona was careful to choose a husband who was a secular Muslim. Nevertheless, he, too, took a second wife with whom he had a child. Mona divorced him and came to live in our home. Later, her father took her on *hajj* (pilgrimage to Mecca), and when she returned she was veiled. After that, she would no longer stay with us. She did not want to risk the chance that my father—her Christian uncle—might see her without a veil.

The Christians in my Syrian community are suspicious of the motives of veiled women. They believe the problem is not with how women dress but with how men determine who is entitled to enjoy looking at their women. The daughter of my Muslim cousin Mona is exquisitely beautiful by Middle Eastern standards. Rasha is blonde with blue eyes and a soft, round face. The bright, upcoming engineer she married demanded that she wear a veil. Otherwise, he said, men "would eat her up in one bite with their eyes." Although she did cover her hair, the beauty of her eyes and face always showed through. The Christian side of the family was appalled.

Ironically, in the beginning, Christian women wore the veil, like their Jewish and Greek predecessors. In every illustration, particularly those of Mary, mother of Jesus, the Christian saints wear head coverings. Moreover, most Catholic and Orthodox nuns in the Middle East still wear the habit, although many in the West have chosen secular clothing since the 1960s. And the history of the veil goes well beyond Christianity and Islam in the region. Among the Canaanites and the Amorites, only slaves and prostitutes—priestesses of Ashtarout—did not cover their heads. Ishtar, the most widely worshiped goddess in Babylonian and Assyrian religion was known in Greater Syria as Ashtarout and in Greece as Aphrodite. She was worshiped under diverse names and forms and her primary role was as goddess of love. Ashtarout's temples were frequented by male worshipers who had sexual relations with her priestesses.[6] These priestesses were distinguished from other free women by their long, loose hair, ornate jewelry, and exposed faces. In contrast, women who belonged to reputable households covered their heads in public as a sign of their high social status.

Arab poets still commemorate Ashtarout as the forceful lover who captures the entirety of men's minds and bodies. In the same vein, in the Arabic language, women's sexuality is perceived as a powerful force that both captivates and corrupts men. The term *fitna*—meaning both beauty and chaos—reflects the belief that women possess a powerful sexual drive that threatens the social order. The "mere proximity of a woman to a man would lead to sexual relations."[7] Some scholars have argued that fitna has been a source of fear for Islamic societies whether it is perceived collectively or within an individual man's psyche. They claim that female sexuality has "always been potent with a predilection to create havoc and chaos in the male" and that therefore, there is a great need to "control the woman in order to preserve order and well-being in society."[8] It is noteworthy that fitna is ascribed to men in a comparable yet dissimilar manner. While a man might be described as a *faten* to denote his physical beauty, he consciously causes fitna in his premeditated actions. A woman is also described as *fatina* to indicate her beauty. But it is this very beauty—not the woman's conscious actions—that causes chaos.

Perceptions of how the veiling of women symbolizes conservatism and social control differ among Muslims. Some Muslims consider all women ʿaura—Arabic for private parts—a word used to describe shame, weakness, and immaturity.[9] Others reject this derogatory term and consider women equal to men in rights and responsibilities. Yet a third group argues that veiling is not an indicator of oppression but a preventive and protective measure for social control. The veil prevents men from looking at women to desire them; therefore it protects their souls from falling into sin and prevents social problems. A fourth group claims that conservative attitudes, including veiling, were reactions to imperialism and colonialism. Western cultures swept away many aspects of Arab and Muslim traditions. The only thing left for them to exercise their jurisdiction over was their girls' honor. They felt that they needed to maintain that as an authentic and pure cultural symbol.

Like their Muslim compatriots, Christians in Syria believe in a woman's fitna, but the veil is used neither to shield men from falling into sin upon seeing a beautiful woman nor to protect women from unwanted sexual predators. Individuals are expected to control their desires and respect social boundaries. With the exception of elderly and evangelical Christian women, who cover their heads during church services, most Christian and Jewish Syrians I knew did not wear the veil. Although the majority of the people I associated with were Christians, Jews were among our acquaintances. Rima was a Jewish girl who went to my Catholic middle school. Unlike many of us, she dated openly in school. We frequently visited my mother's cousin who lived in the Jewish quarter at the eastern end of the *suq* (the market), centrally located between a Christian and a Muslim neighborhood. The Jews I saw in the street and those whose houses I visited were similar to Christians in their dress and interactions.

Generally, middle-class Christians are more conservative than the Christian elites. They are nevertheless thought to be more liberal and Westernized than middle-class and elite Muslims. Yet, in reality my Christian girlfriends were as restricted as my Muslim—veiled—girlfriends in their "going out" and dating. Therefore, I never associated the veil with purity and righteousness; rather, I saw it as a cultural symbol. In 1991, a study by Iranian scholar Homa Hoodfar found that educated and working-class women in Egypt empower themselves by choosing to veil: "Veiling has become an instrument through which women publicly dissociate themselves from some of the culturally disapproved traits and characteristics attributed to the stereotype of the modern woman."[10] In this instance the veil strengthens their access to modern life and serves as a shield to guard their pure image in public. Similarly, Syrian women who wear the veil protect their freedom to work, date, and engage in public life yet maintain their compliance with the mainstream Muslim culture.

In the 1960s, when dating was absolutely forbidden, my Protestant mother disguised herself by wearing a scarf and sunglasses, long skirts, and long sleeves and secretly dated my Orthodox father against her parents' will. Otherwise, relatives and friends who recognized her would have informed my grandparents, who would have punished her. Even today, a woman wearing the veil is less likely to be tainted if she is seen with a man; people are less likely to judge the association as a "relationship."

Eventually, my parents were allowed to marry and when I came of age in the 1980s, they in turn fought to keep me pure and innocent for my future husband. They sent me to Roman Catholic elementary and middle schools, where, under the nuns' scrutiny, my peers and I were not allowed

Figure 12.1.   The author (then Rita Homsieh), *third from left,* cutting up with Muslim and Christian high school classmates in Damascus, Syria, 1990. Courtesy of Rita Stephan.

to talk to boys. Spending any time privately with a young man, particularly a male student, was risky. If we were caught, our parents were notified and our peers would humiliate us. As a result, my small clique of Christian friends and I decided that an all-girls public high school would be our gate to freedom and social amusement (figure 12.1). Cliques were formed based on the sections we attended in high school, the neighborhoods we came from, or familial friendships.[11]

The school was comprised of both liberal and conservative, Christian and Muslim students, but the veil was not what divided us.[12] About ten of the fifty girls in our class covered their heads. Nevertheless, several enjoyed the same flirtations I did. I can recall only four girls who truly did not talk to boys. They were introverted and extremely quiet, even with the other girls in the class. But the rest of us dated secretly—something I did until I went to college.

Dating secretly meant meeting the guy you liked after school. It worked like this: the girls—veiled and unveiled—walked with three or four other girls; the guys would be waiting for us on some corner. We met, stopped a bit. Then each couple moved off in different directions. Some stood behind parked cars and others beside shops to casually talk in private for a few minutes. We called these boys "boyfriends," though we rarely had physical contact with them. The most exciting thing was telling the other girls what we did after school. By physical contact I definitely do not mean sex, but rather holding hands and kissing on the cheeks. An occasional quick kiss on the mouth was something we cherished for weeks. Veiled and unveiled girls all did the same thing.

Getting to know boys happened in many ways. Normally, they waited outside the girls' high school and courted those they liked. Another technique was to stand at special street corners after the siesta time (from five to seven in the afternoon) waiting for the girls to take their afternoon walks. The compliments they gave young women were mostly flirtatious, but remarks could also be mean if the girl did not dress or behave within certain constraints. If a girl ran in the street, her jiggling breasts would elicit comments. She was also ridiculed if her pants were too tight or her cleavage was showing.

These courtship games gave me the impression that I was truly an oversized "knockout." After all, my figure did not stop the men I passed on the street from whistling and making remarks. Did veiled girls also receive catcalls? You bet. Did we feel equally vulnerable to such harassment? I am not sure that any of us realized the depth of those comments beyond their superficial reassurance of our beauty and femininity. My mother tells stories about our visits to the market. Whenever I went with her, she had to protect me from being winked at, pinched, or touched. She hit people with her purse, cursed them, or gave them dirty looks. Men in the street or at the shop asked for my hand in marriage. What a disappointment when I moved to the United States in the middle of my high-school senior year and none of the American boys asked me out or flirted with me.

I was puzzled for a long time, but eventually I realized the discrepancy was not my fault. By Syrian standards, I was attractive and "in demand." In fact, before we moved to the States, I thought I was deeply in love with a young man I met at the evangelical Protestant church in Damascus. Although my mother was Protestant, she was not evangelical. Hence, she disapproved of the church that my brother and I began frequenting when I was in the ninth grade. Unlike other churches, here men and women sat in separate sections and the women covered their hair. My parents and friends disliked the fact that this church converted "normal" (Orthodox and Catholic) Christians into "born-again" Protestants instead of targeting the Muslims. Under *shari'ah* and state law, it is illegal for churches to proselytize among Muslims.

Since most Syrian Christians are either Orthodox or a sect of Eastern Catholic, Protestantism is seen as alien to the region and its churches, despite the fact that most Orthodox Syrian Christians supported the sixteenth-century Protestant Reformation. Protestantism reached the Middle East in the early 1700s. Although proselytizing is unacceptable in Syria, Protestant converts were often financially rewarded by missionaries and scorned by locals. When my mother married my father, she maintained her faith. However, because they did not agree on a common church to attend, my brother and I had a secular upbringing.

I thought that the boy I loved was worth all the pressure I received from the evangelicals to become born-again. After all, what is love without pain? Our "dates" took place at church-sponsored events and when he accompanied me home after church to protect me as I walked late on those dangerous roads filled with flirtatious fellows. He was a devoted "brother" and we always walked with friends—only two steps behind them—so that very few people suspected anything between us.

Alas, we said sad good-byes forever when I left Syria, the country of jasmine and antiquity, big contradictions and warm hearts. At the age of sixteen I moved with my parents to the United States, where I cut off my braids, shortened my skirts, and began to emerge from behind my invisible veil.

NOTES

1. Library of Congress Report http://countrystudy.us/syria/.
2. Acts 9:3 (New International Version).
3. Mel Lehman, "Christians and Muslims show compatibility in Syria," *Ecumenical News International*, August 5, 2005.

4. "SYRIA: Bridging the gap between Muslims and Christians," *IRIN* [a UN humanitarian news and information service], October 17, 2005, www.IRIN-news.org (accessed May 13, 2006)

5. A minority sect in Islam that reached power in Syria in a coup d'état led by the late President Hafez Asad.

6. For more information see E. W. Hirsch, *Sex Life in Babylonia* (Chicago: Research Publications, 1941); C. Olson, *The Book of the Goddess, Past and Present: An Introduction to Her Religion* (New York: Crossroad, 2002); and D. White, *The Descent of Ishtär* (London: Eragny Press, 1903).

7. M. Badran, *Feminists, Islam and Nation: Gender and the Making of Modern Egypt* (Princeton: Princeton University Press, 1995), 5.

8. Yvonne Yazbeck Haddad, "Islam and Gender: Dilemmas in the Changing Arab World," in *Islam, Gender, & Social Change,* ed. Yvonne Yazbeck Haddad and John L. Esposito (New York: Oxford University Press, 1998), 17.

9. Haddad, "Islam and Gender," 3–29.

10. Homa Hoodfar, "Return to the Veil: Personal Strategies and Public Participation in Egypt," in *Working Women: International Perspectives on Labour and Gender Ideology,* ed. Nanneke Redclift and M. Thea Sinclair (London: Routledge, 1991), 321.

11. The French education system is implemented in Syria, where students do not move from one classroom to the other. Rather, they stay in the classroom assigned to their specific section: scientific versus literary; French versus English; or vocational versus academic.

12. Very few Jews lived outside the Jewish quarter or went to public schools in other school districts. My neighborhood was predominantly Muslim with some Christian presence.

13 Drawing the Line at Modesty

My Place in the Order of Things

MICHELLE AUERBACH

I

Other people's religious practices, even whole cultures, are quaint. Think
of the scene in the reality TV show *Amish in the City*, in which one of the
Amish kids looks at a parking meter in Los Angeles and asks, "What is
that? What does it do?" The Angelinos are amused beyond words. It's re-
freshing to be so quaintly out of it. The Amish make nice quilts, have nice
horses and buggies, get written up in the *New Yorker* every decade or so,
but are completely outside the experience of the LA kids on the show and
also outside the experience of a Jewish girl from Cleveland, me, with three
parking tickets to pay. So much so, that the lack of knowledge about parking meters is just plain nice, too.

Other people's religious practices can also be enraging. Think Alice
Walker sitting in California writing about clitoridectomy in Africa, how
awful it is, how destructive. That her daughter is safe from this practice—

removed by generations and location—allows Ms. Walker to be disgusted in a facile, if culturally appropriate, way. So it goes on, these days with the issue of the *burqa* and veiling being the one we see most often debated by the armchair cultural relativists against the absolutist they see as the devil.

Except it is not all fine, on many levels. Sometimes it is our own cultures we are talking about, our own religions. At times in our lives it is easy to be dismissive. In my case that dismissal would be, "Oh, those backwards Jews." An example: a relative of mine was at a wedding filled with Hasidim. The black hat–wearing, strange-dressing, super-religious Jews immortalized in movies like *The Chosen*. It was ninety degrees outside and this relative, oh so very modern guy he was, asked a sweaty elderly rabbi in a black velvet coat and fur hat, "Why are you dressed like that?" The rabbi answered, "Honoring tradition." Our modern guy in a short-sleeved shirt laughed at him and quipped back, "In Poland we dressed like that because it was cold. In New Jersey, we can move on."

Of course, it was a traditional Jewish wedding with all the trappings: breaking glasses and dancing with the bride and groom up on chairs, so how this modern guy made up his mind where to draw the line . . . But for him this smiling rabbi with his curly forelocks and beard was too vulgarly what Woody Allen calls in *Deconstructing Harry*, "professionally Jewish."

II

In the tone of voice one would say "She was raised by wolves," I can say I was raised by cultural relativists. A Jewish mother with a Litvak rabbinic family and an Italian-Catholic stepfather, who were both followers of a Sikh guru in the 1970s in Cleveland, when even being Jewish was considered beyond the pale. As I was told by a cute blonde girl in the lunchroom in junior high, "Don't worry, someday ethnic will be in."

Ethnic was always "in" with my family. My parents meditated, had friends with dharma names before anyone even knew what the dharma was. Our house was decorated in macramé and nouveau hippie India. The only thing not acceptable was Judaism. According to my mom, this was for good reason, because Judaism was misogynist, devoid of meaning, reminded her of her very authoritarian father, and reeked of the establishment. So of course I was fascinated by it. I might be the only person in the history of suburbia who begged to go to Hebrew school, who dragged her parents through the experience of getting bat mitzvahed.

When I finally moved to New York and got to live with actual observant Jews in college, I was in heaven. Through good karma, as my mom would say, I ended up on the Jewish floor of my freshman dorm, appropriately nicknamed "Jew Reid" to rhyme with Two Reid (the second floor of Reid Hall). I made friends who took me home to their parents for Shabbat and I finally got to see what the Judaism I dreamed about was like.

Just one Shabbat dinner with a college friend's parents and I was hooked. That evening in suburban Maryland, I figured out I was not just fascinated, I wanted something from Judaism. All that rushing around to get the food made, the table set, the house ready. The uphill battle to light the candles and then—silence. Complete and total silence in the sepia light of a spring evening. Not the silence of abandonment that Eastern religion had visited upon my siblings and me, Judaism brought companionable silence. I had always seen religious practice as a completely private undertaking. My mother, meditating alone in her closet for hours, waiting for some loosening of the ties to this incarnation. No, Judaism had something else entirely: the communal meals, the synagogue services, and that other time created out of magic and quiet and slowed-down moments.

How far would I take this obsession, my relativist family wondered? How far would I go into the world of the absolutists?

I stepped right up to the veil and no further. That is how far I could go. I could learn Hebrew as an adult. I could keep kosher, learn to pray, learn to be *shomer* Shabbat—that is, to keep the commandments of resting on the Sabbath—I could study Talmud with wonderful Orthodox men who were committed to women's learning. I could become pseudoengaged to a fellow writer who was Orthodox and move across the country for him and his heavenly life of writing and Judaism. But then I reached his synagogue and came smack up against all the lessons of relativism and feminism and I could not go any further.

Admittedly this man had a few issues with Judaism himself. He drove to his synagogue, on the Sabbath, parked a few blocks away, and walked up to the door, shining in his hypocritical sheen of California sweat. He gave me a marble to put in each pocket to keep my hands busy so I would not be tempted to reach out and shake hands with any of the men in the shul. Orthodox men are not supposed to touch women who are not their close relatives or wives. "Won't I be carrying on Shabbat?" I asked. "This is much better than embarrassing yourself, me, and everyone there." So I was enticed to break Shabbat on my first week in California: first by driving, then carrying. This was a huge deal because you are not to work on the Sabbath and one of the descriptions of work is carrying anything besides your clothes. Marbles may not seem like work, but they clearly break the rule. At least I did not shake anyone's hand.

All of this was fine and good until my boyfriend said good-bye to me and sent me to the women's section of the shul. The other side of that divider that keeps men thinking only of G-d and women away from the Torah and unable to see what's going on. "I really don't worry much about it, I like women-only spaces," a friend told me of the *mechitzah,* this dividing wall, in her shul. I had been a part of a women's co-op in college. *That* was a women-only space. This was a frightening ghetto full of strangers, and I could still barely read Hebrew or follow the prayer book. I was alone and angry. I looked out on the sea of married women in hats and single women with no hats, signaling availability to be married, and I seethed with red-hot fury that seeped out a little at a time as tears through my scrunched eyelids. I was one of the modestly dressed unmarried women with no hat, signaling sexual availability, sent over to the dungeon so that my clavicle or ankle bone, which admittedly I found sexy, would not distract my lover, who I had done *it* with, against all convention since we were not married or even really engaged, on the bathroom sink before we left for synagogue. All this misery so that he and his brethren could pray. My prayers did not count. But my modesty did.

After the experience in shul, I set out to understand the laws of *tzniuth,* or modesty. Why married women must cover their heads, why women need to cover themselves from toe to neck, and why this wall is erected in the synagogue that separates me from the men with whom I was taught in college I was every inch an equal. The problem lay not in the laws, but in my inability to get my brain around them. I was supposed to do a list of innocent things: cover my collarbones, cover my ankles, wear clothes that reveal not one interesting bit of information about my body, always keep the door open when I was with a man. "A *tzniusdiggeh* (active form of the word) person is wholesome, dignified," the teacher of this modesty class told me. I was not entirely sure I wanted to see myself as wholesome. I did not want to be the definition of modest—that reads in my mind sexually unavailable. Further, I was told by a woman teaching modesty laws, that the first moment of tzniuth was when Adam and Eve covered themselves after eating from that famed tree. I had been taught previously to think of that moment as shame, not modesty. I was told that the rules are there to make all of our physical life into a spiritual practice, instead it felt like institutionalized shame. I was a child of the women's lib movement and my mother taught me not to be ashamed of my body. Still, my heart told me if I wanted my house and my life to ring with the silence and slow moments of that house in Maryland, I was not really free to be a buffet Jew. "I'll take a little synagogue and some Hebrew, and a smidge of kosher, but no thanks on all the modesty stuff." That was not going to work. It would leave me with the life I already had. I wanted to wake up on Saturday afternoon from a postprandial nap, have a little snack, get ready for *havdalah,* that service we do to break the Sabbath. And I was going to have to do it in a dress that covered my ankles, as well as a wig, if I married this guy. Even if he drove to shul.

III

In college there were girls who followed the letter of the modesty laws without the intent. We called this *"frum* chic," frum meaning religiously observant. They covered themselves from head to toe—in denim skirts and tight fluffy pink sweaters. They looked more girly than I did in my cowboy boots and black miniskirts. They were the ones who got married to the Jonathans and Davids from Columbia University and then wore gorgeous wigs to cover their hair, no nappy old hats for them. They were destined for big diamonds and shiny coiffed wigs. In what way this was modest—any of it— I never figured out. It made me wonder if all this modesty stuff had more to do with sexual shame than with spiritual wholesomeness.

Recently, a rabbinic student friend of mine read me an article on modesty and hair covering from a text by Haviva Ner-David, a woman who is a scholar of Talmud and Torah.[1] Ner-David said, among pages and pages of arguments about why it is important to cover your head, that she does it as a sign that she is both religious and married, thus taking her interaction with everyone else off the level of sexuality and reserving that most sacred of relations for her spouse. Okay, I like that argument, having been recently melted to the floor when a man told me he is very careful about striking up friendships with single women when he is "taken" because of how confusing and potentially hurtful it can be. Still, the feminist activist in me bristled. This sign of the hat is not a privilege allowed to a lesbian couple, to a monogamous couple who chooses not to marry, to an intermarried couple. None of those situations exist in the world Ner-David describes. I can't fault her, she says quite clearly that she is looking for what meaning speaks to her in her own time and place. Her place is Orthodox Judaism, in which the situations I listed have no traction. Covering her head, as a married woman, following all the commandments associated with modesty, these acts infuse her dressing with meaning. Her hat signals, makes meaning, proclaims. She says that icons, statements, have meaning only in a culture that knows what they mean.

One thing my parents and Haviva Ner-David could sit down and agree on is that no one wants to be swallowed up by the vacuous antispiritual and anti-intellectual ooze of American consumer culture. If that ooze is all that informs dress options, then who are you really? What Orthodox Judaism is offering, is an ages-old and well-tested rule-based paradigm for how to escape the gangrene of the shopping mall, and if that cure is a dose of modesty, and it gets me where I want to go, why is it so hard to swallow? Maybe it is the classical liberal education: Locke, Hobbes, Rousseau, Voltaire, Mill. Maybe my mind was formed by hippies and will always rebel.

I told myself it was an issue of loving myself and my sexuality. I hear my mother's voice saying, "We fought hard in the '60s so that you could be anything you wanted," and my mind added in her voice, "and you, my daughter, would choose this?" This being a rayon dress and a synthetic wig and pantyhose in August, and even the delicate hinges of my wrists covered.

Statistics say that daughters of divorce are far more likely to be sexually active (read: inappropriate) at a young age. My parents were divorced when I was eighteen months old. I remember French kissing a blond kid, not Jewish, on the golf course a few blocks away from my house at thirteen and throwing up on the poor guy's shoes. It did not deter me from pursuing this form of attention and gratification for my entire adolescent and early adult life. Perhaps a blue rayon dress with white lapels and a pair of appropriate heels and nylons, along with the rule about not touching any man to whom I am not married or related would solve this inconvenient problem of searching for affection in the bedroom, on the couch, on the golf course, in cars. The rabbis came up with it for a reason.

I wanted to banish the commercial jingles, the to-do lists, the desires for affection from Eurotrash friends from college who flew off to Vietnam to visit cousins or Paris to visit mothers when they were supposed to be meeting me for dinner. I wanted to banish longing and self-pity. There was a very simple six-hundred-and-thirteen-commandment way to do this; I just had to swallow it wholesale. Then I would have grainy freeze-frame religious time instead of Charlie Chaplin super-sped-up, city-girl time. I would have what I saw in that Maryland dining room around the Shabbat table with the white tablecloth and the candles burning down on the sideboard while we argued and laughed at the dinner table. I just kept getting to those modesty commandments and bailing. My mind suspended disbelief, but my body rebelled.

IV

Haviva Ner-David says that a married woman with an uncovered head is not a promiscuous act in this society. Sneaky way of telling us this is not about sex. Her next argument is that you cover your head as an act of worship and of bowing down before G-d, taking your modest place, not before men, but before the eternal. Men are also expected to cover their heads with yarmulkes and hats when they pray, and actually all the time in more observant circles, so really what is the problem? The rule is egalitarian, does not offend the feminist, and if Ner-David is right, then this is not about sex, which I am not convinced but we can grant her for a moment. The problem is that the hat = married. The hat = property and own-

ership. The hat = all that married means outside what you want it to signify. It is the evil underbelly of what seems like a very elegant reclama-
tion of the symbol.

The problem is that a symbol means exactly what the society thinks it
means, no more and no less. No matter what the bearer thinks it means.
This was brought home to me by that tzniuth teacher I found in LA who
said that we can control those leers in the street by dressing modestly. I
think the exact words were "We can control strangers' reactions to us by
how we dress." Unfortunately that is the problem here, we can't. I do not
want to send some of the messages associated with wholesome and dignified. I cannot wear an index card with my reasons pinned on my hat or
my wig, so that I can explain away the parts I find degrading or difficult.
You are taken as you are seen, not as you intend.

For instance, my babysitter when I was a kid—an assimilated Jew from
the suburbs, who got stoned and had sex with her glamorous boyfriend
in my parent's bed—moved to Israel in college and became observant.
When she got married, her mother had to endure many indignities. Being nonreligious to the point of hostile, the mother hated every step of
this process and felt she was losing her daughter to a cult. The worst part
of all was when the daughter first came into the kitchen of her parent's
house after the wedding wearing *the wig*. Her mom cried. This ballbuster
of a fifty-year-old woman, who scared me as a child and still does, broke
down in tears. "My daughter's beautiful hair." In the norms of our secular society, wigs are for cancer patients and old ladies with genetic bald-
ness. So her mother could not read sexual exclusivity into the wig, nor
could she read married and religious, or bowing before G-d. She read *Loss*.
To this day she cries over her daughter's beautiful hair. She will sit in a
restaurant and tell the story of that first morning and cry. Her daughter
had ugly hair with split ends and the wig looks better, the wig has a thick
luxurious French braid, glossy and exactly the same color as the daughter's real hair but the mother will never see that.

Caught in our culture, we do not control how we are seen, nor do we
control what we see. This mother could not have changed her view of the
wig, because if she could, why would she have chosen to go through life
with that much grief?

So there I was trying to shimmy past my biases and get into this world I wanted to be a part of and I was as caught as this mother. Some people do manage to become *ba'al teshuvah*, or newly religious Jews, "masters of the turning" is the direct translation, like the boyfriend who drove to shul and the ex-babysitter, both of whom had much less relativist upbringings than I. They pull off this transformation by turning away from one set of signals for how to read signs and toward another complete set of meanings for everything. Dishes become kosher or not; hats a symbol of married life on women, and on men a symbol of finding modesty before G-d; candles are no longer for a romantic dinner but separate ordinary time from holy time; touching is not affection but a commandment about when and with whom you do it. If you can master this, you can have what I wanted.

V

I can see inside the veil. I can see the light of that Saturday afternoon when I wake up from my nap and the air around me is still. The light outside is fading and the insects are tuning up for evening. I am filled with repose, not just from resting, but from understanding what the poet Mary Oliver calls my "place in the order of things." This is what I assume other people call *grace*. I can see that living as closely as possible to all the six hundred and thirteen commandments observant Jews follow would get me there. If I could have surmounted that obstacle.

Every tradition I have studied has a difficult path to enlightenment. Some sects of Buddhism pride themselves on the difficulty of their path and call it a crooked path up the mountain. There are more ascetic paths of Hinduism. Christianity has its ascetics, too. My parents' brand of practice was very difficult and rigorous. They became vegetarians, went to India to be with their guru, meditated two hours a day, and were expected to follow an ascetic path even as householders. They all say that leaving behind the ego is a necessary step to attaining the very grace I was looking for. It is simply easier to accept the mandates of a religion separate from the one you were born into. One that seems glamorously foreign or is conducted in a language you do not speak. Maybe this is because you

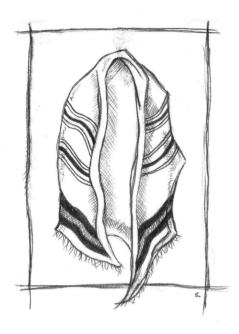

Figure 13.1. A *tallis*, or prayer
shawl, worn by men in traditional
Jewish communities, 2006.
Illustration by Sarah C. Bell.

cannot read the signs. This is what make the Amish seem quaint and the
ultra-Orthodox Jews infuriating. The more Hebrew I learned and the more
Talmud I studied, the more I wanted to argue. Judaism is a living, breathing organism made to grow over centuries, do I really have to do this?

Haviva Ner-David clearly says that symbols, religious acts, need to
speak to us in our time and culture. And this one spoke to me of submission to men, not to G-d. I never did answer the question. I did what religious Jews the world over do, I rabbi-shopped. I found a great thinker
who agreed with me and dropped the whole modesty argument. It is exactly like when a child asks dad and dad says no, so the child asks mom
and voilà, mom says yes. Then I had kids, moved across the country, my
life changed, and I was much more worried about other concerns, and quiet
was not one of them.

My main concern became passing on a living, breathing mess of relativist beliefs even more muddied than my parents' so that my children
can sort it out themselves. My youngest daughter is sure that she is the
incarnation of one of my friends from the first shul I called home, the gay

and lesbian shul in San Francisco, where all my learning paid off. This belief of hers (which I share) is a mix of my parents raising me and my raising her.

I was on the ritual committee of this synagogue and I led services. Certainly there was no mechitzah. There were men in leather yarmulkes and chaps, women in hand-painted prayer shawls, and a rabbi who would say, "We come from a diverse and eclectic tradition." All of our backgrounds were honored. One of the congregants, who acted as cantor, was of Spanish ancestry and chanted in Ladino, not what most of us were used to. Some of us were very observant and led traditional services with a lot of Hebrew. Some were very mellow with guitar and meditating. I found that the commandment to cover my head in prayer, as both men and women are supposed to do, became very important to me when I had an organic reason to consider it. Because of leading services, I was already wearing a *tallis*, the prayer shawl reserved in traditional communities for men, a very plain one that almost every man in Orthodox synagogues wears, off-white with black stripes (not like the silk painted ones I see on many women) (figure 13.1). I did not want my head uncovered when I led services and held the Torah. Once I found it had nothing to do with gender and everything to do with respect, I was free. So I bought a hat.

NOTE

1.   Haviva Ner-David, *Life on the Fringes: A Feminist Journey Toward Traditional Rabbinic Ordination* (Needham, MA: JSL Books, 2000).

On the Road

Travels with My Hijab

MALIHA MASOOD

At first, it felt like a bandage wrapped around my skull. I had trouble hearing people speak unless I faced them head-on and watched their lips move (figure 14.1).

But what a difference it made. Two plus meters of snow-white georgette embossed with little stars. It was a present from my landlady in Cairo. "You must wear the *hijab*," she admonished in a high-pitched shrill. "It is right thing for Muslim girl. You will feel more comfortable here."

Maybe she had a point. From the minute I arrived in my new neighborhood of al-Demerdash, I was conscious of the staring mafia. They just couldn't help themselves. Men, women, and children glued their eyeballs on me or, more precisely, my bare head. Maybe it was the novelty of a stranger's arrival. A Muslim stranger who could barely speak five words of Arabic. I willed the stares to go away. But they assaulted me every waking day, every minute of public appearance. I didn't have the thick skin to ignore them. And I certainly didn't want to remain confined within the

Figure 14.1. A woman wearing
a *batula* or *burgu* appears to be
hailing a cab, 2004. Photo by
Sheryl B. Shapiro.

walls of my apartment. So I reached for the georgette and the headband.
The five-minute walk from my tenth-floor high rise to the nearby subway
station transformed into a stare-free zone. I rode toward downtown Cairo
celebrating my invisibility.

The gleaming tiled floors of the Sadat subway station astound me. They
compete for my attention with a trio of giggly Egyptian debutantes in hip-
hugging jeans, black Spandex tops with matching lacy head scarves. My
eyes gravitate toward the girls. One of them greets a friend who looks like
she has just come from a photo session with French *Vogue*. Stiletto boots,
side-slit skirt grazing the knees, fitted leather jacket, and a knockoff Her-
mès scarf as a head cover. Her face is an airbrushed Lancôme ad. Creamy
beige skin, dark glossy lips, and gobs of mascara paired with pearly gray
shadow. We lock eyes. She breaks into a smirk and elbows her cohorts.
Here we go again. Stares and more stares. This time, it's not that I lack a

hijab. The fashionistas are in shock about my baggy, celery green linen trousers, potato-sack jacket, and those fraying old Tevas. My scarf knots underneath the chin with two long ends dangling on my chest like seaweed. I cannot be bothered with hairpins and makeup or the plain white georgette. After all, I didn't come all the way to Cairo to win a beauty contest.

It's a beautiful station, as far as subway stations go. Clean, bright, and shiny. No one but me seems to notice, much less care. Commuters make a beeline for turnstiles and jam the escalators. The ticket window swarms with human traffic. I stride toward the exit. My ticket slides into a little slot. The turnstile refuses to budge.

I panic and throw my weight against the metal rod. It remains stuck. I try again and again. The only thing moving is my weak little body. No one is behind me, but as I look back, I see a small platoon of witnesses. The sexy hijabis are among them. Their smirks grow bigger along with the requisite stares. A security official watches my predicament and signals me to step into the stationmaster's office near the platform. The inspector volleys heated accusations at me in Arabic that no one bothers to translate. His sidekick squats on his haunches with a look that says, *I know what you're up to.*

"But you don't understand," I plead in English. "I am new in Cairo and made a mistake."

The stationmaster glowers and another stream of rapid-fire Arabic spews forth. The last guttural syllable of his tirade unleashes a wad of spit, the size of a dime, landing squarely on my right jaw. I wipe off the spittle with the back of my sleeve and catch a glimpse of my reflection in the streaky window behind his desk. A petite woman in a white head scarf blinks back. She has big scared eyes the color of espresso and charcoal-thick eyebrows. Her pale complexion contrasts with stray wisps of jet black hair poking from the sides of her veil. It seems to complement the gold pendant on her chain stenciled with the word Allah in stylized Arabic.

Oh no, oh no. A sinking feeling at the pit of my stomach. I know what this is all about. It's about my chameleon face, the kind that morphs into any society's gene pool, bestowing me the dubious honor of "You look so familiar, haven't I seen you someplace before?" It happens everywhere I travel. France, Spain, Italy. And now Cairo. So that's why the stationmaster has been raving like a lunatic. My appearance deceives him into believing the opposite of who I am. In that hijab, I look so, so *local,* for lack of a better word. I cannot possibly be a novice foreign tourist fresh off a transatlantic flight. It's a bit unnerving, the way a piece of fabric on my head erases the American in me. Strange consequences abound. I can't get away with cultural blunders or the failure to understand the intricacies of subway ticketing rules. If I happen to use a wrong token that jams the turnstile, then I must be an Egyptian smart aleck trying to cheat the system.

"Pay this amount." The stationmaster thrusts a form in squiggly Arabic handwriting and draws a big circle in red ink around some cryptic numerals.

Congratulating myself for passing as a local troublemaker, I fork over 120 Egyptian pounds (about $30), assuming it is the bribe for my freedom. The stationmaster orders me to sit back down. I am already twenty minutes late for my first class at the Fajr Arabic Language Institute. Desperation mounts as I rifle through my bag and unearth my U.S. passport and the name of the Arabic school printed on a torn page of the weekly *Al-Ahram*'s English edition. The stationmaster stares at them as if hallucinating.

"You *Amrikeyi?* You no look *Amrikeyi!*"

A speck of light dares to invade his eyes.

"*Merhaba! Merhaba!* Welcome, welcome to Egypt!"

The scowling face gives way to profuse handshakes.

"You come to office every day. I teach you Arabic and you teach me your English, yes?"

He beams like a proud papa.

"You want taxi, yes? Go with Yusuf. He get you nice clean taxi. Very cheap. You pay like Egyptian, not tourist, understand?"

I glance at Yusuf, the sidekick who treated me like a criminal fifteen minutes earlier. He is asleep on the floor, snoring loudly, his gaping mouth an open invitation to buzzing flies.

"You will share with me some *chai,* yes?"

My newfound friend pushes a button under his desk. A minute later, a little barefooted boy in a worn orange sweatshirt produces two chipped glasses of steaming black tea. I sip the heavily sugared brew and straighten out the folds of my crumpled georgette.

We all know that appearances are deceiving. Despite this knowledge, we still judge based on appearances. It is difficult not to when what we see on the outside is initially the only piece of available information about a person. It's not like we can get inside that person's head and figure out where she comes from, why she behaves the way she does, and what makes her tick in general. Appearances are our only clue.

Once when I was pounding away on my laptop at a Seattle public library, I overheard a conversation between two elderly women at a side table. It was about a six-year-old girl whom one of them had seen wearing the hijab.

"Why do they have to wear those things?" The voice sounded horrified.

Her friend responded. "It has to do with their Muslim religion. I hear it's very strict."

I thought of moving to a different part of the library so I wouldn't have to hear about Muslim rhymed with muslin once more. But I was in a lazy mood so I just stayed in my place, pretending to be deaf and ignoring something inside me that wanted to speak out and address those women. The longer I sat, the more conflicted I felt until I finally pushed back my chair and approached the adjoining table.

"Excuse me?"

"Why, hello, dear! Do sit down and join us. What a cute little dress you're wearing. Wherever did you get it?"

"It's from India."

"Ah, India! I just love Indian food. Don't you?" The silver-haired woman elbowed her companion.

"Umm. I wanted to say something."

"Yes?"

"Well, I don't really know how to say this. But I heard what you were talking about that little girl in her hijab. Well, I just . . . "

"To cover up a small child. What an awful thing to do!"

"Yes, it's not an easy thing to understand. I have a hard time understanding it myself. You see, I'm also a Muslim."

"No, you're not!"

"You cannot be!"

"But I am!"

Both women scrutinized my knee-length batik sundress, my hijab-less head, my strappy kitten-heeled sandals.

"Well, you may be a Muslim. But at least you're not fundamental like that little girl."

I winced. And not just because of that mispronunciation again. I am all too familiar with their attitude, and the sadness and anger it evokes in me. As a Pakistani, born and raised Muslim, reared in Seattle for twenty-three years, I have never gotten used to misplaced labels about Islam—not only the fable that wearing hijab automatically equals oppression, but the misapprehension that all Muslim men must be depraved polygamists and that the harsh austerity of our faith condones violence. Not that we Muslims have it all figured out. Some of us are downright allergic to questions and self-examination. But I don't recall a time when I did not feel immense pride in and open-ended curiosity about my cultural and religious heritage. As a teenager, I nearly drove my mother mad with whys.

One of my favorites was the why of veiling. Whenever I raised the issue with Ammi, she pointed me to the verse in the Qur'an advising women to cover their bosoms and hide their adornments.

"But it says nothing about covering the hair!" I challenged her.

"Isn't hair an adornment?" she countered.

"Well I suppose so. But it doesn't clearly say so."

My hijab-clad mother smiled and said, "It is clear enough to me."

That was nearly twenty years ago. Today, Ammi's eyes are just as radiant with faith. Her face continues to glow with *noor,* the sheen of inner light. She still makes it impossible for me to argue with the power of this much belief.

So I had a hard time explaining the significance of veiling to my new-found acquaintances at the library. As our discussion continued, I tried to hammer in the point that wearing the hijab is not an outright sign of the backwardness of Muslim females. It may have to do with cultural values or community peer pressure or at best a personal expression of faith.

The old ladies weren't so convinced. "Then why don't *you* wear it?" one of them asked.

I told her that I didn't think the head cover was religiously mandatory, but many Muslims, including my own mother, considered it otherwise. "How can any religion be so wishy-washy?" they wondered. Either something is required or it isn't. So which is it? I sighed and fumbled for a short answer, which of course does not exist.

The Muslim veil is full of meaning. At any given period of history, time or place, the idea and practice of veiling have led to clashing viewpoints—inclusion, exclusion; progressive, regressive; emancipating, humiliating; erotic, vulgar; trendy—the list goes on and on. One of the most contentious debates in some analytical circles underlies the assumption that feminists oppose the veil and antifeminists don't. That is to say, a covered Muslim woman cannot possibly have a mind of her own, that in order to improve her status and move forward, she has to reject Islamic traditions and adopt Western ways. According to the Egyptian scholar Leila Ahmed, this type of logic is not only ethnocentric and misguided, but it also overemphasizes the wearing or not wearing of the veil as the sole determinant of Muslim women's freedom and mobility or lack thereof. So pervasive is this fascination with the hijab that it inevitably dominates most discussions of women and Islam as if no other factors matter. Ahmed's argument does not negate the importance of the veil. But she compares it to Western women's struggles over gender justice where items of clothing such as bras were briefly in focus as symbols of contention yet did not take over the entire discourse on women's lib.[1]

Another outcome of the veil's hegemony in the public imagination is the idea, whether overtly or covertly expressed, of Islam as oppressor of women and the West as liberator. This idea was also internalized by Muslim rulers who introduced westernizing reforms that forcibly banned the veil, not because of what veiling said about women, but how it reflected on the *men*.

As an instrument wielding the gender politics of identity, the veil may have no equal. Whether enforced or forbidden, obsessive to the point of ridicule, the dialectics of a Muslim woman's head (covered or un-) are not without controversy. But it would be too simplistic to presume that veiling, in and of itself, renders passive submission. "Static" is the one word the veil refutes time and again.

A case in point is the colonial narrative of Algeria. In the initial phase, women wore the veil as a symbol of resistance against French occupation. The veil stood for the dignity and validity of all native customs under fiercest attack, particularly customs pertaining to women, ones the occupier was determined to control. The question of who ultimately controls how women look and dress was in many ways a pivotal battleground. As the Algerian struggle for liberation intensified, the veil was consciously abandoned during the course of revolutionary action in which women actively participated.

The Battle of Algiers (1965) is a film documenting their participation as attractive secret agents, carrying briefcases of false papers and huge sums of money, slinking through the Europeanized city streets where men, young and old, appraise the slim, brunette, bare-legged revolutionaries. When the French authorities discovered this form of militant female subterfuge, it marked a turning point in the Algerian war of independence.

Covert missions became increasingly suspect. As illustrated by the filmmaker Gillo Pontecorvo, in order to conceal packages, women were obliged to alter their body image. They became slouchy and shapeless and took back the protective cover of the veils under which they carried revolvers, bombs, and hand grenades. Enemy raids continued and it was not uncommon for these now-veiled revolutionaries to be shoved against walls to have their bodies passed over with magnetic detectors.

This is not to equate the struggles of Algerian women exclusively with the veil, then or now. The point is that veiling is a dynamic process, and during the Algerian revolution, women themselves dictated their appearances for strategic resistance. In a certain sense, the hard-won independence from France caused a turning back in society, wrestling with values already outmoded. Whereas the veil had been largely eschewed in the prerevolutionary era, it was resumed by many after the revolution and stripped of its traditional dimension. Interestingly, interaction with Western culture, in the form of colonization, also shaped the language of the veil as a distinct by-product of both East and West.

As my hijab and I ventured deeper into the Middle East, we encountered more contradictions. Traveling beyond Cairo in the winter of 2001, I still insisted on wearing the head scarf out of respect for the cultures I encountered, though the preponderance of high-society Arab girls flaunting their you-know-whats in people's faces was rather disconcerting. Don't get me wrong. I would have gladly cheered their right to wear skintight Spandex. But while Spandex paired with veils may appear to be a creative spin on Islamic modesty, my mind couldn't go beyond the hypocrisy.

In the Jordanian capital of Amman, I once saw a woman in full *niqab*, a thick black veil covering her entire face with a six-inch open strip around the eyes. She wore black from head to toe. But there was something odd about her, as she stood alone on a street corner, teetering on stilettos. After a while, a car drove by, screeched its tires, and stopped. A man got out, yelling profanities at the woman who was apparently his sister. She yelled back in defiance, protesting loudly as he clutched her wrist and dragged her toward the waiting car. She refused to get inside and her voice climbed decibels, occasionally breaking midsentence from hoarseness. There was a strange disconnect between the fury coming out of her mouth and her black-cloaked obscurity. Suddenly, she whipped out a cell phone from somewhere underneath her voluminous garments and furiously punched the numbers with a black-gloved finger. She spoke into it through her face veil, which fluttered with the movement of her hidden lips.

The brother went ballistic. He grabbed his sister's hand, yanked away the mobile, and smashed it with his feet. Then he tightened his grip, twisting her hand behind her back. The girl howled and kicked him in the shins with her spiky heels. He smacked her head and tried to push her to the ground. As their fighting continued, another car approached. A sleek white Mercedes with tinted windows. The passenger door opened and a tall, gray-haired man in a double-breasted suit stepped out and gestured to the woman with a curt angling of his head.

She was squatting on her haunches, a whimpering black huddle with teary eyes. The well-dressed stranger helped her up and led the still crying woman into the backseat of his car. Then he went up to the disgruntled brother, who was pummeling his fists on the car's roof. A lengthy speech followed. The older man took a wad of bills from his wallet, slipped them in the brother's front shirt pocket, and patted his cheek in a there, there kind of way.

The brother laughed sarcastically and hurled one final insult at his sister waiting inside the car. The one word I made out was *sharmuta*, Arabic for whore.

The next evening, I returned to the same street corner at the exact same time but there was no more drama. I waited at that spot for five consecutive nights but she never came back. Even if she was a prostitute, I wondered what drove her to it and why she was so heavily veiled. Maybe it was a way of ensuring her protection and anonymity. But that hadn't deterred her brother from recognizing her. Or did her niqab mean that she was in fact a pious woman, forced by circumstances to her current profession? Maybe, maybe not. After that incident, I was less and less sure of the real motives for veiling.

In the old city of Damascus, I was the star entertainment among the flared denims, boot-clad fashionistas snickering at my sensible Birkenstocks and navy *abaya* with cross-stitched embroidery that labeled me a local country hick instead of the American city slicker I wanted them to befriend. What I really wanted was to take pictures of these Damascene hipsters and show them to my American friends back home, who thought of themselves as the epitome of hipster style in Capri pants and tight midriff tops, without the slightest inkling of hipster competition in Syria. Yes, Syria, where I felt like a dork for the sake of Islamic modesty (figure 14.2).

Speaking of modesty, when I lived in Beirut, I had this roommate, Najma, a struggling architecture student, who sat in her room from dawn to dusk, fiddling with straight edges and blueprints. Whenever Najma was stuck on a problem, she would sing. I could have listened to her all day when she belted out classics by the Lebanese diva Fairuz, in a voice as clear as a bell.

Most days, Najma wore a purple paisley print head scarf folded into a triangle and knotted behind her nape. It kept a mass of thick corkscrew curls in check. She wasn't particularly religious. The only time we discussed Islam, Najma pointed out that she was an agnostic and we left it at that. I rarely got a chance to talk to her because she was so busy with

Figure 14.2. The author eschews hipster fashion in favor of traditional *hijab* in the old city of Damascus, Syria, 2001. Courtesy of Maliha Masood.

her studies, often not returning home until two or three in the morning. For my birthday, she gave me homemade tapes of the music she listened to—funky fusion beats with hints of Sufi trance. I liked dancing to them in the tiny living room we shared.

Najma watched my attempts to shimmy my shoulders and wiggle my hips like a real belly dancer.

"You're trying too hard," she said.

"This is impossible!" I was trying to isolate my abs and shake them like Jell-O.

Najma stifled a giggle. *La habibi, la!*

"What then? What am I doing wrong?"

"You must learn to find your center. *Yallah,* I show you."

We wore gym clothes and dressed them up in gauzy veils, doubling as sarongs and bandanas to keep off the sweat. Najma blew me away with her graceful moves. What really surprised me was the smoldering sensuality that oozed from her limbs like sap from a ripe rubber tree. When I asked her how she learned to dance so well, she whispered in my ear, "La Souke."

La Souke turned out to be a nightclub where Najma performed Thursday and Saturday nights. Men went wild over her in thigh-high boots, wriggling in a cage, Madonna style. But she was best in her arousing Arabic numbers, all decked out in sequined halters and hip belts made out of little silver coins. In one routine, she added a sheer black veil, flinging it in the air and letting it fall flat on her face as she swayed and fluttered. Najma's dancing veil reminded me of an untrimmed sail, taunting the wind that fueled its flight. It defied definition. It could be anything one wanted it to be—just like Najma.

Demure student by day and sexy dancer by night—it was not my business, nor anyone else's, to judge her. The club gig paid well and Najma needed the money for college and rent. She could have had a "safer" job, but dancing was so much more lucrative. Wasn't she bothered by all those leering men, total strangers who probably went home and jerked off fantasizing about her pretty, dancing image? Najma laughed and said she could not care less. She was having a good time on that stage, proud of her sculpted body, and it emboldened her confidence to dance in public, to let people have fun, but the real entertainment was for herself! In a way I guess she was calling the shots.

When I left Beirut and vacated the apartment, Najma's good-bye present was a postcard-sized bundle and she told me not to open it until I got home. Five years later, I still have that chiffon veil of hers. Sometimes, I press my face into its black softness just to breathe the lingering scent of sweet tobacco smoke and Chanel No. 5.

By the time I reached Turkey, I had flung away my hijab. Yet there I met Turkish women who were clamoring to wear the head scarf in universities and government institutions where veiling was banned by law, making it a contentious battleground between individual self-expression and government policy. In the eyes of Turkish women demanding the right to cover their heads, the issue at heart was a matter of free will to dress as they pleased. And they were demanding this right even as they studied to be doctors, lawyers, and diplomats. Given Turkey's campaign to get into the European Union, the Turkish state has reinforced its anti-hijab laws, blatantly devoid of the concept of choice.[2]

If only choice could ever be simple. Back in the States, my traveling veils have converted to fashionable neck scarves and shawls. I have quite a collection in shades of burgundy, turquoise, and amethyst with patterns of polka dots and spiral chains. Most of them have been donated to my mother. We no longer argue about the whys of veiling. And she doesn't chide me for my uncovered head because she knows my faith is strong. Strong enough to muster the discipline to pray five times a day in a country where the *azan* or call to prayer does not blare from a neighborhood minaret but echoes inside the heart. What Ammi and I both resent are the judgment calls within our own Seattle community where an unveiled Muslim woman automatically earns the "secular" label, meaning she is nonobservant of practice. Is the presence of the hijab a surefire indicator of inner belief? Does the lack of hijab therefore signify none? Instead of an emphatic yes or no, my answer would be "it depends."

Recall the deceptiveness of appearances and our penchant to judge by them. In the United States, just as I discovered in the Middle East, appearance is everything. My ability to blend in has a reverse effect on my own home turf. Here, people have a hard time believing that I'm a Muslim just because I don't cover. They can tell by my funny sounding, hard-to-pronounce-name that I must be a "foreigner," but that's about it. The emphasis on image is so strong that if you don't look like a caricatured Muslim, you simply cannot be one.

A caricatured Muslim woman is undoubtedly veiled. But what are the implications behind that veiled image? Is she subservient, helpless, and weak? Feisty, determined, and ambitious? Not too long ago, I saw a PBS Frontline broadcast reissued from the 1980 film *Death of a Princess*. It is a dramatized documentary based on the true-life account of a Saudi princess, who was publicly executed for adultery. Justification for the punishment oscillated on the grounds of "Islamic law" and a violation of family tribal honor. The film suggested that the princess's murder was instigated by her own grandfather. Saudi uproar over the allegedly insensitive airing of their dirty laundry enflamed the controversy.

One unforgettable scene was especially criticized. The film describes how bored Saudi princesses cruise the desert highways in their chauffeured cars to pick up men. They could be married, young or old, beautiful or hideous. Black abayas and niqabs camouflage their identities, just as they did for that woman I had observed in Jordan, who may have been a prostitute. But unlike her, these rich royals are not at work. They are on a desert raid exploiting the anonymity of their covering for promiscuity. The car slows; the princess rolls down her window to eye a potential mate. Or she might sit inside a parked vehicle with a trio of others like her, silently observing men who are dancing for her pleasure with their swords, men wanting to please, men wanting to be chosen by the predatory veiled women who can see without being seen.

Much of the media attention and Saudi offensive centered on this scene's crudeness, which was said to be fiction and to have cheapened the film and insulted Saudi women, especially members of the royal family. Watching the scene unfold, I was struck by the image itself, for it made me think of how much power those Saudi royals wielded by virtue of being covered.

As a physical barrier, the veil denies men their usual privilege of discerning whomever they desire. By default, the women are in command. The female scrutinizes the male. Her gaze from behind the anonymity of her face veil or niqab is a kind of surveillance that casts her in the dominant position. It enables a woman to uncover with her eyes, to make visible that which is forbidden. So there seems to be an acute relationship between veiling and vision that undercuts the legacy of social, cultural, political, and religious meanings associated with the Muslim veil. It continues to fascinate me, the Rubik's cube of identities the hijab conceals and reveals.

A year of traveling alone in the Middle East and my upbringing as a Pakistani Muslim American have shown me that there is no formulaic way to describe the hijab. Even though I don't wear one as a rule, a part of me is stitched from its threads. Just because those threads are not always visible doesn't mean they don't count. The white georgette cloth that first felt like a bandage still floats in my eyes, sweeping layers of memory. We've had a long relationship, fraught with love, hate, confusion, and plenty of surprises. We've journeyed together and served each other well as travel companions—for the most part. My hijab gave me refuge from prying stares and possibly averted more serious dangers. It adopted me at subway stations and rejected me in trendy cafés. It has kept me warm on cold winter nights, it has wowed, titillated, and amazed, and it has also made me laugh, dance, sulk, and complain. As with most relationships, my hijab and I have had our spats and dramas. These days, we're in a mellow groove, content to leave each other alone, but always on the lookout for a rousing debate.

NOTES

1. Leila Ahmed, "The Discourse of the Veil," in *Veil: Veiling, Representation and Contemporary Art*, ed. David Bailey and Gilane Tawadros (Cambridge, MA: MIT Press, 2003).

2. In a noted case in 1999, politician and member of the Islamist Virtue Party Merve Kavakçi became the first veiled woman to be elected to the Turkish Parliament. She was prevented from making her parliamentary oath when she wore her head scarf to a swearing-in ceremony in defiance of the secular Turkish constitution. She was eventually stripped of her Turkish citizenship when it was discovered that she had earlier that year taken dual American citizenship.

THREE

What is this pictured form, this monarch and this prince?
What is this old wisdom? They are all veils.
The remedy against veils is ecstasies like this.

—Maulana Jalaluddin Rumi

15 Purdah, Patriarchy, and the Tropical Sun

Womanhood in India

JASBIR JAIN

There is a mystique attached to the word *purdah* and its multiple aspects, meanings, and practices. Attitudes toward it fluctuate, not only in accordance with the rise and fall of fundamentalisms and ethnicities, but also through the different purposes it fulfills in language. It is part of many idioms and indicates emotions ranging from belonging to privacy to coyness. There are a whole range of synonyms and metaphors attached to it: *ghunghat* (a veil pulled over the face) (figure 15.1), *odhni* (a head scarf that is used for the ghunghat), *chunri,* and *chadri* (sheet, mantle, cloak) are only some of them. As part of a dress, its manner of use is often indicative not only of the religion one follows but also one's caste, class, and perhaps region. And from being a mere part of a dress, it has the capacity to signify a relationship between the self and the other.

The real significance of purdah lies not in these external signifiers, but in its impact as a social construct. It affects men and women alike and defines the notion of both masculinity and femininity. It touches even those

Figure 15.1.   A woman in India cuts grass wearing *ghunghat.* Photo by Vijay Kutty.

of us who have always believed that we are outside its influence. In a larger sense it sustains the idea of patriarchy. Primarily, it is about space—about segregation and division, signifying a conjunction of power and space. In its implied meanings it goes much beyond the covered face and the hidden body to encompass notions of respectability·and virtue, class and caste, protection and exposure.

When I ask myself what purdah means to *me*—daughter of a Sikh household, married into a conservative Jain family (both outside Hinduism), an educated professional who has traveled extensively—I experience conflicting responses. At the outset, I am outside it and have been able to negotiate the boundaries of my physical and emotional spaces fairly well. But a deeper reflection shows it has affected my code of behavior and my sense of moral values. True, purdah was much more real for my grandmother and, to some extent, my mother. Both my grandmothers always wore full-sleeved and loose baggy shirts that fully hid the contours of the body. They moved around with their heads covered, especially in male presence. My mother often recalled her journeys in a horse carriage with a chadri stretched across the rear to protect the women from the bazaar gaze. This kind of purdah was seen as a social necessity and sought to protect the women from public view.

Marriage revealed to me another aspect: discrimination between daughters and daughters-in-law. My husband's mother insisted that daughters-in-law should not sit on the front seat of a horse carriage or wear *salwar kameez*.[1] Marriage brought additional responsibilities that affected the code of behavior. It was easy enough to tolerate and laugh at these restrictions, as our visits home were of a short duration. None of them really meant anything in our social circle. But the linkage with social roles was underlined in more than one way. It implied prohibition, exclusion, and hierarchy.

Ordering of space into the private and the public introduces the notion of ownership and belonging. It has implications for sociocultural, as well as intellectual, mobility. For a moment, if we place purdah in the center, we can see the different controlling mechanisms it unleashes. It controls a woman's mobility, her morality, her sexuality, and her intellectual freedom. Purdah, in some form or other, is shared by almost all societies, in West or East.[2] Differences in economic and political histories mark the difference in external manifestations. In India itself, the manner in which purdah may be practiced by the same caste and economic group may differ with the location (whether rural or urban, open countryside or crowded cityscape), class (aristocracy, peasantry, working class), woman's status (wife, courtesan, or mistress), and the degree of power she wields. At times of cultural encounters, whenever there is a threat to cultural survival, the hardening of attitudes often takes place and a revivalist, protectionist approach is adopted. Similarly, colonial India rushed into restrictive practices where purdah was concerned in order to protect its cultural identity and prevent British intrusions into the personal sphere.[3]

The practice of purdah has a long history in India and, across time, myths have accumulated around it. These have usually been passed on by word of mouth, through oral traditions and interpolations in written texts. Sometimes, this took place through translation, and other times through political manipulation. Of these, there are four such myths I propose to discuss: that purdah came to India with the Muslims and owes its origins to the defense against Muslim invaders; that, in the Ramayana, Lakshmana drew a circle defining the protected area for his sister-in-law Sita's movement during the absence of men; that purdah is identifiable primarily with sexual segregation in social space and defined by the dress code; and that it is always negative and oppressive. (There are many more, but four should suffice.) These beliefs are interwoven and overlapping and at times contradictory. For instance, the first and second say very different things. While the first emphasizes religious opposition, the third makes a subtle distinction (an unwarranted one) between moral sphere and dress code, between protection and denial of freedom. The Hindu mind wills itself to believe they are necessary and different.

Purdah in its sense of patriarchal control is native to the Hindu. The laws of Manu (*Manavdharma Smriti*) subordinate woman to man, whether a father, husband, or son, and deprive her of free agency.[4] The very fact that a woman's dharma (her sense of duty) is defined through obedience to her husband denies her free access to the outside world. Other defining constructs like *sati* (one who is pure and chaste), and *pativrata* (committed / devoted to the husband), also place a woman within limited loyalties and freedom.

The Ramayana is one of the two Indian epics—the second being the later Mahabharata—that have defined Indian society. It depicts the character of an ideal son and king, Rama, who is referred to as *maryada purshottam,* the best of men in his adherence to normative traditions. The eldest of the four sons of King Dashratha of Koshala, Rama was exiled to the forest for fourteen years. His stepmother, Kaikeyi, had extracted a promise from the king to grant her one boon: she wanted Rama to be exiled. In order to honor his father's promise, Rama willingly proceeded to the forest. His wife, Sita, and his younger brother Lakshmana accompanied him. The Ramayana describes the battle between the forces of good and evil. Rama, who earned his godhood through his behavior, represents the forces of good, while Ravana is the demon king who abducted Sita. It is this abduction that led to war between the two. Sita was rescued, the war was won, but as the legend goes, she was subjected to a purity test, *agnipriksha*, the trial of chastity by fire.

The story of the Ramayana survives as a living tradition, written or rein-terpreted by successive generations across the length and breadth of not only India but the whole of South Asia. Its concepts have become part of everyday language and the collective unconscious. It has lived through different mediums—recitals, *kathas* (tales), Ram-lilas (annual enactments normally held in October every year leading to the celebrations of Dussehra and Diwali), ballets, movies, and tele-serials.

It also inhabits the political imagination. Mohandas Gandhi, in his search for an ideal society, projected the concept of Ram-Rajya, the golden period of history when a king was responsive to the people's needs; Rama placed moral duty above personal desire.[5] Fundamentalists and protes-tors alike have used the story. In the 1980s, a tele-serial, Ramanand Sagar's *Ramayana,* so trapped the country's imagination that trains were halted at the time of its telecasting.[6] The political agitation surrounding the dis-puted site of the sixteenth-century Babri Masjid, said to have been built on the ruins of a Hindu temple, led to its demolition in December 1992. The right-wing Bharatiya Janata Party periodically raises the issue of the temple's reconstruction on the same site in Ayodha, insisting that this temple is the birthplace of Ram-lalla, the baby Rama. Deepa Mehta's 1997 film *Fire* uses the Ramayana as background narrative to illustrate gender oppression.[7]

The Ramayana is a living reality for the Hindu mind in personal and political terms. Thus the contradiction between purdah as a result of in-vasions and the myth of the circle Lakshmana drew needs to be examined more critically. There is no denying the fact that every threat, no matter from where, or every war, no matter in which country or age, has led to the protection of women, who constitute a vulnerable group. The idea of family honor, more particularly male honor, and that of purity of lineage are linked with the bodies of women. The British presence, in its own way, was also instrumental in the hardening of gender-based space divisions.[8] As for the *Lakshmana-rekha,* neither Valmiki's *Ramayana* (700–500 B.C.E.) nor Kamban's (900–1200 C.E.), or even Tulsidas's *Ramcharitmanas*[9] (six-teenth century) make mention of this. *Ramcharitmanas* belongs to the Bhakti period and is written in Avadhbhasha, a language of the people. It is the one most popularly recited in the Hindi-speaking heartland of India.

Lakshmana is supposed to have drawn the demarcation line, the *Lakshmana-rekha*, around his sister-in-law Sita, when she compelled him to go to his brother Rama's rescue. The popular legend goes that because Sita crossed this boundary, stepping outside the line, she was abducted by Ravana, the demon king who lusted after her. This abduction generated the rest of the story: war, Ravana's defeat, Sita's return, and her agnipriksha. A Hindu woman's life, whether she likes it or not, every now and then comes up against Lakshmana-rekha and agnipriksha. In Valmiki's *Ramayana*, Lakshmana leaves Sita to the care of the forest deities.[10] In Kamban's *Ramayana*, she is left to her dharma, her sense of inner control, and to the overlordship of Jatayu, the eagle.[11] In *Ramcharitmanas*, Sita is again given to the care of the forest deities and the four directions of the sky, that is, the world of nature.[12] Ravana enters a leaf cottage, disguised as an ascetic. Step by step, the tale progresses through desire and the yielding or resistance to temptation. Rama thwarts the advances of Ravana's sister, Surapankha, resisting her attempts to seduce him. Sita, however, is charmed by a golden deer and desires to possess it, so that first Rama, then Lakshmana, must pursue it. On the face of it, this is not very different from Eve's yielding to Satan's persuasion, but dissimilarities soon creep in. Sita's resistance to Ravana renders her a victim of oppression by both her abductor and her husband. The trial by fire signifies both subjugation and purification.

The Ramayana story, in its multiple readings, reinterpretations, and retellings, defines first the limits of legitimate sexuality and the violation of those limits. The controlling figure remains male: definitions and purificatory rites are male prescriptions. Passed on through oral tradition, these two episodes—the mythical Lakshmana-rekha and agnipriksha—define Indian womanhood within Hinduism and form a part of the socialization process, working at both the conscious and unconscious levels.[13]

Documentary sources are hard to come by, but needle and thread are mentioned in early Sanskrit writings and stitching of wounds and the like were not unknown to the Hindus. But saris, dhotis, and other garments were draped round the body, and a length of cloth was either knotted or thrown across the upper body. Stitched clothes, like shirts and trousers, were not in vogue until the seventh century c.e., when Kushan invaders brought tailoring to India. Purdah, in the sense of segregation and subordination of women, is a homegrown product symbolizing the relationship between self and the other.

During the British period, purdah was reinforced in two different ways. The first was through legislation and codification of half-forgotten cultural memories and beliefs. In its attempt to introduce a written code for legal interpretation in the courts of law, the British government turned to *Manusmriti* for the purposes of defining Hindu "personal law" (as supplementary to the general law).[14] *Manusmriti* prescribed a strict code of control over women and evoked outdated gender behavior.

The second came from nationalists' defense of women as custodians of culture. This led to a division into public and private space, the former being the outside world of political life and the latter of domesticity and women.[15] Purdah as segregation began to appear as the last bastion of culture against both modernization and Westernization. Indian women, however, carried on a parallel discourse. While Pandita Ramabai took it upon herself to interrogate *Manusmriti* clause by clause, Rokeya Sakhawat Hossain wrote a fantasy, *Sultana's Dream*, where she put the men behind purdah, and several essays (anthologized in *Avarodhbasini*) describing the accidents that the observation of purdah or a false sense of womanly conduct could lead to.[16]

Segregation of space depicted in fiction, as well as in autobiographies, often led to comedies of errors, fatal accidents, and tragic turns over mistaken identities on account of the bride's ghunghat. Rabindranath Tagore narrates one such story in his novel, *Nau Durghatna* (translated into English as *The Wreck*). Two newlywed couples, who had not seen each others' faces at their weddings, end up with the wrong partners as the result of a shipwreck.[17] The veil with its intermingling of mystery and desire itself calls forth romantic associations of hide-and-seek in the game of love. Many a Punjabi folk song expresses the mischief and playfulness behind the ghunghat. In one, a young man in search of a bride wants to marry a girl who winks at him through the veil (*Aasan kudi O laini jihri khund vi-*

chon akh maren). Another describes the relationship between daughter-in-law and father-in-law, when the young bride observes purdah but shows off by leaving the side of the ghunghat with the hair clip open to his view (*suhre koluun khund kad-di, nanga rakhdi clipwala pasa*), thus satisfying a need to appear attractive to others. There is no end to the songs and *ghazals* that build romance around purdah/ghunghat as it symbolizes the desire for the unknown other with all its pain, longing, and restraint. Well-known Indian poets lyricize over the imagined beauty of the veiled woman. The framed relationship between men and women, with all its decorum and restraint, is often the mainstay of a family. In a powerful feminist novel, *Mitro Marjani* (Damn You, Mitro), Krishna Sobti tells the story of a daughter-in-law who lets her *dupatta* (cotton stole or scarf) slide off her head as a gesture subversive of his authority.[18] This act is seen as a sign of rebellion.

These worldly, material aspects of purdah are matched by its spiritual intensity in fourteenth- to eighteenth-century Bhakti poetry and in the verses of the Sufi poets.[19] The Rajasthani poet Mirabai's religious hymns refer to the ghunghat as the veil between God and his devotee. It is only the devotion, concentration, and meditation of the devotee that can help him cross the distance to God. The devotee must bring about the required change within his heart, to remove the veil—"Transcend the veil and ye shall find God" (*ghunghat ke pat khol, tohe piya milen ge).* Sufism, a parallel movement with its roots in Islam, again expresses similar emotions. We find references to the ghunghat in the verses of Amir Khusro and of Bulle Shah, both Sufi poets who treat the devotee as female and are desirous that the veil be lifted between the devotee and the beloved.[20] It is significant that one of the Hindi words for revelation is *darshan*. During certain hours, a curtain is drawn across the idols in a temple and pulled aside at the time of worship. The word also carries within it the right to accord an audience. The impact of both Sufism and the Bhakti movement can be seen in the rise of Sikhism, a faith that provides space for a woman to relate directly to God (and not through her husband, as with Hinduism). Sikhism does not perceive woman as subservient to man. Neither does it exclude her from priestly tasks on the grounds of bodily impurity.[21]

Spatial divisions are reflected in purdah-observing households. It is not only the Muslim households who had their *zenana* and *mardana* (women's quarters); Hindu households, especially in Bengal and Rajasthan, also had separate living spaces. As Malvika Karlekar observes, the *antahpura* (the inner quarters) distinguished itself from outer spaces, defining a separate sphere of function and influence.[22] Rama Mehta's *Inside the Haveli,* a semi-autobiographical fictional narrative, describes a similar division of space in the *haveli*s (mansions) of Rajasthan. Set in the princely state of Udaipur, it focuses on a three-hundred-year-old haveli, the ancestral home of the protagonist's husband. The first chapter, with its dominantly socioanthropological tone, describes the physical and social environs and the protected and secluded inner courtyards. Lest the reader assume that this seclusion would allow more privacy, the chapter ends with the observation, "There are no secrets, there could be none in the haveli."[23] Even the communities (heterotopias) that are created in the women's world abound with eavesdroppers, messengers, observers, and manipulators.

Working through the mind of a young, city-bred girl called Geeta, who has come to the haveli as a new bride, the novel examines the effects purdah has on the body, the mind, and relationships with others. Husbands and wives do not meet during the day; there is no normal social life that includes mixed gatherings; cajoling, confidence sharing, and persuasions are all carried out through servants and have their moments of frustration and suppression. A double discourse runs right through the narrative. The upper layer is one of a gradual growing into the purdah tradition and of accepting its priorities of family and tradition over individual aspirations. This endorses and attempts to capture traditional values. The underlying discourse expresses the frustrations of suppression and resentment against the compulsions of tradition.

Geeta extends her world by creating an informal class for the servants' children, with both negative and positive results. While it opens her world, as well as that of the children, it also disrupts existing feudalistic structures. Again, the excessive decorum and restraint in the behavioral code among women of equal status dampen all emotional expression and spontaneous impulses. The loyal haveli servants, no matter how well treated, are also like bonded slaves. The flow is against democratic setups and encourages reticence, restraint, and secrets; none in the haveli dare express their feelings.[24] Behind the latticed windows, women are like caged birds, without control over their lives, their aspirations, or their relationships.

Seclusion and subsequent female resentment are themes found in myriad Indian novels across languages, religions, regions, and generations. Attia Hosain's autobiographical *Sunlight on a Broken Column* takes up the story of a Muslim *taluqdar* (landholding) family in 1940s Lucknow. The novel opens with the lines, "The day my aunt Abida moved from the zenana into the guest-room off the corridor that led to the men's wing of the house, within call of her father's room, we knew that Baba Jan had not much longer to live."[25] Abida's physical move marks the shift of authority in the household from a secondary into a male role. But as soon as her brother comes home, she is demoted, married off to an elderly widower, and expected to bury herself in the countryside.

Again in *Suvarnlata*, a novel describing life in a 1930s Bengali household, Ashapurna Devi explores gender subordination through seclusion in the tale of a nine-year-old child bride growing up in a middle-class Bengali joint family, where several generations live together. As Suvarnlata grows up, the mother-in-law's strict control does not allow the young couple to meet during the day. When her husband looks surreptitiously for opportunities to spend time with her, she begins to feel disgusted at his single-minded obsession with physical desire. She is fond of reading, but when she borrows magazines, she is criticized. Interested in the nation's struggle for freedom, she is upset by her family's indifference. Throughout she longs for a little privacy, a little space, and the opportunity to express her creativity. Finally, they move into a house of their own and Suvarnlata gets an uncle-in-law to publish her book. But when it arrives, the family's laughter that greets this publication drives her to make a bonfire of all five hundred copies.[26]

In the Kannada novel *Phaniyamma*, M. K. Indira recalls the real-life history of a great-great-aunt, Phani, born in 1840 in South India, where purdah as ghunghat or covering the head is virtually nonexistent.[27] Widowed as a child, Phani lived to the age of 112. Her marriage was never consummated, and the moment her husband died—when she was only nine—she was deprived of all ornaments and condemned to a life of widowhood. Her lifelong task would be to minimize her needs, secluded in dark rooms, dark corners, and kitchens. At the age of thirteen, with the onset of menstruation, she was raised to the status of a *madi*. Madi women avoided the touch of others and had to take extreme precautions about purity, uphold all orthodox traditions, and observe all rituals. More than a religious necessity, madi women were an economic necessity in large households, where they carried out household chores.

Widows were not allowed to drink milk or consume any other kinds of passion-generating food. They were required to live on one meal a day. Phani's life was spent with no idea of sex and it was only when she was forty that she realized the meaning of copulation. But she was not without her own responses. Over the years, she began questioning these restrictive practices and resisting their imposition on women of the younger generation. Many works similar to *Phaniyamma* are fictionalized accounts of personal experiences; the frustrations and struggles they recount of women sacrificed to family and tradition are real.

The practice of purdah has its origins in an overriding social concern with a woman's purity—whether she is a child, married, or widowed. Purity is a multilayered concept, including nonviolation of the body, moral decency, and sexual abstinence. The sanctification of the kitchen area, the idea of pollution through touch, the need for frequent baths—and consequently the health risks involved when women must often work wearing wet saris—are all fallouts of this concern with purity. The idea is to protect a woman's sexuality, perceived as a threat to masculine supremacy. Male ownership offers protection and respectability: public women, like courtesans, mistresses, or *devadasi*s (prostitutes) fall outside the notion of this social respectability and send the message that a woman without a man is available to be sexually exploited.

The question naturally arises: what about purdah today? Does it still exist despite increases in education, use of technology, shifts in architectural design, and the disintegration or near extinction of the joint family? The answer is yes. Regardless of shifts in fashion or excessive bodily exposure, despite the acceptance of unmarried couples living together in metropolitan areas, purdah continues. It persists in both the male and female mind-set, though proportionally more in the male. It still allows for facile

Figure 15.2. Modern purdah, as young
women veil against the sun's rays. Photo
by Jasbir Jain.

divisions between who is respectable and who is not. It is evident in the
violence against women and in the gender-based moral values voiced publicly. It is supported by religious fundamentalists of all faiths, Hindu, Muslim, Sikh, and Christian.

Purdah as a face covering offers women anonymity and defense against
sexual harassment. It also provides them with an unobserved observer's
position. Amusingly, it has even returned as a protection from the increased
heat of the tropical sun that has come with the drop in ozone levels (figure
15.2). Nowadays, with sun damage to bodies becoming more widespread,
young women with their faces covered and only their eyes visible can be
seen in India riding scooters, driving cars, going to work or shopping, performing whatever activities require them to be outdoors.

Ranging from the mundane to the spiritual, from the personal to the
social, purdah continues to occupy an ambivalent space, difficult to accept in its totality, equally difficult to reject completely. In its oppressive

aspects and the bodily and mental restrictions it imposes, the exclusion it defines, it is a reprehensible social practice. But—where the repression of the *burqa* or ghunghat is *not* relevant—as a symbol of social grace and decorum, purdah continues to be a desirable part of social life.

NOTES

1. Trousers *(salwar)* and a long shirt *(kameez* or *kurta)* were more liberating than draped garments and were Muslim in origin. Until the mid-1980s, salwar kameez was not much in vogue in South India. The whole of North India wore salwar kameez, but married women elsewhere did not.

2. In literary representations, women in most cultures have been shown as the protected sex, in need of chaperonage, moving around in salon chairs, and with roles limited to domestic life. In the nineteenth century, Victorian England had both camouflaging robes and moral prudery. James Tod, in his *Annals and Antiquities of Rajast'han* (1829; New Delhi: Rupa, 1997), repeatedly draws attention to the common element between Indian lifestyles and Western constructs concerning women. The differences were of degree and details and not of kind. The Ramayana and the biblical story of Eve's seduction by Satan would form an interesting comparison of desire, temptation, resistance, trial, and exile. The transgression of a taboo leads to the exile of Adam and Eve. At the very outset of the Ramayana, the stepmother's longing for power leads to Rama's exile. But later, the narrative becomes a psychodrama where contrary desires result in the conflict.

3. Barbara Daly Metcalf, in her introduction to *Perfecting Women*, writes, "The Indian woman was to be the bastion against all that was corrupt in the west" (Delhi: Oxford University Press, 1992), 12.

4. Clarisse Bader—in her introductory chapter to *Women in Ancient India* (New Delhi: Radha Publications, 1988), 12–13—identifies the beginning of binaries between the male and the female principles with the recognition of Brahman as the universal spirit and the primary cause, which led to a lower placement of the forces of nature creating hierarchical divisions such as nature/culture, irrational/rational. In Hindu thought, the division between *purush* (man) and *prakriti* (woman) subordinated shakti, the female energy, to the regulatory overlordship of the male.

5. For a detailed elaboration of Ram-Rajya, refer to my essay, "The Utopian Vision and Colonial Experience," in *The Utopian Imagination* (Jaipur: Printwell, 1992), 181–82.

6. Religious revival was at its height in the 1980s with the telecasting of the *Ma-*

habharata and the *Ramayana*. I recall how the actors playing the roles of Rama and Sita were literally worshiped by people and how meetings and programs were rescheduled to facilitate the Sunday morning viewing of the *Ramayana*.

7. Deepa Mehta's controversial film *Fire* works with multiple discourses, primarily that of repressed sexuality turning to lesbianism placed against the intermittent narration of the Ramayana with its advocacy of woman's purity. There is also the ascetic-householder husband's constant self-trial at sexual abstinence. The institution of marriage, the claustrophobic environments of Hindu households, and the sexual attitudes of a society bred on control, restraint, and repression are critiqued. The women's wings of the Shiv-Sena and Bajrang Dal parties protested violently against the film, whose title indicates fire in all its literary, figurative, and referential senses. It is the final *agnipriksha* that a woman must endure and it is also the burning of the bride that had almost become the prescribed end for dowryless women in the 1970s and 1980s.

8. Partha Chatterjee's *The Nation and Its Fragments* (Delhi: Oxford University Press, 1994), 130, comments on this situation, which led to a new subordination for women.

9. I treat the Gita Press publication as the definitive edition. There are many different versions and rewritings in addition to the reinterpretations. There are folk Ramayanas, as well as Sitayanas, the narratives of Sita, and other popular publications.

10. Valmiki, *Ramayana* (New Delhi: Penguin, 2000), 274.

11. Kamban, *Kamba Ramayana* (New Delhi: Penguin Books, 2002), 141.

12. William Buck in his "retelling" (not translation) of the Valmiki *Ramayana* (New York: New American Library, 1978), 137, writes, "[Lakshman] drew a circle around Sita on the ground, with the tip of his bow."

13. See Sudhir Kakar, *The Inner World: A Psycho-Analytical Study of Childhood and Society in India* (1978; Delhi: Oxford University Press 1988), 56–68. Kakar is of the view that the Sita myth persists despite modernization, urbanization, and education.

14. *Manusmriti*, also known as *Manavdharma Sastra*, was one of the earliest texts to be translated into English (in 1794). In the introduction to *The Laws of Manu* (New Delhi: Penguin, 1991), ix, the translators write, "Under the British, the text become instrumental in the construction of a complex system of jurisprudence in which 'general law' was supplemented by 'personal law' determined by one's religious affiliation."

15. Chatterjee has commented on this division in *Nation and Its Fragments*. It grew as concern for cultural values intensified in the 1880s, when Western-mediated modern intellectuals joined the national struggle. Home was woman's place; the world of business was the male space. Mohandas Gandhi would later turn this division upside down.

16. See Pandita Ramabai, *The High Caste Hindu Woman* (1888; New Delhi: Inter-India Publications, 1984). And Rokeya Sakhawat Hossain's utopian tale about the reversal of purdah, *Sultana's Dream*, first published in English in 1905 and reissued as *Sultana's Dream and Padmarag* (New Delhi: Penguin 2005), places the subject within the framework of fantasy. Another slightly later work, *Inside Seclusion: The Avarodhbasini of Rokeya Sakhawat Hossain* (1931; Dacca: Women for Women, 1981), comprises a 47-page report documenting purdah customs. These essays are humorous and satirical and at times, bitter, as they point out the various restrictions that purdah brings with it.

17. *Nau Durghatna* is a story about arranged marriages, originally written in Bengali (Delhi: Adarsha Prakashan, 2004).

18. Krishna Sobti's Hindi novel, *Mitro Marjani* (New Delhi: Rajkamal, 1967), is about a joint family with three sons and three daughters-in-law. Mitro is the second daughter-in-law whose unfulfilled sexuality leads her to flaunt her body and move about with her head uncovered.

19. The Bhakti religious movement sought direct relationship with God, sidelining Brahmin control. Several of the *bhakts* (devotees) belonged to marginalized groups and had no direct access to temples and other centers of worship on grounds of caste restrictions. The movement spread throughout India and allowed social mobility not possible in upper-class society. Two of the best-known women bhakts are Bahinabai and Meera. Meera (1498–1565) was married to the king of Mewar and was a devotee of Lord Krishna. Constant harassment by her husband's family drove her from home; she moved to Dwarka and became an itinerant singer. Meera's worship of Krishna can be seen as an alternative to marriage or as resentment against male impotency or as a need for greater freedom than a woman's life permitted. There have been various fictional and nonfictional accounts of Meera's life, including films.

20. Bulle Shah (1680–1757) was born in Punjab to the family of Syed Shah Muhummad and was well versed in Arabic and Persian. His verses are still very popular across religions. In these verses, the devotee is a female who seeks to please God, her lover. His *kafi*s (midnight ragas) speak of submergence, frenzied emotions, and a game of hide-and-seek, a search for identity in God and of union with him. He uses god-names like "Shyam" (identified with Krishna) with ease. In many of his verses, he reprimands God for hiding himself ("why do you peep from behind the veil?") and celebrates total abandonment and surrender in front of the lover, discarding all inhibitions. *Bulle Shah* (New Delhi: Hind Pocket Books, 2006), 152, 136.

21. See J. S. Grewal's *Guru Nanak and Patriarchy* (Shimla: Indian Institute of Advanced Study, 1993), 6–9, 16–18.

22. Malvika Karlekar's detailed study of Bengali women's autobiographies and lives in the *antahpura*s is *Voices from Within: Early Personal Narratives of Bengali Women* (Delhi: Oxford University Press, 1991).

23. See Rama Mehta, *Inside the Haveli* (New Delhi: Penguin, 1996), 6. Princely states were ruled by royal families and spread throughout India, although the British, especially in terms of succession, exercised the overarching control. After independence in 1947, these states became part of the Republic of India. James Tod's 1829–32 *Annals and Antiquities of Rajast'han* (see note 2 cite) records the history of Rajasthan, an area littered with princely states. *Inside the Haveli* is located in one of them, the state of Udaipur, spelled in Tod's time Oodipore. It describes the manners of the people. Tod constantly compares these practices with history, architecture, traditions, and ancestry of the land and toward the end of the first volume also portrays the festivals of North India and those in other parts of the world with Islamic and Christian traditions (483) and comments favorably on the practice of female seclusion (485). Even in Muslim families, the divisions of space clearly demarcated roles.
24. Mehta, *Inside the Haveli*, 32–33.
25. See Attia Hosain, *Sunlight on a Broken Column* (New Delhi: Arnold Heinemann, 1979), 14.
26. See Ashapurna Devi's *Suvarnlata* (New Delhi: Bhartiya Jnanpith Prakashan, 1989).
27. M. K. Indira, *Phaniyamma* (New Delhi: Kali for Women, 1989).

REFERENCES

Bader, Clarisse. *Women in Ancient India* (1867). Translated from French by Mary E. R. Martin. New Delhi: Radha Publications, 1988.
Chatterjee, Partha. *The Nation and Its Fragments.* Delhi: Oxford University Press, 1994.
Devi, Ashapurna. *Suvarnlata.* Translated by Hanskumar Tiwari. 1979. New Delhi: Bhartiya Jnanpith Prakashan, 1989.
Grewal. J. S. *Guru Nanak and Patriarchy.* Shimla: Indian Institute of Advanced Study, 1993.
Hosain, Attia. *Sunlight on a Broken Column.* 1961. New Delhi: Arnold Heinemann, 1979.
Hossain, Rokeya Sakhawat. *In Seclusion: The Avarodhbasini of Rokeya Sakhawat Hossain.* Edited and translated by Roushan Jahan. 1931. Dacca: Women for Women, 1981.
———. *Sultana's Dream and Padmarag.* 1905. New Delhi: Penguin, 2005.
Indira, M. K. *Phaniyamma.* Translated by Tejeswani Niranjana. 1976. New Delhi: Kali for Women, 1989.
Jain, Jasbir. "Evolving Traditions, Retreating Modernities: Women and Gendered

Social Reality." In *Feminism, Tradition, and Modernity*, edited by Chandrakala Padia. Shimla: Indian Institute of Advanced Study, 2002.

———. "The Utopian Vision and Colonial Experience." In *The Utopian Imagination*, edited by Jasbir Jain and Santosh Gupta. Jaipur: Printwell Publishers, 1992.

Kakar, Sudhir. *The Inner World: A Psycho-analytic study of Childhood and Society in India*. 1978. Delhi: Oxford University Press, 1988.

Kamban. *Kamba Ramayana*. Translated by P. S. Sundaram. New Delhi: Penguin Books, 2002.

Karlekar, Malvika. *Voices from Within: Early Personal Narratives of Bengali Women*. Delhi: Oxford University Press, 1991.

The Laws of Manu. Translated by Wendy Doniger O'Flaherty and Brian K. Smith. New Delhi: Penguin, 1991.

Mehta, Deepa. *Fire*. 1997. Film.

Mehta, Rama. *Inside the Haveli*. 1977. New Delhi: Penguin, 1996.

Metcalf, Barbara Daly. Introduction to *Perfecting Women*. A partial translation of Maulana Ali Thanawi's *Bihisti Zewar*. Delhi: Oxford University Press, 1992.

Ramabai, Pandita. *The High Caste Hindu Woman*. 1888. Delhi: Inter-India Publications, 1984.

Shah, Bulle. *Bulle Shah*. Presented in two scripts, Urdu and Hindi, by Harbhajan Singh and Shoab Nadvi. New Delhi: Hind Pocket Books, 2006.

Sobti, Krishna. *Mitro Marjani* [in Hindi]. New Delhi: Rajkamal, 1967.

Tagore, Rabindranath. *Nau Durghatna* [in Hindi]. Translated from Bengali by Shri Ramnath 'Suman.' Delhi: Adarsh Prakashan, 2004. Originally published as *Nauka Doobi* (1906). An English translation by Surendranath Tagore under the title *The Wreck* is also available (1921).

Tod, James. *Annals and Antiquities of Rajast'han*. 2 vols. 1829–32. New Delhi: Rupa, 1997.

Tulsidas. *Ramcharit Manas*. Commentary by Vidyaratan Pandit Jwala Prasadji Parashar. Mumbai: Ramayana Press, 1986.

———. *Shri Ramcharit Manas*. Gorakhpur: Gita Press, 2002.

Valmiki. *Ramayana*. Edited and translated by Arshia Sattar. New Delhi: Penguin, 2000.

———. *Ramayana*. Retold by William Buck. New York: New American Library, 1978.

The Veil *From* Persepolis

MARJANE SATRAPI

From *Persepolis: The Story of a Childhood,* by Marjane Satrapi. Translated by Mattias Ripa and Blake Ferris. Paris: L'Association, 2003. Used by permission of Pantheon Books, a division of Random House.

17 Concealing and Revealing Female Hair

Veiling Dynamics in Contemporary Iran

ASHRAF ZAHEDI

*My hair and my face are my means of displaying my
disagreement with the Regime.*

Mina Nikzad, a Tehran University student, 2005

*The Islamic government may overcome the U.S., but
it will never succeed in telling Iranian women what
to wear.*

Tehran shopkeeper, 2004

Female hair, revealed or concealed, has always been an intriguing aspect
of woman's image and identity, worldwide.[1] In contemporary Iran, female
image and identity are highly politicized. Iranian political regimes, past
and present, have constructed ideal images of Iranian women congruent
with their ideology and presented women as symbolic of the country—
modern or Islamic. In constructing new icons, each regime has used encouragement, legal measures, and physical force to impose its political will
on Iranian women. The compulsory nature of unveiling and reveiling has
deprived women of the right to choose individual identities and violated
their human rights. These violations have politicized Iranian women and
inspired them to challenge authority (figure 17.1).

Control over female hair has not been confined to Iran. It has a long
history and draws on the social meanings of female hair and its sexualization. Human societies are fascinated with head hair. It is the only part
of the human body that continuously grows and can be shaved, cut, and

Figure 17.1.   A fearless young woman in Tehran, Iran, is
pulled over by the morality police but continues talking
on her cell phone, 2005. Her arms and hair are exposed,
although she wears minimal *hijab*. The female police wear
chadri. Photo by Satyar Emami. Courtesy of the Iran Times
International.

shaped without harming the body. Though there is nothing inherently sexual about female hair, most societies throughout history have assigned
sexual symbolism to it, letting it determine a woman's attractiveness and
power over men.

   In some cultures, wild, uncontrolled hair is associated with uncon-
ventional, uninhibited women and is frowned upon. Witches are often portrayed with untamed hair. Traditionally in Japan, a proper woman wore
an elaborate, highly controlled hairstyle. In India, widows' heads were
shaved to desexualize them and curb their appeal.

   Cutting the hair has been used to punish women who did not comply
with social norms and behavioral codes. In World War II Vichy France,
for example, the heads of women who took German soldiers as lovers
were shaved. Stripping women of their hair cast them as "recognizable"
undesirable elements of society.

   Men in power have sexualized, theologized, and politicized female hair.
They have written and drawn from theological and legal texts to justify

its concealment. Central to this justification was the need to control female sexual power and in turn, the male gaze. Hence responsibility has shifted from men's uncontrollable sexual appetites to women, who must diminish their own sexual appeal to protect men. Women acquiesce by internalizing popular beliefs.

The need to curb the sexual power of female hair can be traced to places of worship where genders mix. Women are expected to wear hats or scarves in Christian churches. In contrast, men are expected to remove their hats in church. Men's headgear is not intended to curb their sexual appeal but is usually a marker of social status. Female headgear serves a dual function: on the one hand it is meant to hide her sexuality, on the other, it is meant to beautify and enhance her attraction. The social meanings of head coverings worldwide are as diverse as the cultures they come from. In Iran, the social meaning of the veil is a contested one and continues to be the subject of religious and political disagreements.

Iranians commonly believe that veiling began with the Islamic conquest of Iran in 637 C.E. The veil, however, goes back to the Persian Empire, from the Achaemenid (ca. 500–330 B.C.E.) through the Sassanid (226–651 C.E.) dynasties. But the pre-Islamic veil had a different social meaning. As in the ancient Mesopotamian and Mediterranean cultures, veiling in the Persian Empire was a status symbol enjoyed by upper-class and royal women, who led secluded lives and wore the veil in public to protect themselves from the impure gaze of commoners. Common women were forbidden to wear the veil.

The first known reference to veiling is believed to be in an Assyrian legal text of the thirteenth century B.C.E.[2] The veil signified class distinction. Assyrian law prohibited peasant women, slaves, and prostitutes from wearing the veil and violators were punished.[3] Women who wanted to choose an identity different from the one the authorities assigned to them were disciplined.

Contrary to common beliefs, Islam did not invent the veil, nor was it compatible with Arab lifestyles. Early Muslims adopted veiling as a result of their exposure to the cultures they conquered.[4] The Islamic veil was neither used as a marker of social status nor limited to any certain class of women. The Islamic veil signified modesty.

Islamic veiling, as a social and religious requirement for all women, was a new concept. Veiling took a long time to institutionalize in Iran and for the most part it remained an urban practice. Moreover, Turkic tribes who migrated to Iran between the tenth and sixteenth centuries led nomadic and pastoral lives, incompatible with veiling.[5] Indigenous paintings show that tribal women did not wear the veil.[6]

"Italian travelers to Iran [in the sixteenth century] wrote that women were shockingly exposed."[7] But during Persia's Safavid dynasty (1501–1736 C.E.), religious authorities gradually gained more power and actively advocated the veiling of women. Nevertheless, the practice did not spread to Iran's rural and tribal women. They have always had an active role in social production; veiling curtails their activities and movements. And although tribal and rural women have their own, local, forms of head coverings, even in today's Islamic Republic of Iran, they wear the veil only when they travel to cities. Head coverings are part of traditional clothing for women and men in Iran, serving to mark their ethnicity and signifying their social status. Women wear caps, shawls, and scarves or combinations thereupon. Head coverings partially conceal female hair, but their shapes, colors, and decorations are intended to enhance female beauty. Tribal women have always had some degree of freedom to adorn their head covers and in turn beautify and express themselves, even today.

The exposure of the Iranian elite to European societies in the late eighteenth and nineteenth centuries and their socioeconomic advancements inspired many to seek reforms. Unveiled European women and their status within society highly impressed these reformers—men and women—who sought many changes in Iran, including improvement in the condition of women. They began demanding access to education, changes in marriage laws, and unveiling. In the 1920s and early 1930s, activist Iranian women published magazines and formed organizations to raise awareness and sensitize the public to the injustices they faced.

Prevailing reformists of the time tied seclusion, veiling, and women's education together, in part influenced by Western perceptions about Muslim societies. For the West, the veil was—as it continues to be—the symbol of women's oppression, signifying backwardness. Modernist Iranians called the black veil (or *chadri*) *kafan-e seeyah*, meaning "black shroud," a play on the word *kafan*, the white burial cloth. The reformists were strongly opposed by secular and religious conservatives.

The reformists hoped for a strong ally who could stand up to conservatives, and they found him in a new king, Reza Shah Pahlavi, a soldier who rose through the ranks to depose the last shah of the Qajar dynasty (1781–1925). Reza Shah was influenced by the modernist visions of Mustafa Kemal Atatürk, president of Muslim Turkey. Among his secular reforms, Atatürk encouraged unveiling of Turkish women. Reza Shah, however, took a different path in unveiling Iranian women.

In 1935, Reza Shah established Kanoun-e Banovan or Ladies Center and, with the support of women's advocates, waged a campaign to prepare public opinion in favor of unveiling. Nevertheless, conservatives' opposition remained strong. In 1936, the shah legally abolished the veil or chadri. The abolishment of the veil was called *kashf-e hijab*. The word *hijab* at this point and in this context was used only in reference to the veil. Many educated upper- and middle-class men and women welcomed unveiling. Soon, Iranian women appeared in public unveiled and in Western clothing. Some revealed their hair; others wore European hats, often as a substitute for a head scarf, but many simply as fashion statement. Ironically, Iran was the "first Muslim country to impose Western dress on women."[8]

The shah also initiated a number of other reforms benefiting women, but it was the unveiling that polarized society. Unveiling was a progressive measure and provided many women with the choice of public attire. This choice, however, was for unveiling proponents only. Advocates of the veil were left with no choices. Unveiling was an important part of Reza Shah's modernization efforts and he was not to be deterred by conservatives' strong opposition. He employed the use of physical force, ordering soldiers to remove women's veils, sometimes tearing them off in public.

The imposition of unveiling—not only the violence—was highly offensive to those who believed in the veil. For women who were unready or unwilling to appear in public unveiled, it was a major religious and emotional challenge. Forcefully unveiled women felt naked and shamed. Many refused to leave their houses and avoided public places. Even using the public bath was a trial. Unveiling was particularly painful for older Iranian women.

Reza Shah ordered theater, restaurant, and hotel owners not to allow entry of veiled women. Even wearing a head scarf was not permitted.[9] For women with limited resources, unveiling was a financial burden. They could conceal their modest clothing under the veil, allowing them to blend in with others. Unveiling required proper—Western-style—clothing, which they could not afford.

Compulsory unveiling outraged the clerics and secular conservatives. They had tied women's moral character to the veil. It symbolized the identity and chastity of Muslim women. These men saw themselves as the guardians of morality and social decency and used mosques and public spaces to oppose unveiling. Bazaar merchants, who stood to lose lucrative sales of the black chadri, supported them. Many violent confrontations took place between proponents of the veil and the shah's army. The army suppressed all opposition.

Complications now arose about who should be unveiled. At issue were the prostitutes. Sex workers were not to represent the image of modern Iranian women. According to the authorities and prevailing beliefs, prostitutes lacked the moral character of decent women. But how could the new laws be enforced without allowing the prostitutes to unveil like other women? Thus it was recommended that "if the prostitutes would take husbands, they could then remove their veils like other respectable women."[10]

Unveiling presented a new image of Iran. For the shah and modern Iranians, the image of veiled women was synonymous with backwardness. This image had to be removed from the Iranian stage. Women who wanted to veil, and for whom the veil was part of their identity, were marginalized while modern, educated women emerged as a symbol of the new Iran. With their educations and modern looks, they were well suited for various governmental jobs. Veiled women, even if educated, were not allowed to work wearing the veil, not even the head scarf.[11]

Teachers were not allowed to teach if they wore the veil and some of them left their jobs. Likewise, conservative advocates of girls' education who did not support unveiling no longer allowed their daughters to attend school. Unveiling, in some cases, effectively undermined education. In short, compulsory unveiling provided modern women with the choice of identity and access to education and employment, yet it simultaneously deprived veiled women of the same choices and opportunities.

The whole period of forced unveiling lasted only four to five years. In 1941, Allied forces removed Reza Shah from power, accusing him of favoring Nazi Germany, though Iran remained neutral during World War II. His young son Mohammad Reza Pahlavi became the new king. With his more flexible approach toward the veil, compulsory unveiling came to an end. Some religious leaders sought to reimpose the veil universally. Others merely encouraged women to reveil. Some women, either because of religious convictions or pressure from their families, took up the veil. Thus women appeared in public as *ba hijab,* veiled, or *bee hijab,* unveiled, and were referred to as such. Veiled women were also called *chadori.*

Many women—among them those who experienced the freedom of movement without the veil yet did not want to appear in public with revealed hair—chose to wear head scarves. The head scarf gave them a medium to negotiate between ba hijab and bee hijab, veiled and unveiled. In so doing they constructed a new symbol of cultural identity. Now all women had the freedom to make a choice of public attire and self-presentation.

From 1941 to 1978, veiled and unveiled women were present in public. But the image and the social meaning each group put forward was totally different. Though veiled women were seen in public, unveiled women had social and political "presence." The issue, however, was not just the veil. The physical indicator of modernity was "revealed" hair. Women in scarves and with "concealed" hair, wearing modest fashionable Western clothes, were still viewed as "traditional."

Shah Mohammad Reza Pahlavi implemented a number of reforms in the 1960s and 1970s. Some, like his father's, benefited women. But his policies were often ill-conceived and improperly implemented, leading to uneven economic development, social disparity, and growing gaps between rich and poor. He carried out his reforms without taking into consideration people's sentiments and building national consensus. Some questioned his modernization program, which was accompanied by Westernization.

For them, Westernization was merely a new disguise for political domi-
nance and cultural imperialism, a threat to Iranian and Islamic culture.
The Western way of life was viewed as vulgar and decadent. Opposition
to the shah, his policies, and his alliance to and dependency on the West
increased and as it did, so grew his determination to suppress it. The shah's
expanding military might was, to some extent, aimed at his internal opposition. Over the years, his regime became increasingly undemocratic
and dictatorial.

In the 1970s, many Iranians raised questions about the negative impacts
of rapid social change. Some Iranians, like some Turks and Egyptians, directed their criticism at political leaders. The failure of regimes espousing
capitalist, socialist, and nationalist ideology led many to doubt the merits of these imported ideologies. Instead, the religious critics found an ideal
paradigm in Islamic ideology and authentic Islamic culture. They glorified
Islam as a social remedy to all social problems. Turning to Islam and so-
called authentic culture had a great appeal and came to be known as the
authenticity movement.

Proponents of cultural authenticity believed cultural imperialism had
corrupted Iranian women. These women, instead of following their own
Islamic culture, had adopted Western values and allowed themselves to
be seen and used as sexual objects. With revealed hair and makeup on
their faces, they had made themselves inauthentic to Iran, becoming "Western dolls" and slaves of Western fashions, obsessed with consumerism and
lacking social and political consciousness.

Women were pivotal to the political construction of the authenticity
movement of the 1970s, whose image was shaped by Dr. Ali Shariati, a
French-educated Iranian sociologist. By setting Fatemeh (also Fatema or
Fatima), the daughter of Prophet Muhammad, as a role model, Shariati
inspired women to emulate her modesty. He encouraged women to distance themselves from the ideology and fashion that objectified them, to
challenge traditional customs, and to take active roles in the pursuit of
education. What's more, he urged them to respect their bodies and minimize
their sexual appeal by wearing a long and loose manteau, or jacket, and
cover their hair with a *rusary*, or scarf. This outfit symbolized the modern
Muslim woman. Before the authenticity movement, the veil was synony-

mous with the chadri, the black, head-to-toe veil. The manteau and rusary provided a modern meaning for hijab and a more practical way of observing the Islamic dress code of modesty, while simultaneously remaining active in public life. A new image and identity were constructed.

Inspired by Shariati's teachings, some women took up the veil, while others used the manteau and rusary to indicate their identities as authentic Muslim women. The outfit had not only religious but political meaning. In the mid-1970s, these women had active presence in universities and the society at large. They were self-confident and charged with the ideology of cultural authenticity. Needless to say, the shah did not welcome this politicization of women. Shariati and his followers were harassed by SAVAK, the shah's brutal secret police. Nonetheless, he left them to choose what they wished to wear.

Decades of discontent with the shah led to the Iranian Revolution of 1979. Massive numbers of Iranian women participated. The image of thousands of veiled women demonstrating against the shah captured the world's attention. The veil had found a new political meaning. No longer a symbol of backwardness and oppression, it now signified resistance. Even many secular and modern women, who did not believe in wearing the veil, put it on in solidarity with religious women and in opposition to the shah.

Iranian women, veiled and unveiled, played an important role in the revolution and its victory. Though they did not participate in the revolution as women advancing their own cause, they hoped to benefit by supporting it. But their symbolic use of the veil came to haunt them as the postrevolutionary regime of the clerics set into motion the Islamization of Iran.

Women were the first targets. Shortly after the revolution, the clerics' regime entertained the idea of officially reveiling Iranian women. And veiling was good for business. Among the clerics' supporters were the aforementioned conservative bazaar merchants, who could recapture the huge market they had lost during the Reza Shah era and only partially regained during his son's reign.

On March 8, 1979, thousands of Iranian women—many of whom had veiled to express their dissent and support the revolution—marched in the streets in the first of many protests against the veil. They were often violently attacked by Islamic zealots. Ironically, they were not supported by secular and leftist organizations that had, in principle, favored women's rights and social advancement. In the name of revolutionary unity, these organizations viewed women's protests as diversionary and chose not to support them. This was a sobering experience for secular and modern women. Without the support of men and secular political organizations, they could not succeed.

In July 1980, the Islamic regime began implementing "compulsory" veiling as part of the regime's agenda to institutionalize and exploit the female identity espoused by the authenticity movement. It promoted wearing the veil as "moral cleansing." Concealing female hair became the clerics' immediate political project. The regime capitalized on all mass media to justify veiling. It propagated the links between veiling, morality, and Islamic virtue. Women who did not comply with veiling or the new hijab were subjected to harassment, violence, and imprisonment.

The meaning and symbolism of hair again took the center stage. Female hair was publicized as seductive and alluring. According to a prevailing Islamic view, "it has been proven that the hair of a woman radiates a kind of ray that affects a man, exciting him out of the normal state." Even Abolhassan Banisadr, Iran's first elected postrevolution president, allegedly shared this view.[12] Concealing female hair says more about men's sexual anxiety than about the seductive power of women. In other words, "fear of the power of female sexual attraction over men" justifies any device that can protect men against female power.[13]

The regime orchestrated a major campaign to institutionalize veiling, using the same tactics that Reza Shah exploited to unveil women. The clerics used force as well as their legal authority over business to enforce reveiling. Shop, restaurant, and hotel owners were ordered not to serve unveiled women. Just as veiled women had once been barred from employment, unveiled women were now not allowed to work. With the Islamization of Iran, proponents of veiling and hijab would now be the ones to benefit. For them, the veil would be liberating, providing opportunities they did not enjoy under the shah. In veils or the manteau/rusary, the daughters of traditional religious families, who would otherwise not have been permitted to study and work, filled the seats in universities and found employment in the public sector, even taking night shifts, once taboo for traditional Iranian families. The veil has increased the social presence of these women, paradoxically bringing them *out of* seclusion.

Meanwhile, women who found the veil oppressive were fired from their jobs and lost their livelihoods, becoming socially and politically marginalized. They faced a contradiction between their own identity and the emerging female identity constructed by the regime. Some resented the imposed veil/hijab to the degree that they moved to rural areas where veiling was more relaxed or simply left the country altogether. Most Iranian women living in the West cite imposed veiling as the main reason for their migration.

As much as the regime hoped to actually reveil Iranian women and impose head-to-toe chadri, in practice most women have chosen to wear manteau and rusary. They believe in modesty and view manteau/rusary as compatible with Islam. But the regime's obsession is not so much with modesty as it is with female hair. The slightest showing of female hair, even for modestly dressed women, can lead to their punishment. Self-appointed Islamic vigilantes along with the "morality police," commonly referred to as Kommiteh, report violations of the modesty code to the authorities and the violators are fined or punished with penalties ranging from seventy-four lashes to two years' imprisonment. In the same way that Reza Shah sanctioned unveiling and revealing of women's hair by the use of force, the clerics' regime has used force to reveil and conceal women's hair.

Despite the regime's efforts, resistance to the veil and Islamic dress codes continues. Women raise constant questions about the merits of concealing female hair in any form, whether beneath the veil or a head scarf. Compulsory concealing of hair has led many women to create different styles of head coverings. Inspired by tribal and ethnic head coverings, women have fashioned new scarves and different ways of wearing them. Women's creativity in styling trendy-yet-acceptable Islamic attire is a manifestation of their desire for self-expression and their quest for a new identity and image.

During the 1997–2005 government of President Mohammad Khatami—

who came to power with the support of youth and women—pressure on women became less intense. They therefore felt freer to express themselves, to construct a new image and identity through fashion. The dark color, shape-concealing manteau was transformed into a shorter, colorful, shape-revealing garment. Gone were the long dark pants, replaced by three-quarter-length trousers that hint at shapely ankles. The big dark rusary was discarded in favor of small, brightly patterned, and transparent head scarves. Stray strands of highlighted hair peek from the fabric, illuminating the women's faces.

Iranian designers capture women's quest for self-expression with smartly constructed "Islamic" clothing, displayed at fashion shows (figure 17.2). Women express themselves and slyly defy the authorities with makeup. Indeed, sales of cosmetics, once associated with the "Western doll," are on the rise. Despite the regime's efforts to enforce modesty, Iran is the third largest consumer of cosmetic products in the Middle East.[14]

With female hair and body already covered, a higher emphasis is placed on the face. The use of makeup is complemented with plastic surgery. It is believed that Iran now has the highest rate of nose surgery in the world.[15] Nose surgery costs at least one million tomans ($1,200). Though highly expensive for middle-income Iranians, nose surgery has been highly popular. Even those who could not afford the surgery wear nose plasters as status symbols.

Nose surgery is an urban phenomenon of the upper and middle classes. They often say, "it is the fact that they have to wear head scarves: a big nose stands out and even more when you are not allowed to show your hair."[16] In a country that does not allow social and political changes, Charlotte Wiedemann remarks, "people are willing to manipulate in an area where change is possible. It is easier to correct a nose than an entire system."[17]

With the 2005 recapture of political power by more conservative clerics and the presidency of Mahmoud Ahmadinejad, pressure on women has again increased. The clerics and Ahmadinejad recently started a fresh campaign against "social corruption and social indecency" within the Islamic Republic of Iran; women have been its main focus, labeled as sym-

Figure 17.2. Iranian designers, "Islamic" clothing, displayed at fashion shows, 2005. Photo by Satyar Emami. Courtesy of the Iran Times International.

bols of public corruption and Western influence. Those women not fitting the regime's ideal image are once again warned, fined, and punished. According to Tehran police chief Brigadier General Morteza Talaie, "30 percent of complaints to police involve cases of women not covering up properly."[18] These women are called *bad hijab*, or improperly veiled, and shopkeepers are ordered not to serve them. Shops selling Western fashion and serving improperly veiled women are occasionally closed.

During the past twenty-eight years, the regime has been trying hard to confine the image of Iranian women to the one congruent with its ideology. Recently, the Iranian parliament has been discussing the idea of fashioning a new style of Islamic attire. Should the uniform be approved, it will be enforced at schools, universities, and government offices.

The regime has a vested interest in enforcing the black veil (figure 17.3). It supports the conservative merchants of the bazaar, who have enjoyed annual sales of $30 million in chadri fabric imported from Korea and Japan.

Figure 17.3. Women and a little girl in various states of covering peruse materials that encourage veiling, outside a mosque in Shiraz, Iran, 2004. Photo by Sheryl Shapiro.

In the past few years the sale of black veils has reached $40 million.[19] With such financial gains, these merchants will continue to support the regime and push for keeping the veil mandatory.

Iranian women's concerns are not about whether to veil, but about their right to choose veiling. From 1936 to 1941, this right was violated for women who wished to be veiled and inversely, the rights of women who wish to be unveiled have been violated since the establishment of the Islamic Republic in 1979. This violation, indeed, dates back to imposition of the veil following the Islamic conquest of Iran. Women's resistance to unveiling and reveiling has been resistance to assigned identity, assigned image, assigned symbolism, and assigned gender roles. Compulsory unveiling and reveiling and revealing and concealing of female hair have deprived Iranian women of choice about their identity, self-presentation, and place in society. Violations have only intensified women's determination to challenge these regimes. Women's quests for self-determination and human rights will continue to play out in the Iranian political scene.

NOTES

1. The first epigraph comes from Mina Nikzad's interview with the author in Tehran, Iran, 2005; the second, from "Islamic Government Tight Control on Women's Dress," *Iran Focus*, August 25, 2004, www.iranfocus.com/modules/news/articles.php?storyid = 92.

2. Nikki R. Keddie and Beth Baron, eds., *Women in Middle Eastern History: Shifting Boundaries in Sex and Gender* (New Haven: Yale University Press, 1991), 3.

3. Fadwa El Guindi, *Veil: Modesty, Privacy and Resistance* (Oxford: Berg, 1999), 11, 14; Keddie and Baron, *Shifting Boundaries*, 3.

4. Guity Nashat, "Women in Pre-Islamic and Early Islamic Iran," in *Women in Iran: From the Rise of Islam to 1800*, ed. Guity Nashat and Lois Beck (Urbana: University of Illinois Press, 2003), 28.

5. Nashat, "Women in Pre-Islamic," xiii, 5.

6. Keddie, *Shifting Boundaries*, 12.

7. Keddie, *Shifting Boundaries*,12.

8. Hadeih Moghissi, *Populism and Feminism in Iran* (New York: St. Martin's Press, 1996), 39.

9. Guity Nashat, ed., *Women and Revolution in Iran* (Boulder, CO: Westview Press, 1983), 27; Parvin Paidar, *Women and the Political Process in Twentieth-Century Iran* (Cambridge: Cambridge University Press, 1995), 107.

10. Camron Michael Amin, *The Making of the Modern Iranian Woman* (Gainesville: University Press of Florida, 2002), 99.

11. Nashat, *Women and Revolution*, 27.

12. Azar Tabari and Nahid Yeganeh, eds., *In the Shadow of Islam: The Women's Movement in Iran* (London: Zed Press, 1982), 110.

13. Fatema Mernissi, *Beyond the Veil* (Indianapolis: Indiana University Press, 1987), 31.

14. *Kanon-e Zanan-e Irani* [Iranian Women], March 2005, www.irwomen.com/print.php?id = 1527.

15. Robert Tait, "Nose Plastic Surgery Fever Grips Iranians," *Dawn*, May 8, 2005, www.dawn.com/2005/05/08/int16_htm.

16. Charlotte Wiedemann, "Plastic Surgery in Iran: Man-Made Nose; Man-Made Flower," *Qantara.de*, April 2006, www.quantara.de/webcom/show_article.php/_nr-414/i.html?PHPSESSID = 13309.

17. Wiedemann, "Plastic Surgery."

18. "Tehran Police Launch Campaign to Keep Women Covered Up," *Iran Focus*, April 19, 2005, www.iranfocus.com/modules/news/articles.php?storyid = 896.

19. Bahman Ahmadi Amoui, "27 Years Import to Observe Islamic Dress Code," *Kanon-e Zanan-e Irani*, 2005, www.irwomen.com/news_en_cat.php?newsid = 5.

REFERENCES

Ahmadi Amoui, Bahman. "27 Years Import to Observe Islamic Dress Code." *Kanon-e Zanan-e Irani*, 2005. www.irwomen.com/news_en_cat.php?newsid = 5.

Amin, Camron Michael. *The Making of the Modern Iranian Woman*. Gainesville: University Press of Florida, 2002.

El Guindi, Fadwa. *Veil: Modesty, Privacy and Resistance*. Oxford: Berg, 1999.

"Iran Sevomin Masraf Koonandeh Lavazam-e Arayesh dar Khavarmiyaneh" [Iran is the third consumer of cosmetic products in the Middle East]. *Kanon-e Zanan-e Irani*, 2004. www.irwomen.com/print.php?id+1527.

"Islamic Government Tight Control on Women's Dress." *Iran Focus*, August 25, 2004. www.iranfocus.com/modules/news/articles.php?storyid = 92.

Keddie, Nikki R., and Beth Baron. "Deciphering Middle Eastern Women's History." In *Women in Middle Eastern History: Shifting Boundaries in Sex and Gender*, edited by Nikki R. Keddie and Beth Baron. New Haven: Yale University Press, 1991.

Mernissi, Fatema. *Beyond the Veil*. Indianapolis: Indiana University Press, 1987.

Moghissi, Hadeih. *Populism and Feminism in Iran*. New York: St. Martin's Press, 1996.

Nashat, Guity. "Women in Pre-Islamic and Early Islamic Iran." In *Women in Iran: From the Rise of Islam to 1800*, edited by Guity Nashat and Lois Beck. Urbana: University of Illinois Press, 2003.

———, ed. *Women and Revolution in Iran*. Boulder, CO: Westview Press, 1983.

Paidar, Parvin. *Women and the Political Process in Twentieth-Century Iran*. Cambridge: Cambridge University Press, 1995.

Tabari, Azar, and Nahid Yeganeh, eds. *In the Shadow of Islam: The Women's Movement in Iran*. London: Zed Press, 1982.

Tait, Robert. "Nose Plastic Surgery Fever Grips Iranians." *Dawn*, May 8, 2005. www.dawn.com/2005/05/08/int16_htm.

"Tehran Police Launch Campaign to Keep Women Covered Up." *Iran Focus*, April 19, 2005. www.iranfocus.com/modules/news/articles.php?storyid = 896.

Wiedemann, Charlotte. "Plastic Surgery in Iran: Man-Made Nose; Man-Made Flower." *Qantara.de*, April 2006. www.quantara.de/webcom/show_article.php/_nr-414/i.html?PHPSESSID = 13309.

18 That (Afghan) Girl!

Ideology Unveiled in National Geographic

DINAH ZEIGER

What is it about a veil that poses such a threat to Western women? Once symbolizing reverence or mystery in Western culture, veiled women today signify tyranny, and lifting the veil has become a metaphor for freedom and democracy. As liberated women, we identify covered faces and bodies as constrained, but we fail to question how or why we see them that way. An issue of *National Geographic* prompted me to consider the implications of the rhetoric of the veil and how it plays in the ideological war being waged between Western and Muslim values.

Shortly after the United States–led invasion of Afghanistan in 2001, *National Geographic* sent the photographer of its most famous image—"the Afghan girl," published in 1985—back to Pakistan to find her. Several problems loomed: seventeen years of almost constant warfare, coupled with chaotic conditions in Pakistani refugee camps, reduced the odds of finding her, especially since no one apparently knew her name—she was simply "the Afghan girl."[1] In his haste or indifference when he took her picture, photographer Steve McCurry had not asked the girl's name. She symbolized the brutalizing effects of war, but the June 1985 *National Geographic* story never referred to her directly. In fact, the only reference to her appears in the caption on the cover, next to her photo: "Haunted eyes tell of an Afghan refugee's fears" (figure 18.1).

The resulting documentary of McCurry's January 2002 mission, *The Search for the Afghan Girl*, was published in *National Geographic* magazine and aired on the *National Geographic Explorer* series on cable television in March 2002. The search became something of a cultural sensation, with appearances by McCurry on Oprah Winfrey's daily television talk show and articles about the search and discovery in other media. As I looked at that March 2002 cover of *National Geographic* featuring a *burqa*-clad woman holding the 1985 photograph of "the Afghan girl," two thoughts struck me: one concerned the way the subject of this search was exploited as "evidence" of some kind of truth; the other raised a question about why anyone would look at a photograph of a veiled face. Presumably we cannot know who it is since we cannot see individual features, so what is the use of such an image? Both issues point toward the political nature of images of veiled women.

Veiled women—swathed head to foot or behind the barred windows of the harem—have been the subject of photographs and paintings since Westerners began exploring and claiming the "exotic" East. These hidden faces frustrate expectations; they cannot or will not communicate—yet we claim they convey volumes about the condition of women, the repressive nature of traditional religious practices and the backward (as opposed to Western progressive) nations in which they live. We seldom if ever consider the possibility that a variety of motives might exist for veiling, ranging from resistance to Western colonialism, to privacy, to the sense of liberation, of being "seen for their minds rather than as sex objects."[2] Instead, we regard the veil as a prison and the women as the oppressed victims of gender or religious practice passively awaiting rescue.

This perception of veiled women as simultaneously readable and unreadable helps explain how the *National Geographic* photographs participate in the construction of the "woman question" as an ideological issue. The photographs, which appeared at a moment of profound crisis

Figure 18.1. The framed drawing, *top,* in a shop in Kabul, Afghanistan (photo by Soraya Omar), and the mural in Seattle, Washington (photo by Jean Thies), evoke the mysterious Afghan girl from a 1965 photograph in *National Geographic,* an icon for wartime suffering and diaspora.

following the events of September 11, 2001, derive their power from two sources: first, the status of the magazine itself, which exists for most Americans as one of those institutions charged with saying what counts as true; second, the status of photography, which retains an aura of truth, even though we know how easily photos can be (and frequently are) manipulated, retouched, and staged.[3] Photographs reflect a hierarchy of attention, a system of values, whether consciously or unconsciously articulated— what they are juxtaposed against, where they are placed on a page, to focus our attention—that affects how we perceive the significance of the information.[4] Most of us rely on photographs as evidence and a way to measure difference—this NOT that. We accept them as part of the apparatus of scientific examination, used in everything from medicine to astronomy, and increasingly, as a tool in systems of social and political control— employed for police identification, passports, and military intelligence.[5]

When *National Geographic* began its search for the Afghan girl, it took extraordinary pains to make certain that the person claiming to be that girl was the real thing. Rigorously gathered forensic evidence verified the woman's authenticity—the unassailability of its proofs resting on the exposure of an attempted fraud. *National Geographic* needed to establish scientifically that the woman eventually identified as Sharbat Gula was the girl in the photograph. That need lay partly in the magazine's own history and its claims of publishing irrefutable truth, mainly through the evidence of photographs. *National Geographic's* origins within the National Geographic Society, an amateur scientific organization begun by Gardiner Greene Hubbard in 1888, situate it within several historical trends of the late nineteenth century, in particular, the rise of mass journalism and new printing and photographic technologies and the emergence of new academic disciplines.[6] The society's founding members belonged to a nineteenth-century elite whose interests in education and science coincided with new philanthropic institutions such as public libraries, national galleries of art, and museums dedicated to science and natural history.

Catherine Lutz and Jane Collins, in their book-length study of *National Geographic*, trace the magazine's role in mapping American national consciousness, first by literally making maps, later by showing the world to its readers through photographs. The society conceived its mission as explaining cultural differences, and *National Geographic,* through innovations in photographic technology, became its vehicle for "[purveying] 'primitive' peoples for Western perusal." Its articles initially focused on "scientific" undertakings, recounting treks to map borders and catalog the geographical features of terrain. Eventually, it turned to the people occupying those places, and its stories assumed the quality of adventure in exotic locales. From this position, *National Geographic* carved its niche as an arbiter of American culture by revitalizing natural history as a topic of popular culture, which, in turn, provided the material for stories about the world, above all, the peoples of the world.[7]

Thus when *National Geographic* set out to find "the Afghan girl" in 2002, it hired a team of experts, including a forensic pathologist, who constructed from the original photograph a model of the girl's face seventeen years later. In addition, it sent the photograph to John Daugman, inventor of automatic iris recognition, a technology that uses iris patterns much as we use fingerprints to determine identity. The actual search for the unknown woman relied more on luck than science, but once located, the careful accumulation of evidence began.

Despite the Afghan cultural practice of isolating women from unrelated men, a male optometrist, in the presence of her husband, carefully examined Sharbat Gula's eyes. His forensic examination would be familiar to anyone who watches the CBS television series *CSI: Crime Scene Investigation,* which week after week reveals criminal evidence in microscopic detail. The doctor removes her veil and places her on a chair at an angle to, not facing, the camera. In the video, we look at her, but she does not look back at us. For viewers and experts alike, Sharbat Gula becomes an object for scrutiny rather than an identified subject; McCurry even gazes on her through a crack in the door, literally spying on her. The camera focuses an extremely tight shot on her eyes, but she still does not look directly at it or us. Later, other experts examine her image, deploying all the technologies of surveillance available: we see her eyes enlarged to billboard size and tacked on a wall surrounded by macroimages of parts of her face; we observe as Daugman, the iridian specialist at Moorfield Eye Hospital in London, takes meticulous measurements and finally declares a perfect match. Conclusive evidence—based on the accurate measurements and photographs of her eyes—provided the proof that she was the Afghan girl photographed seventeen years before.

Finally, we watch McCurry pose Sharbat Gula for a photograph, this time holding the June 1985 issue in her hands the way a suspect in a police photo holds an identification board at chest height for a "mug shot." Nameless and undifferentiated then, *National Geographic* scientifically established Sharbat Gula's identity in 2002. Her face still symbolized a nation, but it was the face of a woman hidden behind the veil, not the frank, fearful gaze of the girl.

The 1985 and 2002 *National Geographic* photographs frame a narrative of Afghanistan that conforms to an American ideological position that links Islamic fundamentalism and terrorism but ignores the historical and cultural roots of the 1979–88 Afghan-Soviet conflict and United States involvement in promoting it. In both photographs, women's bodies represent a national narrative, but it is a fiction constructed to bolster an American ideal of nation, illustrated by juxtapositions of a contradicting lack—lack of freedom, lack of education, lack of choice. In the original photo, the girl with the fierce gaze is framed as fearful yet hostile to an invader, the Soviet Army. In the 2002 cover photograph, the girl exists only in the portrait held by a shrouded figure, a woman made inaccessible by the outcome of that invasion. In both pictures, she represents the innocent victim, first of war, then of the aftermath of war. For many Americans, the decision to bomb Afghanistan in 2001 was linked through photographs like these as much to "the woman question" and women's treatment at the hands of the Taliban as it was to the war on terror and the fundamentalist organization's role in the events of 9/11.

Yet the position of women in Afghan society has been at the center of nationalist conflicts since the early twentieth century. Feminist scholar Valentine Moghadam points out that the concepts of nation-state and national identity are weak in Afghanistan, except among the urban elites. Afghanistan's traditional social structure resists centralized civil authority or regulation and denies the state exclusive control over the means of violence. Moghadam correctly argues that the patriarchal nature of Afghan social relations, combined with a weak central state, undercuts attempts at modernization and emancipation.[8]

Afghan nationalism, such as it is, emerged from British attempts in the nineteenth century to expand its sphere of influence from India and block the aspirations of Germany and Russia, which saw the region as a gateway to warm-water ports. Fear of Russian ambitions, which appeared to threaten Britain's interests, provoked two Anglo-Afghan wars in 1839 and 1879.[9] However, traditional tribal structure, with its ties of kinship and loyalty, never permitted more than a weak state to form; a strong monarch would emerge periodically, but he usually depended on the tribes for military support and often competed with the Muslim religious establishment for control. Even in the twenty-first century, Afghanistan remains a country fragmented by warring tribal factions who fight over land and water and sometimes over women and "honor." One of the few things that unite these diverse people, Moghadam points out, is Islam, but even then it is a blend of *shari'ah* (Islamic canon law) and tribal customs, primarily *Pashtunwali,* the tribal code of the Pashtuns who make up about half of the Afghan population.[10]

What many Westerners fail to understand is that it is not the veil alone but the way geographic, economic, and social relationships in Afghanistan intertwine to oppress women. Geography constrains its development: vast mountain ranges surround Afghanistan, making road building difficult and costly, limiting access to raw materials and manufactured products, while its thin, rocky soil and arid climate make large-scale agriculture laborious. Geography, therefore, partially dictates Afghanistan's feudal-tribal economy. It is an economy based on land ownership, water rights, and tribal connections, tying most of its population to tenant-landlord relationships and bonds of blood.[11] Women function within this social structure as chattel, whose labor is bought and sold through marriage, and as representatives of a family's honor.

Marriage arrangements figure prominently in the nation's economy as part of the complex web of the tribal system of exchange, a practice that Moghadam argues has been abused in Afghanistan, keeping many rural households in a state of perpetual indebtedness. In the Qur'an, the *mahr* (a dowry payment from the groom to the bride that is an essential part of the formal Islamic marriage contract) comprises only a nominal fee, providing a kind of social insurance for the wife in the event of divorce or

widowhood in many Muslim countries. However, in the Afghan patriarchal context, the mahr constitutes compensation to the bride's father for
the loss of his daughter's labor in the household unit.[12] A woman's father
or husband controls her labor power, deciding when, where, and how she
works; others manage the product of her work, for which she receives no
wage. Women in rural areas work primarily as farm laborers or weavers,
while some in urban areas are employed in factories. Economist Hafizullah Emadi points out that women work in industries that require little physical strength and less education, such as the cotton and textile industries,
or in agriculture, which is labor intensive and demands the efforts of all
members of the household.[13] In Afghanistan, women are regarded as resources, reproducers of labor, part of the property of the male-dominated
household. In common with most patriarchal societies, female education
and literacy rates are low, while fertility is high.

At the same time, an ideology linking family honor to female virtue
controls women's activities through restrictive codes of conduct and rigid
gender segregation.[14] Part of the complex Afghan value system derives
from the belief that humans struggle between conflicting inclinations—
'aql or reason, and *fitna* or chaos, which results when desires are not
checked. Women are equated with desire and fitna, from which men must
be protected. Thus, the virtuous woman behaves appropriately by covering her head and body and living separately, in purdah or seclusion.
Veiling assumes cultural status connected to a woman's, and thus her family's, honor and respect for social order.[15]

These restrictive codes, combined with the notion of marriage as an economic transaction, conflict with Western capitalism and modernization.
This conflict precipitated women's emancipation movements in Afghanistan in the 1920s, the 1950s, and the 1980s. Each time, reform efforts col-
lapsed when confronted by deeply entrenched traditions and tribal
loyalties that forcibly blocked attempts to universalize education and
change marriage practices. Some leaders publicly supported unveiling,
hoping to encourage more opportunities for women, but it was mainly
urban women of the upper and middle classes who adopted it.

According to anthropologist Louis Dupree, in his 1980 edition of
Afghanistan, "Village and nomadic women seldom wore the *chadri* [burqa] . . .

Figure 18.2.   Despite Western claims to the contrary, after the Taliban was routed from part of Afghanistan in 2002, women there still wear the *chadri,* or *burqa,* as it is sometimes called. Photo by Sheryl B. Shapiro.

because it would have interfered with their many daily economic functions. Now, however, if a village grows to town status, complete with a bazaar, and a man gains enough wealth to hire servants, his wife often insists on wearing a *chadri,* for she believes the custom to be sophisticated and citified—not realizing her city cousins have opposite attitudes. In addition, many young girls in the cities and towns wear the chadri briefly after puberty to indicate that they have become bona fide women, ready for marriage."[16] (Figure 18.2)

In urban areas, customs began to change during the reign of King Amanullah (1919–29). At a public function attended by his wife, Queen Soraya, Amanullah declared that Islam did not require women to wear a veil. According to contemporary accounts, Queen Soraya immediately "tore off her veil, and the wives of other officials present at the meeting followed her example." Afterward, the queen often appeared in public unveiled but usually wearing a wide-brimmed hat with veil attached. However, as was to become a pattern throughout the twentieth century, Amanullah's reforms mobilized opposition in rural strongholds, mainly instigated by tribal leaders and mullahs, which eventually drove him from power. In the 1950s, Prime Minister Mohammad Daoud Khan, in pursuit of economic reforms, once again brought women's issues to the fore—women were encouraged to be economic contributors. Daoud declared veiling a "voluntary option," and at the fortieth anniversary celebration of Afghan independence in 1959, he asked the wives of his ministers to attend unveiled. When religious leaders complained, he challenged them to cite verses in the Qur'an that specifically required women to cover their bodies. When they kept complaining, he jailed them. By the mid-1960s, women had achieved the right to vote, and one held the post of health minister.[17]

Again, a fundamentalist backlash—largely rural and Islamist in origin—gained momentum, triggering a five-year-long civil war that ended in 1978, when a military coup ushered in a period of socialist reforms aimed at restructuring Afghanistan socially and politically. The most ambitious elements proposed by the People's Democratic Party of Afghanistan called for reforming land mortgage practices, confiscating and redistributing land, forbidding the payment of bride price, and giving women the freedom to choose a marriage partner. The most contentious proposal, however, proved to be the literacy program aimed at educating women, which included conducting classes in every village. The literacy campaign fueled rebellion in rural regions, as party members forced men to send their wives and daughters to classes, which many saw as increasingly political and polemic. Conservative traditionalists opposed women's education on the grounds it would morally corrupt them.[18] Rebellion escalated nationwide, leading to internal fighting and the eventual intervention of the Soviet Union in December 1979. But opposition forces—supported by Pakistan, the United States, China, Iran, and Saudi Arabia—continued their lethal campaign, literally undermining the country.

Despite the escalating war, the ruling socialist party, backed by the Soviets, continued to push land reform and women's education, fanning the opposition of the Islamist mujahedin, freedom fighters. Yet Western media accounts of the 1979–88 Soviet-Afghan civil war largely ignored its gender dimensions, focusing instead on the ideological struggle between capitalism and communism. Stories appearing in popular Western media focused on boy warriors, and the bombing and strafing tactics of the Soviets forces. When the Soviets pulled out of Afghanistan in 1988, Western media shifted attention to the plight of refugees, but as the Taliban—fundamentalists trained in Arab religious schools in Pakistan—overran its opponents, journalists fixated on the brutality of that regime as epitomized by its treatment of women. In these accounts, Western complicity in arming and funding the mujahedin generally passed without comment. It is within the context of the battle to eject the Soviet Union from Afghanistan that the photograph of "the Afghan girl" appeared.

One reason the 1985 *National Geographic* cover photograph appealed so widely was because the girl's face was uncovered and accessible. To drive home its point about the suffocating conditions under Taliban rule, the April 2002 *National Geographic* cover photograph constructs an eerie scene of a completely shrouded figure holding a copy of McCurry's original portrait, with the headline "Found! After 17 Years, an Afghan Refugee's Story." The *National Geographic* photographs and narrative frame the burqa as a political issue and reinforce a Western way of seeing that contributes to our sense of the United States as civilized. By implication, American power is clean, rational, and constructive, while barely understood Muslim society is shown as oppressive—wracked by irrational, random violence involving personal assault, hatred, and fanaticism. We assume our system is benevolent and nonideological, which blinds us to our responsibility in creating the conditions that aggravate the violence.[19]

Both *National Geographic* photographs are dense with connotations; every detail of the images coalesces to form an ideological structure called "oppression." In the original, the girl with the fierce green eyes symbolized "an Afghan refugee's fears," but she remained unknown, unidentified, and unremarked in the accompanying story. The 2002 cover photograph visually ties the pictures together physically and ideologically. In the context of America's war on terrorism, *National Geographic* "found" this anonymous girl-woman, whose cover portrait now cannot reveal the "haunted eyes" that captured the Western imagination seventeen years earlier. The ideological conception of oppression is literally "fleshed out" in these photographs: the absence of the visible fleshly body and the presence of the veil prove the oppression. Sharbat Gula's face is revealed on the inside pages as she is documented, measured, and identified, even to the extent of holding the evidence of the earlier photograph up to her face. Yet even in these revealing photos, her body and head remain engulfed in the voluminous folds of the burqa. Although she is ultimately named, our acceptance of this ideological conception linking veil and oppression leads us to "see" Sharbat Gula as representative of all veiled women.

This highly aestheticized treatment sustains a nineteenth-century photographic convention depicting the eroticized, unattainable, and exotic "Oriental" woman. Imprisoned behind the veil, she became the central figure in a romantic fantasy of conquest and possession.[20] Removing the veil marks the ultimate form of colonization, fusing, as it does, narratives of oppression, desire, and imperialist expansionism. Historian Kumai Jayawardena connects the Western obsession with lifting the veil to economics: capital needs free, unconstrained bodies for work, and anything that restricts women's mobility or enforces seclusion damages capitalism's chances for a source of cheap labor.[21]

Jayawardena's argument helps explain how and why the issue of veiling has become enshrined as part of American foreign policy. Unveiling as articulated by prominent Western feminists as part of emancipation and justice movements is co-opted as an expression of American democracy and freedom, of "our way of life," on behalf of global capital-transnational corporations, which need sources of cheap labor to produce a range of products, especially textiles, where women are the primary workers. At the same time, these women become consumers of mostly imported manufactured goods. Thus, unveiling is a move to free women to work while educating them into particular class positions and social roles as laborers and consumers.[22] It is no accident that antiveiling campaigns have had a high degree of success in countries where they were attached to Western notions of progress. Reformers (both in the nineteenth century and today) regard dress reform as a sign that indigenous institutions and practices reflect "modern" Western values.

In the pages of *National Geographic*, the Afghan girl symbolizes the Afghan nation for most Americans—an oppressed, imprisoned, brutalized state. She represents the national boundary marker against which

America measures its own cultural values, not hers. The photographs separate Sharbat Gula from the long arc of Afghan history and its particular
cultural practices. By aestheticizing her face—and the lack of her face in
the 2002 cover photo—the photographs mask American complicity in undermining Afghan women's ongoing struggle for justice and equality. Instead, they are used to mobilize Western sympathies for women victimized
by the "backward" practices of nations in need of instruction. In post-9/11
American ideology, the veil has become an overtly political symbol for
the oppression and violence of Islamic beliefs, and unveiling is seen as a
corrective action. Thus, the photographs fuse Western feminist goals and
language with post-9/11 American national interests, linking the oppressive treatment of women, visible in the veil, to the "uncivilized" cultural practices of the male-dominated Islamic society of Afghanistan in
particular, and all of the Middle East in general. Popular media like *National Geographic* play a key role in describing and disseminating this linkage to the public. The removal of the veil from the women of Afghanistan
constitutes a necessary step in the American nationalist agenda to remake
the Middle East in the Western capitalist mold.

NOTES

1.   Debra Denker, who wrote the original June 1985 story, did know the girl's
      name, according to an e-mail exchange. "We did our field work in Novem-
      ber 1984 and the article was then published in June 1985. I got lots of letters,
      some of them asking about the young girl in the picture. I went to the school
      where the picture had been taken when I was in Afghanistan in late 1985, and
      asked about her. People told me her name and that she had been married at
      age 14 and they did not want to be disturbed, so I respected that. I passed
      that info on to Lauren (Stockbower, Steve McCurry's then partner, in an April
      1986 letter) and asked her to let Steve know. He was usually on the road and
      I was not particularly close to him, so thought that was the best way to get
      info to him. Perhaps it never got to him or perhaps he forgot. [*National Geo-
      graphic* contacted her in January 2002 to chat.] . . . I was quite shocked when
      a story came out a couple of months later about the 'search' for Sharbat Gula."
      April 10, 2006, e-mail to author.
2.   Leila Hessini, "Wearing the Hijab in Contemporary Morocco: Choice and Iden-
      tity," in *Reconstructing Gender in the Middle East: Tradition, Identity, and Power*,

ed. Fatima Gocek and Shiva Balaghi (New York: Columbia University Press, 1994), 53.

3. John Tagg, *The Burden of Representation: Essays on Photographies and Histories* (Minneapolis: University of Minnesota Press, 1988), 2–3.

4. Esther Parada, "C/Overt Ideology: Two Images of Revolution," in *The Contest of Meaning: Critical Histories of Photography*, ed. Richard Bolton (Cambridge, MA: MIT Press, 1989), 223.

5. John Berger and Jean Mohr, *Another Way of Telling* (New York: Vintage International, 1995), 98.

6. Catherine Lutz and Jane Collins, *Reading National Geographic* (Chicago: University of Chicago Press, 1993), 16.

7. Lutz and Collins, *Reading*, 16–23.

8. Valentine M. Moghadam, "Nationalist Agendas and Women's Rights: Conflicts in Afghanistan in the Twentieth Century," in *Feminist Nationalism*, ed. Lois A. West (New York: Routledge, 1997), 77, 76.

9. Angelo Rasanayagam, *Afghanistan, A Modern History: Monarchy, Despotism or Democracy? The Problems of Governance in the Muslim Tradition* (London: I. B. Tauris, 2003), xvii.

10. Valentine M. Moghadam, "Reform, Revolution and Reaction: The Trajectory of the 'Woman Question' in Afghanistan," in *Gender and National Identity: Women and Politics in Muslim Societies*, ed. Valentine M. Moghadam (London: Zed Books, 1994), 84.

11. Hafizullah Emadi, "State, Modernization and the Women's Movement in Afghanistan," *Review of Radical Political Economics* 23, nos. 3–4 (1991): 224–25.

12. Moghadam, "Nationalist Agendas," 77.

13. Emadi, "State, Modernization," 231.

14. Moghadam, "Nationalist Agendas," 78.

15. Audrey C. Shalinsky, "Women's Roles in the Afghanistan Jihad," *International Journal of Middle East Studies* 25 (1993): 662.

16. Louis Dupree, *Afghanistan* (Princeton: Princeton University Press, 1980), 247.

17. Huma Ahmed-Gosh, "A History of Women in Afghanistan: Lessons Learnt for the Future, or, Yesterdays and Tomorrow, Women in Afghanistan," *Journal of International Women's Studies* 4, no.3 (May 2003): 4, 6.

18. Moghadam, "Nationalist Agendas," 85, 87.

19. Parada, "C/Overt Ideology," 225.

20. Sarah Graham-Brown, *Images of Women: The Portrayal of Women in Photography of the Middle East 1860–1950* (New York: Columbia University Press, 1988), 9.

21. Kumai Jayawardena, *Feminism and Nationalism in the Third World* (The Hague: Institute of Social Studies, 1982), 9.

22. Jayawardena, *Feminism*, 9.

REFERENCES

Benjamin, Walter. *The Arcades Project*. Translated by Howard Eiland and Kevin McLaughlin. Cambridge, MA: Belknap Press, 1999.

———. "The Work of Art in the Age of Mechanical Reproduction." In *Illuminations: Essays and Reflections*, edited by Hannah Arendt. New York: Schocken Books, 1968.

Berger, John, and Jean Mohr. *Another Way of Telling*. New York: Pantheon, 1982.

Dupree, Louis. *Afghanistan*. Princeton: Princeton University Press, 1980.

Emadi, Hafizullah. "State, Modernization and the Women's Movement in Afghanistan." *Review of Radical Political Economics* 23, nos, 3–4 (1991).

Foucault, Michel. "The Political Function of the Intellectual." *Radical Philosophy*, Summer 1977.

Graham-Brown, Sarah. *Images of Women: The Portrayal of Women in Photography of the Middle East, 1860–1950*. New York. Columbia University Press, 1988.

Jayawardena, Kumai. *Feminism and Nationalism in the Third World*. The Hague: Institute of Social Studies, 1982.

Lutz, Catherine A., and Jane L. Collins. *Reading National Geographic*. Chicago: University of Chicago Press, 1993.

Moghadam, Valentine M. "Nationalist Agendas and Women's Rights: Conflicts in Afghanistan in the Twentieth Century." In *Feminist Nationalism*, edited by Lois A. West. New York: Routledge, 1997.

———. "Reform, Revolution and Reaction: The Trajectory of the 'Woman Question' in Afghanistan." In *Gender and National Identity: Women and Politics in Muslim Societies*, edited by Valentine M. Moghadam. London: Zed Books, 1994.

Rasanayagam, Angelo. *Afghanistan, A Modern History: Monarchy, Despotism or Democracy? The Problems of Governance in the Muslim Tradition*. London: I. B. Tauris, 2003.

Sekula, Allen. "The Body and the Archive." In *The Contest of Meaning: Critical Histories of Photography*, edited by Richard Bolton. Cambridge, MA: MIT Press, 1989.

Shalinsky, Audrey C. "Women's Roles in the Afghanistan Jihad." *International Journal of Middle East Studies* 25 (1993).

Smith, Anthony D. *Nationalism: Theory, Ideology, History*. Cambridge: Polity Press, 2001.

Stocking, George. *Victorian Anthropology*. New York: Free Press, 1987.

Tagg, John. "The Currency of the Photograph: New Deal Reformism and Documentary Rhetoric." In *The Burden of Representation: Essays on Photographies and History*. Minneapolis: University of Minnesota Press, 1988.

Viroli, Maurizio. *For Love of Country: An Essay on Patriotism and Nationalism*. Oxford: Clarendon Press, 1995.

19 Burqas and Bikinis

Islamic Dress in Newspaper Cartoons

KECIA ALI

As a Muslim woman and academic who specializes in the study of gender issues in Islam, I have a well-developed response at the ready whenever I'm asked about the veil: I plead battle fatigue. I'm just really, *really* tired of talking about it. Since the day a fellow Muslim panelist pounded the table and started yelling at me about apostasy at a conference session, I am no longer astonished by the intensity of the sentiments the topic provokes. I try to avoid becoming embroiled in the endless debates about whether or not the *hijab* is obligatory and what it "means" when Muslim women cover. There are many eloquent essays and cogent analyses of the topic, but the very act of analysis unavoidably places more weight on the veil. Still, there are intriguing issues associated with veiling beyond its place in the tired polemics over Muslim women's "status" or "position," including Who decides what something signifies? How can assigned meanings be subverted? Given my interest in these questions, I am drawn to the depictions of Islamic dress in an unlikely place: the comics (figure 19.1).[1]

Since the events of September 11, 2001, a number of comic strips and editorial cartoons in my local paper, the *Boston Globe*, have featured veiled figures prominently. Occasionally someone wearing a head scarf appears in a comic strip as a nod to diversity, or in an editorial cartoon as a short-hand way of making clear that the woman depicted is Muslim. The comics I focus on here differ in two ways from these more ordinary images. First, the garb they show is not a simple head scarf, but rather a flowing *chadri, burqa,* or *abaya,* including a face veil. Second, those who appear thus covered are almost never Muslim women; the use of Islamic dress is a device to call attention to something else entirely.

In one episode of the sports-oriented *Tank McNamara,* the main panel shows four women playing beach volleyball. Three wear athletic-style biki-nis, while the fourth is dressed in unmistakably Islamic robes that also cover her head and face. In the upper left-hand corner, a small inset box shows two men conversing in the stands. One asks, "Is she, like, making some sort of political statement?" The other responds, "Nope. She just had her first skin cancer removed."[2] The cartoonist, of course, is playing for the readers' laugh at the unexpectedly utilitarian purpose ascribed to the woman's clothing. In this respect, it is a simple enough, and funny enough, gag. However, the men's reported dialogue raises further questions, acknowledging the possibility that her gesture could, in fact, be political. She might be making some sort of statement about the objectification of female bodies or their subjection to the male gaze (incorporated into the comic by the positioning of the two men who survey the game from above). The man's response, however, denies this interpretation at the same time it affirms a male prerogative to assign meaning (or its lack) to female attire.

An editorial cartoon depicting a mother and daughter back-to-school shopping trip displays a similar contrast between highly revealing attire and total concealment, but with a more overt message. In the first panel, the mother's expression shows resignation at her scantily clad teenage daughter's interest in the skimpy fashions on display in the store windows. In the next panel, the outfit on display is downright slutty, the daughter fascinated and the mother furious. In the third, with another revealing outfit enthralling the daughter, a lightbulb appears over the mother's head in the universal illustrators' shorthand for inspiration. In the fourth and final panel, the mother and daughter exit the mall, the mother now smiling contentedly while her daughter, clad head-to-toe in a voluminous black gown, with only eyes visible, seems perplexed.[3]

Like the *Tank McNamara* strip, this cartoon speaks to a utilitarian covering function for Islamic dress. Here, though, the veil's purpose relates implicitly to sex and sexuality. Though the bikinis worn by the volleyball players show skin, the athletes there are depicted in a way that is not meant to convey sexual allure; their bodies and postures are muscular, even menacing, in contrast to the slender, seductively posed mannequins in the mall displays. This back-to-school cartoon plays on the irony of a Western (and therefore supposedly liberated) female adopting the veil as a solution to the overexposure of flesh found in American popular culture. (Is it reading too much into the comic to note that the third mannequin is wearing a cross around her neck, above the exposed cleavage, perhaps signifying the permissiveness of mainstream Christianity as practiced in the United States?)

A depiction of the flip side of this cultural borrowing is present in a strip where no female or veiled figure makes an appearance, but the presumed contrast between Western and Iraqi (read: Muslim) standards of dress and comportment is central. In an installment of *The Boondocks*, the main character, Huey, says to his sidekick, Caesar: "Well, the American way of life is coming to Iraq. And you know what that means." After a moment of silent contemplation, Caesar turns back to Huey and queries, "Iraqi Girls Gone Wild?" "Iraqi Girls Gone Wild," Huey confirms.[4] This cynical take on the liberation that is assumed to come with "the American way of life" encapsulates the centrality of sex and sexuality to both cultures, while insinuating that the values the United States exports are not primarily those of democracy.

The presumed contrast between the West and the Muslim world is played out with a different twist in a *Bizarro* panel that appeared not long after the U.S. invasion of Afghanistan. One burqa-clad figure, eyes covered with mesh, turns to a similarly dressed companion in a marketplace and says: "I'd *love* to live in the West." The reader has just a moment to let conventional assumptions about the female desire for freedom from Taliban-imposed seclusion rise to the surface before they are shattered, as the speaker continues: "Being a transvestite here is *pointless*."[5] (Figure 19.1)

These cartoons deflect major controversies about the veil and, in doing so, attest to the instability and insufficiency of the categories veiled/unveiled and their assumed linkage with oppression/liberty. Even as they rely on certain stereotyped assumptions about Muslims and the West, they undercut these assumptions by revealing gags that defy expectations. Thus, the burqa-wearing Afghan is not the epitome of oppressed Muslim womanhood, but a man in drag. The adoption of Islamic dress is not a clerically imposed measure but a solution to the hypersexualization of American teen fashions or a preventive measure against skin cancer. And the U.S. "liberation" of Iraq will bring debauchery rather than political and economic freedom.

A March 2005 editorial cartoon threads together themes of clash between civilizations and gender—and makes an explicit mention of Islam—as it addresses the 2004 appointment of former presidential advisor Karen Hughes to the State Department for a role in public diplomacy. In the picture, President Bush is seated behind his desk in the Oval Office. Speaking into his telephone, he declares, "We think Karen Hughes will be perfect for projecting the Bush administration image to the Islamic world." A woman—presumably Hughes—stands on the carpet nearby, clad in black with only her eyes and her high-heeled shoes visible. The word "secrecy" is printed across her robe; the cartoonist is making a point about government policy, linking secrecy with a literal cover-up in the form of Hughes's chadri.[6]

But what else might he have intended by depicting a powerful American political figure clad as she is? Is it a commentary on what Hughes, and by extension the administration, will have to do to ingratiate herself with "the Islamic world," her intended target audience? Is her acquiescence to Islamic dress a marker of the administration's willingness to overlook restrictions on women's rights for the sake of other policy priorities? While there is no reason to think that Hughes's gender had anything to do with her being chosen for this post, the way she is depicted in this image is a direct result of her femaleness. Had Colin Powell been selected for the role, it is a safe bet that he would not have been depicted in traditional Arab men's dress, let alone clad in black robe and veil.

Whatever role Hughes's gender did or did not play in her appointment, it was to be a crucial feature of her brief tenure in the role of envoy; her visit to the Middle East in the fall of 2005 included special audiences with groups of women in the region. In these events, Hughes presented herself as the embodiment of the free American woman and addressed the freedoms (to vote and drive, in the case of Saudi women) that she felt her Muslim listeners lacked. Her audiences objected strenuously and, in the case of Turkish women, proclaimed their concern with American foreign policy above gender issues. Many members of the American media seized on the incidents as evidence of a yawning cultural gap between the United States and the Muslim world (portrayed, contrary to reality, as monolithic). The imagery of veiling appears as shorthand for this cultural distance in the *Slate* column that Fred Kaplan devoted to dissecting the Bush administration's misstep in sending Hughes to the Middle East. A savvy (male) "Muslim leader" would not, he asserts, "send as his emissary a woman in a black chadri who had spent no time in the United States, possessed no knowledge of our history or movies or pop music, and spoke no English beyond a heavily accented 'Good morning.' Yet this would be the clueless counterpart to Karen Hughes."[7] Although the substance of Kaplan's remarks concerns Hughes's lack of language skills, cultural knowledge, and firsthand experience of the societies she visited, the first differentiation he makes between her, as an American woman, and her Muslim "counterpart" is that the latter would appear "in a black chadri."

The cartoon and columns referring to Hughes discuss the "Islamic" or "Muslim" world but only allude to religious norms governing female dress. An editorial cartoon appearing in the *Boston Herald*—the *Globe*'s more conservative competition—in 2002 more directly ties veiling to Muslim doctrine. The cartoon depicts the Statue of Liberty standing in the middle of New York Harbor swathed in a burqa with only a small, darkened slit for her eyes. To the side, a speech bubble proclaims, "Muslim fanatic terrorists struck at the Statue of Liberty last night . . ."[8] At first glance, this image seems simply to reinforce stereotypes. If taken at face value, the cartoon would be merely a transparent reproduction of the usual symbolism: Islam = veil = oppression; America = unveiling = freedom. The unveiled statue personifies liberty; veiling her, or any female, is tantamount to submitting to Muslim fanaticism: veiling *becomes* a terrorist act. However, I think the cartoon delivers another level of meaning, proclaiming the utter futility of investing the veil with such importance. A closer look at the image shows that the Twin Towers are noticeably absent from the skyline in the background. Their absence serves as a reminder of the 2001 attacks that destroyed buildings and killed thousands of people. On reflection, it becomes obvious that a comparison between that mayhem and murder, on the one hand, and covering a statue with a piece of cloth, on the other, is ludicrous.

Consideration of this Statue of Liberty cartoon alongside a composite illustration that accompanied a thoughtful editorial on women's rights in the new Iraqi constitution suggests that perhaps there is simply something about the cartoon format that allows a fresher approach to issues usually dominated by polarized perspectives and clichéd arguments. In this composite, a front-facing image of the head of the Statue of Liberty, its ragged bottom edge making clear that it was ripped from a larger picture, has been superimposed on a photo or realistic illustration of a woman in a chadri facing sideways. The illustration suggests that in order for Iraqi/Muslim women to attain legal rights, they must adopt a Western/American model of liberty. Additionally, the mismatch between the two images implies that such a transplant will be difficult and likely unsuccessful. While the accompanying editorial discusses the diversity of the Islamic legal heritage and cultural practices in Muslim societies, the illustration draws on conventional images in a way that reinforces rather than subverts stereotypes linking unveiling directly to liberty and Americanization.[9]

Although it seems to me that cartoons often allow a fresher and less polarized approach to difficult topics, they do not always subvert the dominant order. Two other cartoons about Iraqi women and democracy implicitly link the (un)covering of women's faces (though not hair or bodies) with democracy. A cartoon from August 2005 depicts American antiwar activist Cindy Sheehan standing before a cluster of microphones, demanding "Give me one good reason my son died in Iraq!" Standing behind her, not speaking, a Muslim woman in flowing robes and head covering, but with her face unveiled, holds up a finger as if to interrupt while, in her other hand, she holds a ballot box.[10] The implicit message is that not only has American military involvement brought democracy to Iraq, but it has led to women's participation in the electoral process. (Notably, Iraqi women obtained the franchise in 1980, under Saddam Hussein, and have been both voting and running for office, though in less than fully free elections, since that time.) Another editorial cartoon, published a month earlier, displays less confidence in Iraqi democracy, or at least women's participation in it. It shows a group of Iraqi men—two in robes and turbans, three in Western apparel—clustered together around a large parchment labeled "Iraq's Constitution." One of the men (wearing a turban) is writing, two are looking on approvingly, and another is glancing over his shoulder at two entirely veiled women standing some distance away, watching the proceedings. The last man, with one foot planted firmly in the men's semicircle around the constitution, has turned around to face the women, one of whom has her eyes showing, while the other's face is obscured with mesh. Grimacing, his arms outstretched as if to ward them off, he declares "Don't worry . . . we're protecting your right to privacy!"[11] For the previous cartoonist, women's participation in electoral matters is compatible with an unveiled face; the woman's loose head scarf and robe are probably depicted to identify her as Iraqi rather than to emphasize her covered dress. For this cartoonist, however, the burqa/abaya/chadri symbolizes the barriers to Iraqi women's substantive participation in constitutional democracy.[12]

Whereas these two cartoons present fairly standard depictions of Muslim women, the comics and cartoons where the veiled figures are *not* Muslim women (the volleyball player, the teenager at the mall, Karen Hughes, and the Statue of Liberty are not Muslim; the Afghan transvestite is Muslim but not female) defy neat resolutions. These cartoons demonstrate that anxieties about female bodies and sexuality are not solely Muslim. Furthermore, they show that American cultural imperialism cannot be separated from internal Muslim debates over women and gender, in both private and public spheres. As Joan Jacobs Brumberg and Jacquelyn Jackson point out, "The female body—covered in a burka or uncovered in a bikini—is a subtle"—and, I would argue, sometimes not so subtle— "subtext in the war against terrorism."[13] The furor over burqas and bikinis dodges the basic problem of respecting women as human beings, not as symbols of any civilization's values. Other elements of these cartoons, in fact, illustrate comparatively restricted female agency: other than Sheehan, the women in these cartoons are entirely silent; the only veiled figure to speak is the male Afghan in a burqa. As one way of commenting on the world, editorial cartoons and comic strips alike can be important tools for social critique and reflection, but they also merit discussion and criticism—and not only when, as in the Danish Muhammad cartoon fiasco of 2005–6, they shock and offend. By using images susceptible to multiple interpretations they can humorously point to both minor foibles and major failings in a way that is at once more immediate and less threatening than can be conveyed by words alone.

NOTES

1.   Portions of this essay first appeared in *Bitch: Feminist Response to Pop Culture* 27 (Winter 2005): 11–12. My thanks to Andi Zeisler, for encouraging that early version; to Jennifer Heath, for her insightful comments on several drafts since

then; and to Sam Watkiss, for editorial assistance at a critical juncture. Of course, any errors of fact or interpretation are my own.

2. *Tank McNamara,* by Jeff Millar and Bill Hinds, June 29, 2003.

3. Cartoon by Signe Wilkinson, published in the *Boston Globe,* September 3, 2003.

4. *The Boondocks,* by Aaron McGruder, April 29, 2003.

5. *Bizarro,* by Dan Piraro, March 27, 2002. The words appearing in italics here were capitalized and underlined in the original.

6. Cartoon by Jack Ohman, published in the *Boston Globe,* March 23, 2005.

7. Fred Kaplan, "Karen Hughes, Stay Home! What on earth is she doing in the Middle East?" *Slate,* September 29, 2005, www.slate.com/id/2127102/; viewed May 16, 2006.

8. Cartoon by Jerry Holbert, published in the *Boston Herald,* 2002.

9. Editorial by Ellen Goodman, "Women's Rights in a Shi'ite Iraq," and illustration by Tim Brinton, both published in the *Boston Globe,* February 17, 2005.

10. Cartoon by Doug Marlette, published in the *Boston Globe,* August 28, 2005.

11. Cartoon by Joel Pett, published in the *Boston Globe,* July 28, 2005.

12. An interesting parallel cartoon by Rob Rogers (*Pittsburgh Post-Gazette,* published in *USA Today,* February 4, 2005) shows a woman in a head scarf and two men in turbans outside a building labeled "Iraqi Polling Station." All three are wearing buttons reading "I just voted!" The woman asks "So . . . Is this American-style democracy?" "No," responds one of the men; "We won't fully experience that until we have voter apathy."

13. As quoted in Amir Marvasti and Karyn D. McKinney, *Middle Eastern Lives in America* (Lanham, MD: Rowman and Littlefield, 2004), 51.

Dress Codes and Modes

How Islamic Is the Veil?

AISHA LEE FOX SHAHEED

> *If [man] orders us to veil, we veil, and if he now de-*
> *mands that we unveil, we unveil . . . [man may be]*
> *as despotic about liberating us as he has been about*
> *our enslavement. We are weary of his despotism.*
>
> Malak Hifni Nassef (1886–1918), Egyptian feminist, writer, and activist

"Do they make you veil?"

It's a question I'm frequently asked when people hear I'm traveling to visit family in Pakistan. It has always caught me off guard. No individual, religion, or state has ever dictated that I—as a secular person of mixed heritage—must veil. Nonetheless, when the subject of Muslim women's clothing arises, the discussion inevitably veers toward the veil.

Given the profound differences between styles of dress and conceptions of female modesty across Muslim communities—from northern Nigeria to Uzbekistan, the suburbs of Paris to Indonesia—I find the terms "Islamic dress" or "Muslim clothing" ironic, as if there were a singular uniform prescribed by Islam (figure 20.1).

My grandmother is an Indian Muslim who migrated to the newly created state of Pakistan following the partition of 1947. To me, a Muslim woman always wore a *sari* and covered her head only when she prayed in the privacy of her room. In downtown Karachi, I was well aware of the

Figure 20.1.   A 2007 photo, *left*, of a Yemeni woman wearing a *sharshaf*; and, *right*, a 2007 photo of the colorful *sitarah*, said to have been introduced by Ottoman rulers, that traditional women still wear over it in Sanaa. Photo by Sheryl B. Shapiro.

variety of women's clothing within the Islamic Republic of Pakistan, from the baggy and brightly colored *salwar kameez* (trousers and tunic) worn by Muslims, Christians, and Parsis (South Asian Zoroastrians) to neutral-colored cloaks that we call *arabis*, and face veils.

As a child, I asked my grandmother if she had ever worn a veil and was laughingly told how she and her sisters were among the first generation of Muslim girls in Lucknow to go to college, a move encouraged by their father. He permitted all his daughters to study, reminding them that their behavior would be the key to whether other young women of the community would be allowed out subsequently. My great-grandfather did not want his daughters to veil their faces, although as the first women to attend the previously all-male Muslim University at Aligarh, they donned the Indian-style *burqa* (a slim black cloak); so they did not veil. In order

Figure 20.2.   Painting of the author's grandmother and
great-aunt, by her father, Asad Shaheed, 2004, from a 1965
photograph. They usually wore saris, emblematic of South
Asian heritage, culture, and history (older generations
still wear saris today, as younger women do on formal
occasions). Courtesy of Aisha Lee Fox Shaheed.

to reach the college, my grandmother and her sisters had to ride bicycles
through the crowded market: a foray into public space that, even for the
most liberal of Muslim Indians at the time, required girls to dress modestly. With their heads covered by their *dupattas*, they cycled to school and
attended lectures in classrooms where the female students sat at the back
behind a black curtain. (Figure 20.2)

The thought of my grandmother in a burqa is foreign to me. No one in our family now ever covers their heads or faces. When I asked my grandmother why, she replied, "We did so you wouldn't have to."

My great-grandfather, she explained, had not supported the cloistering of women, which in South Asia is called purdah or *chadri aur chardivari* (literally, a curtain and four walls). Of greater importance to him was that his daughters become educated to the same degree as his sons, and this would require them to leave the home and participate in public. By veiling for a specific period of time, related to their daily routine and their life stage as unmarried women, my grandmother and her sisters were able to overturn social norms by attending college and to observe the sanctities of public space or private honor. For our family, veiling was tied to our identity as a religious minority in India and symbolized familial honor but was never viewed as a religious injunction or a requirement of Islam.

Every person with Muslim heritage has a different experience, precisely because what we wear—including the veil—depends on our specific culture(s), the historical moment, and prevailing conceptions of female modesty and sexuality. Islam, like most religions, has been interpreted in different ways across communities, and what is deemed appropriate clothing for women varies accordingly. Whether Islam requires women to cover their heads and/or faces is perhaps less pertinent to women's lived experiences than whether their families, local religious authorities, and government require them to cover themselves. For this reason, contemporary debates around the veil should begin with politics rather than theology, as both state-level and nonstate groups further their own agendas by exercising control over people's clothing in the name of religion, culture, and authenticity. In the context of Muslim women, this control can be played out through the imposition, or the banning, of the veil.

Ayesha Imam and Nira Yuval-Davis assess the links between gender and fundamentalisms:[1]

> Definitions of collective identity are increasingly hinged on definitions of gender, so that the construction of a "Muslim woman," a "Christian woman" or a "Hindu woman" is therefore integral to the construction of "Muslimness," "Christianity" or "Hinduism"; this explains in part the emphasis on controlling women's sexuality and other aspects of their lives.[2]

The fluctuations of women's clothing are apt material for mapping the history of politics and the politics of history. A politically grounded approach to Muslim women's histories moves toward finding a vocabulary with which to better approach current issues of veiling, secularism, and fundamentalisms.

Clothing, like language, varies according to time, place, and the individual. The process of dressing oneself may not incur much consideration, yet the most plainly visible indications of any social, political, and historical context are "read" through the clothing of its people. Clothes can create boundaries between people and shape collective identities. In this way they are a visual means of creating community. A police uniform or a nun's habit signals belonging to a specific group. The standardization of clothing creates a semblance of homogeneity, projected to those inside and outside the group. Just as often, however, clothing indicates the wearer's social position, marital status, region, ethnicity, profession, rank, religion, and so forth. So while clothing can be used to give an impression of oneness on the surface, it can also be used to mark differences within a community.[3] Exploring the metaphor of clothing as a language, Alison Lurie (1981) reflected, "Besides containing 'words' that are taboo, the language of clothes, like speech, also includes modern and ancient words, words of native and foreign origin, dialect words, colloquialisms, slang and vulgarities."[4]

If clothing is a silent language, the *practice* of veiling among Muslim women becomes a context within which we can more deeply explore sundry examples of the veil and the women who wear them. Symbols of dress are always contingent upon a specific community, and so the denotations of a firefighter's costume or a sex worker's footwear may be visibly apparent to those familiar with a region but incomprehensible to those outside. At times, social codes, such as adherence to modesty, are expressed through the cultural specificities of dress. For example, under colonial rule when British women encountered Indian women in saris, many were astonished by the apparent immodesty of an exposed midriff and bare feet, even at formal occasions. Conversely, as clothing restrictions relaxed in the wake of Victorian conventions, Indian women were shocked by the British women's naked calves and décolletages.[5]

The language of veiling is equally slippery and taking "the veil" as a starting point for discussion can be problematic given the term's many uses. This slippage arises from the difference between the veil (which is an item of cloth) and the practice of veiling, implying modesty and moral conduct. In the (Christian) West, the term "veil" is usually used with reference to a woman's face covering, most often associated with brides (white) and widows (black). In Arabic, the term *hijab* simply means "barrier"; in Farsi and Urdu, purdah refers to a "curtain." While some scholars take such terms to mean creating a general distance between unrelated people of the opposite sex, others have sought to define which parts of the body are permissible in public spaces.

In practice, to some Muslim women, veiling may simply mean tossing a scarf or the end of a sari over the head or, as currently to female flight attendants with Pakistan International Airlines, draping a sheer scarf over hair tied into a bun. To some, the primary requirement of veiling is that the hair be completely covered while others take this to include the wearer's ears and neck. For Muslim women, the covering of the face can be measured in degrees, ranging from the white, filmy *yashmak* (face veil) popular in late Ottoman society, to a *niqab,* which allows only the eyes to be visible, to the all-enveloping burqa.

What may be assumed to be acceptable Muslim clothing in one place may not be so in another. In Tunisia, women are liable to undergo police intervention if they veil, while in Saudi Arabia, they are punished if they do not. This suggests that we should broaden our scope away from notions of a single "Islamic culture," to encompass women in multiple Muslim contexts: in Islamic states, in secular Muslim-majority states, in Muslim families and communities in the diaspora, among migrant Muslim communities, for non-Muslim women who are subject to Muslim laws because of their country of residence or their children's, and for women who do not identify as Muslim but who are automatically categorized as such because of their family heritage or the laws of their country.[6]

This wider conception of Muslim women's experiences and a recognition of the need to share this information with our sisters in other contexts, has informed the transnational solidarity network, Women Living Under Muslim Laws (WLUML) since its inception in 1984. For more than two decades, WLUML has built alliances and provided information, support, and a collective space for women to work toward gender equity and social justice and now has a presence in more than seventy countries. WLUML networkers represent a wide variety of backgrounds, experiences, and political views, and they address themselves to equally diverse groups of women. Most of their work has been focused around urgent-action campaigns, human rights lobbying, promoting legal reform, grassroots support, and international alliances. Some might take their interest in the history of clothing for a frivolous pursuit. However, after years of experience, the network recognized that women's lives, livelihoods, and mobility are shaped by prevailing political forces, often under the guise of a return to religious tradition. In this way, Islam has been used to deny women the choice to veil or not veil in order to further political agendas. WLUML also acknowledges that factors other than Islam—local customs, colonial history, and fluctuating gender norms—also contribute to Muslim women's dress.

In the mid-1990s, WLUML networkers began voicing the need for a politicized display of the history of dress codes and styles—a fundamentally visual topic. Specifically, they were interested in documenting what women in each region over time wear every day; what their communities deem "decent" apparel; and what they and/or their communities consider "Muslim" dress. The result was an international touring exhibition titled "Dress Codes and Modes: Women's Dress in Some Muslim Countries and Communities," featuring about twenty panels, each ten feet high, of color and black-and-white images, analytical text, and historical quotations, accompanied by items of clothing.[7] The primary goal was to provide a portable tool for WLMUL networkers to use at conferences or seminars, in classrooms, and in other venues worldwide.

The twentieth century witnessed a proliferation of multilateral politics and waves of decolonization, resulting in a complex cross-fertilization of culture. For example, female migrant workers from Sri Lanka and Southeast Asia, employed in the Arabian Peninsula, are increasingly returning home strictly veiled and in Arab-style garb, which in turn fuels the fashion industry and alters local culture, redefining what is considered appropriate Muslim dress in that context. In an increasingly globalized world with easy access to long-distance travel and a plethora of local, regional, and international media, there is a heightened need to redefine oneself, with regard to culture, ethnicity, religion, and nation.

Denying that all Muslims share a common history and a unified identity, WLUML wanted to stress the cultural diversity of Muslim women, who are often unaware that their specific historical contexts shape their local construction of Muslim-ness and differentiate them from women in other Muslim contexts. "Dress Codes and Modes" reintroduced women to their histories, using clothing as a visual example of political control while simultaneously offering plentiful examples of women's agency and activism in all regions. To this end, the group decided to organize the material on a regional, comparative basis rather than thematically. Although many more could have been selected and the possibility for expansion still exists, the countries represented at the outset included Egypt, Iran, Nigeria, Pakistan, Sri Lanka, and Turkey.[8]

"Codes and Modes" underlined the fact that practices of veiling have been uneven within and across regions and throughout history. In fact, Muslim women rejecting the veil are not a recent phenomenon. For instance, in Mecca in the early eighth century C.E., Aisha bint Talha (a niece of the Prophet Muhammad's wife, Aisha) chose not to veil. Although veiling then was not prescribed for all ranks of society, it was sometimes expected that women of a lofty rank would cover their faces. Aisha bint Talha refused, countering criticism by explaining, "God has honored me with beauty. I want the people to understand what rank I enjoy before them. I will not veil myself. Nobody can reproach me with a fault."[9]

Throughout history, rural women have veiled far less strictly and ignored seclusion when it impeded their physical labor. On the other hand, head coverings have often been worn during work outdoors in many regions, including western Europe, for environmental reasons, which begs the question whether religion or circumstance determines what we wear.[10]

Analyses of clothing in Muslim contexts usually emphasize women and the veil, yet Muslim men have also been subject to clothing regulations. While Islam advocates some degree of modesty of dress for men (which some, not all, take to mean covering their legs and torsos), like women's, men's dress codes are often politically imposed. The Ottoman Empire (1299–1923), for example, used official dress codes to mark the rank, profession, religion, and ethnicity of its citizenry, and many of these regulations pertained to men. In a move toward social cohesiveness, and confronted with increasingly Westernized fashions among the ruling classes, Sultan Mahmud II (1808–39) imposed a universal male dress code. At first, the fez, now synonymous with Turkey, was worn only by the military, but by 1829 it was compulsory for all men. While some were pleased with the promise of social leveling, others, whose headgear had illustrated elevated social rank, had more to lose. Then, in a drastic reversal, the fez was banned in the twentieth century by Mustafa Kemal Atatürk, the first president of the Republic of Turkey (1923–34), and all citizens were required to wear European-style hats and clothing.[11] Where once the fez was regarded as a culturally alien imposition by the Ottoman state, it now stood as a marker of Muslim Turkish identity.

In the 1990s, Afghanistan's fundamentalist Taliban rulers imposed salwar kameez, turbans, and beards of a certain length on Afghan men, even jailing them when they did not comply.

Minimizing the element of religion in analyses of the veil can offer certain insights into the heated debates concerning Muslim women and clothing. It is not simply that Muslim women are hindered by their religion. On a basic human level, clothing is about the beautification of the body and is designed to attract the opposite sex for the purposes of procreation. Female sexuality is harnessed for the furtherance and integrity of any community, and women's clothes, therefore, are functionally designed to simultaneously conceal and attract attention according to prevailing local standards of beauty, modesty, and gender roles.

With this in mind, it is easier to see how veiling among Muslim women—incorporating diverse styles and varying degrees of modesty—is also about making them inaccessible (to some people on some occasions). The question at stake is whose honor is being protected: that of the woman beneath the clothes, her father's, her husband's, her family's, her community's, or her state's? As in Europe, women in Muslim contexts historically have not controlled wealth and so their clothing and jewelry have been indications of their fathers' and/or husbands' status.[12] Sexual control of women is fundamental to patriarchy in both Muslim and non-Muslim societies, and codes of honor are represented in women's clothing.

When political objectives require a degree of social control to maintain their legitimacy, women's behavior gains new social meaning. This control can take different forms: for example, in Iran and Saudi Arabia, all women are legally required to veil, while restrictions have been placed on veiling in Turkey and Tunisia. The divergence of such policies across Muslim states reflects the underlying political nature of clothing regulations. Women's sexuality is also controlled in other ways and often just as inconsistently as through policies on veiling. For example, in Algeria, polygyny is permitted but in neighboring Tunisia it has been banned since 1956. Tellingly, both laws regulate women's sexuality and both countries justify their laws with recourse to Islam. The politics of clothing and the politics of fundamentalisms cannot be extricated. As collective cultural identities are formed and re-formed, women's sexuality is controlled through legal impediments (such as access to safe abortion), through violence (such as so-called honor killings, also called in some cultures "crimes of passion," which are often decriminialized), and through their public appearance (such as enforced veiling). For those who impose their agendas upon others under the guise of a return to some mythical pan-Muslim past, gender is a key site for cleaving communities and fostering collective identities.

Fundamentalist movements—by which I refer to those exploiting the discourses of religion, culture, and ethnicity to further their political objectives—have a vested interest in projecting an impression of homogeneity, arguing that there is an authentic, traditional, morally correct, and essential form of "Islamic dress" for women.[13] Comparing regions, Imam and Yuval-Davis argue that "control over sexuality is a central theme of the social programs promoted by fundamentalist movements everywhere" and find that sexual control is often exercised through dress codes.[14] Typically, the clothing fundamentalists advocate is justified as "traditional" or "religiously correct," although many times the dress code is alien to the context in which it is introduced, as with Iranian-style chadri in Sudan. Countries such as Iran and Saudi Arabia are examples of state-level politicized religion, but there are other forms of fundamentalisms perpetrated by nonstate actors with as much impact upon the liberties of a community.

The Algerian example gives some indication of how sexual control through enforced veiling has been carried out by nonstate fundamentalists. Having won independence from French colonial rule in 1962, for more than twenty-five years Algeria operated as a single-party state, under the leadership of the National Liberation Front. Despite federal attempts to monitor rising Islamist groups, the Islamic Salvation Front won local elections in 1991, just two years after its formation. The Algerian Islamists had targeted women since the early 1980s, preaching against Western clothes and campaigning to make public space increasingly more segregated. The more dogmatic Islamic Front leaders argued for installing religiously based laws, and in the boroughs under their control, workplaces were segregated and the hijab was made mandatory for all female employees.[15] When the Islamic Front won the first round of national elections in 1991, the government cancelled the elections and declared the party illegal, resulting in a brutal and violent conflict beginning in 1992. Thousands have been killed in the wave of terror instigated by the armed appendages of the Islamic Front: the Army of Salvation and the Armed Islamic Group. The first to be targeted were those who represented the state, then intellectuals and teachers, and, within a year, civilians in cities and countryside alike.

The ideological program of the Islamic Salvation Front necessitated a great degree of social control, so the monitoring of female sexuality escalated. Some were targeted for harassment and violence merely for living alone and/or retaining custody of their children; others were killed because they refused to wear the hijab. In a well-publicized case, sixteen-year-old Katia Bengana was shot dead by armed Islamists in the street on her way home from school. Outraged, women's rights activists struggled to organize themselves in response to the escalating violence and repression, and a public women's meeting was organized by the Collective of Algerian Democratic Women in March 1993, to commemorate International Women's Day. When the collective instituted an annual prize for resistance against fundamentalisms in 1999, the prize was posthumously awarded to Katia Bengana. It continues to be given to a different recipient every March 8. Reflecting on the nature of the atrocities in Algeria, women's rights activist Louisa Ait-Hamou insists that despite media portrayals to the contrary, this was not a civil war between "religious fundamentalists" and "secular civil society." She argues that the conflict is neither ethnically nor religiously based but that the Islamists are fighting to establish a new political order predicated upon theocracy and patriarchy.[16] Here, the veil is a word in the language of fundamentalisms that signifies sexual control, limited access to public space, and social homogeneity.

Regulating the veil and other aspects of Muslim women's autonomy can also emanate directly from the state. Is control over the bodies of women always tied to religion? The Islamic Republic of Pakistan does not mandate the veil, but in the Islamic Republic of Iran even tourists must cover their heads. Does this mean that one state is more "Islamic" than the other? Perhaps there are more political justifications for state-decreed clothing regulations. In a provocative thesis, Shaya Nourai contrasts the instances of dress codes in postrevolutionary China and Iran: both exemplify the profoundly undemocratic cultural revolutions of the twentieth century.

Positing that the Mao suit in the People's Republic of China and the hijab in the Islamic Republic of Iran are both "symbols of social standardization," Nourai views their enforcement by the state as "barometer[s] of a nation's level of commitment and adherence to the ruling powers."[17] In the process of representing a cohesive society—to itself and to outside observers—the inheritors of revolutionary powers must secure their political legitimacy. By situating these examples in the context of nation building and state control, Nourai also questions the notion that religiously based arguments are always at the root of dress codes. One conclusion she draws is that, in a classic example of using discourses of liberation to garner political support, both Communist China and Islamic Iran claimed to liberate women through dress, despite the forceful nature of their clothing regulations. In China, for example, the masculinization and militarization of women's dress facilitated their entry into the public sphere in the service of the state; in Iran, it was argued, the hijab allowed women to have more access to public space while still adhering to the newly defined parameters of modesty.

Even where the state does not impose a dress code, clothing has been used as a nation-building tool, as in the 1920s during India's struggle for independence, when Mohandas Gandhi's boycott campaign (the *swadeshi* movement) involved eschewing British-made products including textiles, to be replaced by homespun cloth (*khadi*). The significance of the homespun movement was to challenge colonial rule by using locally produced, non-Western products with very specific (peasant) class connotations.

Of course, individuals also approach veiling and clothing regulations creatively; there exists a rich history of opposition to dress codes. Nourai notes that in Maoist China women wore brightly colored socks under their drab military-style uniforms, and in Iran women shaved their heads to obey the injunction against showing their hair (and also stopped wearing hijab), much like a protesting schoolgirl in France, who in 2005 explained that she didn't wear hijab because there was no hair to hide.[18]

Just as people demonstrate their resistance and agency through clothing, reappropriation of the Muslim veil—often represented as an oppressive obligation—can be a conscious decision. Muslim women from myriad backgrounds and varying degrees of religiosity actively choose to veil, an issue brought to a head in 2004 with heated debates about banning head scarves in French schools. These fights still rage throughout Europe. In the West, Muslim women may opt to wear some form of hijab as an act of identification and solidarity with a specific regional community and/or to signal their inclusion in a pan-Muslim community (*ummah*). Women may also choose to veil in the name of cultural nationalism, as in regions of Central Asia where the local veil (*parandja*) was banned under Soviet rule. Following the collapse of the Soviet Union, increasing numbers of Central Asian women returned to the veil as a marker of their cultural—not religious—identity.[19]

As my grandmother learned at a young age, women may consciously choose to veil to facilitate their access to public space. Regarding contemporary Turkey, Aynur Ilyasoglu argues that for Islamist women, veiling (*tesettür*) represents a transition from the private to the public and provides social sanction for their participation in higher education and the workforce. While wearing modest clothes, she argues, these women enjoy a heightened degree of public freedom without radically altering their familial/domestic sphere.[20] Likewise, following the 1979 Islamic Revolution in Iran, the chadri was imposed upon some women who had never, and would otherwise never have, worn it, except to demonstrate their solidarity against Shah Mohammad Reza Pahlavi. Others who had been unable to leave their homes were in effect given official license to participate in the public world.[21]

By equating dress codes with religion we obscure the fact that clothing worn by Muslims is as varied and culturally specific as clothes worn by Jews, Buddhists, or atheists. A politically informed analysis moves us beyond theological debates (an arena where women are structurally disadvantaged in any respect) and into the realm of lived experience.

I'm asked, "What do you wear in Pakistan?" and I hastily explain that I'm not representative of Pakistani womanhood, because of my hybrid outfits: blue jeans, a tunic-style *kurta,* and a bare head. But then I pause. Is my grandmother's sari, accompanied by European high heels, more authentic than my blue jeans? Is that designer blouse any less traditional than the black arabi that covers it? Long flowing skirts have been worn by the nomadic women of the Punjab for centuries, but does that make them more Pakistani than the increasing number of women in face veils I encounter each time I visit downtown Karachi? My grandmother's generation is the last to remember Pakistan in its infancy: a new state predicated upon secularism, diversity, and equity. She veiled so I wouldn't have to ... What can I do for future generations of girls and women who are taught that Islam requires women to cover themselves without denying the Muslimness of a Muslim woman's sari?

Searching for authenticity will always prove elusive, but a thorough excavation of our histories—through the colors of our creativity and the dark moments of control—unmasks the forces that dictate how we clothe our bodies for the world.

NOTES

1. I use the term "fundamentalisms" throughout this chapter, recognizing its ambiguities, to refer to any state or nonstate actor that exploits the discourses of religion, culture, and/or ethnicity to further its political objectives. The chapter's epigraph, by Malak Hifni Nassef, is cited in Leila Ahmed, *Women and*

Gender in Islam: Historical Roots of a Modern Debate (New Haven: Yale University Press, 1998), 181–82.

2. Ayesha Imam and Nira Yuval-Davis, introduction to *Warning Signs of Fundamentalisms,* ed. Ayesha Imam, Jenny Morgan, and Nira Yuval-Davis (London: WLUML, 2004), xiii.

3. Homa Hoodfar, "Politics of Clothing" (paper, 1999), 2, 5.

4. Alison Lurie cited in the introduction to *Languages of Dress in the Middle East,* ed. Nancy Lindisfarne-Tapper and Bruce Ingham (London: Curzon / CIMEL (SOAS), 1997), 2.

5. Lucy Moore, *Maharanis: The Lives and Times of Three Generations of Indian Princesses* (London: Penguin, 2005), 131.

6. WLUML, *Introducing Women Living Under Muslim Laws* (London, n.d.).

7. Fostering a space for sharing and exchange between women throughout the scores of countries linked through the Women Living Under Muslim Laws network has been a key impetus for many of the network's collective projects, such as organizing "Feminism in the Muslim World Training Institutes" to bring together women activists from around the world to not only learn from each other's experiences but to also witness how the intersections of culture, politics, and Islam are manifested in other Muslim contexts. See Anissa Hélie, *Feminism in the Muslim World Training Institutes* (London: WLUML, 2000).

8. Farida Shaheed and Aisha L. F. Shaheed, *Great Ancestors: Women Asserting Rights in Muslim Contexts—The Narratives* (Lahore: Shirkat Gah, 2004), 2.

9. WLUML exhibition catalog, *Dress Codes and Modes: Women's Dress in Some Muslim Countries and Communities* (2002).

10. Hoodfar, "Politics of Clothing," 5–6.

11. Shaya Nourai, "Dressing Up the Nation: The Imposition of the Dress Code during the Cultural Revolutions in the People's Republic of China and the Islamic Republic of Iran" (master's thesis, McGill University, Montreal, 2003), 12.

12. Hoodfar, "Politics of Clothing," 7.

13. For example, in spite of the fact that Western-style clothing has been adopted by many socioeconomically elite groups in non-Western regions, the predominant image portrayed in Western media outlets still tends to equate the "quintessential Muslim woman" with a veil. Alternately, the media often refer to local dress in language stressing the otherness of the Muslim subject: "ethnic," "folkloric," "rustic," "traditional," "their local costumes," and so on. In this way, class distinctions and the rural-urban divide are erased—by indigenous media sources as well—and the result is a deceptively narrow impression of the dress habits of a nation. By representing women in Muslim contexts who wear Western-style clothing as merely striving to be-

come "more like the West," the media ignore other crucial factors, such as variations of class and status, discourses of modernity, the histories of colonial rule, and the nature of indigenous Muslim women's movements, as well as the decision as to who can speak "as" a Muslim woman.

14. Ayesha Imam and Nira Yuval-Davis, introduction to *Warning Signs of Fundamentalisms*, ed. Ayesha Imam, Jenny Morgan and Nira Yuval-Davis (London: WLUML, 2004), xiii.

15. Louisa Ait-Hamou, "Women's Struggle against Muslim Fundamentalism in Algeria: Strategies or a Lesson for Survival?" in *Warning Signs*, 117.

16. Ait-Hamou, "Women's Struggle," 120, 121, 118.

17. Nourai, " Dressing Up," 5.

18. Nourai, "Dressing Up," 10.

19. Marfua Tokhtakhodjaeva, *Between the Slogans of Communism and the Laws of Islam: The Women of Uzbekistan*, Sufian Aslan, trans., Cassandra Balchin, ed., (Lahore: Shirkat Gah / WLUML, 1995).

20. Aynur Ilyasoglu, "Islamist Women in Turkey," in *Deconstructing Images of 'the Turkish Woman,'* ed. Zehra F Arat (New York: St. Martin's Press, 1998), 255.

21. *Dress Codes and Modes.*

REFERENCES

Ahmed, Leila. *Women and Gender in Islam: Historical Roots of a Modern Debate.* New Haven: Yale University Press, 1998.

Bauer, Jan, and Anissa Hélie. *Documenting Women's Rights Violations by Non-State Actors: Activist Strategies from Muslim Communities.* Montreal: WLUML, 2006.

Hélie, Anissa. *Feminism in the Muslim World Training Institutes.* London: WLUML, 2000.

Hoodfar, Homa. "The Politics of Clothing." 1999. An expanded version is available in French as *"Le voile comme espace de négociation de l'identité et de la modernité: du Moyen-Orient au Canada"* (Montreal: UQAM/Concordia, 2001).

Arat, Zehra, ed. *Deconstructing Images of "the Turkish Woman."* New York: St. Martin's Press, 1998.

Imam, Ayesha, Jenny Morgan, and Nira Yuval-Davis, eds. *Warning Signs of Fundamentalisms.* London: WLUML, 2004.

Lindisfarne-Tapper, Nancy, and Bruce Ingham, eds. *Languages of Dress in the Middle East.* London: Curzon, 1997.

Lurie, Alison. *The Language of Clothes.* London: Heinemann, 1981.

Moore, Lucy. *Maharanis: The Lives and Times of Three Generations of Indian Princesses.* London: Penguin, 2005.

Nourai, Shaya. "Dressing Up the Nation: The Imposition of the Dress Code during the Cultural Revolutions in the People's Republic of China and the Islamic Republic of Iran." Master's thesis, McGill University, Montreal, 2003.

Said, Edward. *Orientalism.* New York: Vintage Books, 1979.

Shaheed, Farida, and Aisha L. F. Shaheed. *Great Ancestors: Women Asserting Rights in Muslim Contexts—The Narratives.* Lahore: Shirkat Gah, 2004.

Tokhtakhodjaeva, Marfua. *Between the Slogans of Communism and the Laws of Islam: The Women of Uzbekistan.* Translated by Sufian Aslan and edited by Cassandra Balchin. Lahore: Shirkat Gah, 1995.

Women Living Under Muslim Laws. *Introducing Women Living Under Muslim Laws* [network brochure]. London, n.d.

———. *Dress Codes and Modes: Women's Dress in Some Muslim Countries and Communities.* International touring exhibition catalog, 2002.

21 From Veil to Veil

*"What's in a woman's head is a lot more
important than what's on it"*

SHERIFA ZUHUR

I have just wriggled out of my *abaya* in my airplane seat. This long robe
was made in Kuwait and has a slightly ethnic look with gold trim on the
hems and borders. The synthetic material of my *shayla*, or head scarf, has
been choking me since I left my hotel room in Riyadh early in the morning, and I happily fold it and place it in my briefcase.

An American contractor who began talking with me in the business
office of the hotel suggested that I was wearing the abaya only to please
a Saudi boyfriend or husband. Irritated, I pointed out that when I had
breakfasted sans head scarf, the waiter brought over several notes from
men in the restaurant. One, written on a napkin was fairly innocuous,
"Have a beautiful day!" But another was more to the point. There were
few other single women guests at the hotel. And besides, this American,
the contractor, unlike Saudi or other women, had not experienced harassment by the *mutawain* (the bearded religious "police," an unofficial,
yet troublesome group). He didn't seem very convinced.

I was visiting Riyadh in 2005 to get a sense of whether winds of change were in the air. The first municipal elections since the 1960s had just been held. An antiterrorism campaign was under way; billboards blazed, "My Country . . . Did You Do This?" against a background of bombed buildings. I spoke with and interviewed various men and women and was in turn interviewed by Safi Abdullah, a lively Somali lady from South Africa, longtime resident in the Kingdom of Saudi Arabia, and veteran radio host. Academics and officials of the Diplomatic Institute of the Foreign Ministry adroitly graced me with their opinions, while polling mine.

A former college classmate, wearing his white *thob* and red-and-white head covering, came to meet me in my hotel. He said, "You look like a princess in this abaya." Then, reassuringly, he added, "I tell you, see, we are the same. My head is covered too." But the degree of covering for men and women is not quite equal. Women are completely clothed under their abayas. They must wear long sleeves, their necklines must be high, their hemlines low. That we were not the same was made clear when, as we left the building, he cautioned me: "Fix your abaya well"—meaning that too much of my hair was showing.

A group of Saudi businesswomen met with me in a pleasant coffee shop on the ladies-only floor of the Kingdom Mall. Inside the coffeehouse, we all unwrapped our head scarves, took off our abayas, and relaxed. They did not mention covering at all but conversed about their own backgrounds and how they had chosen their particular professions and about the municipal elections, when women were excluded from voting or standing for office. They spoke of the previous need for a male gofer but added that government ministries were now instituting women's desks, meaning that women could conduct their business without an intermediary. However, a year later, I learned that many of these desks weren't in place or did not actually facilitate doing business since women had to wait for staff for far too long.

The women's group talked about the numbers of Western women who seem to be making Saudi women their cause. They insisted that I should attend the national cultural festival, the Jinadiriyya, held about forty-five kilometers outside Riyadh. Could someone secure me an invitation? From cell phone to cell phone, woman to woman, and with instant generosity, it was arranged.

A small group of mutawain stood in the parking lot outside the

Jinadiriyya festival grounds hurling caustic comments and criticisms at the women disembarking from their chauffeur-driven vehicles and entering the zones designated to represent the Hijaz or Asir areas of the country. The mutawain were barred from entry on these "ladies days," so they were especially eager to correct female abuses of modesty before the women moved beyond their sight lines. One woman in our party had no abaya. She had tried to borrow one before we set out for the festival, but to no avail. A tall, bearded young man in his twenties zeroed in on her. "She is a disgrace. She doesn't respect us!" he screamed. "She has to know . . . you must tell her . . . she is violating the norms of our women. She has to wear abaya!"

The woman in question had just spent four years in Amman but pretended not to understand. The diminutive, angelic woman who had obtained our tickets—clad in trousers and a white *hijab*, with a Jordanian embroidered abaya, instead of the black Saudi style—clucked back and pushed our group along, ignoring our moral savior, while I argued with him to no avail.

"Saudi ladies are used to the mutawain," said one passerby. "Don't pay attention to him!"

Female guards wearing hijab-topped abayas with special black glittering hats guarded the entry to the main hall. A shoving match among would-be-entrants caused one woman to lose her temper in response to the guard's call for manners. I caught only the tail end of an uncharacteristic rant about how this nonsense would not be tolerated "when they give us all our rights." When, I wondered, would that be?

Inside the main reception hall, scarves were abandoned and abayas opened. Women smiled as ladies in shiny folkloric dress circulated trays of tea, coffee, and attractive bread bowls filled with treats. We were presented to a princess hosting the event and treated to a formal program with poetry, singing, and dancing.

The dances of the eastern province of Saudi Arabia feature another "veil," a huge, fancy, diaphanous polyester thob, in blue, green, and violet or other colors embroidered with gilt decorations, which envelops the body and can be pulled up over the head. It is worn over another dress. This thob from Sharqiyya serves as an abaya for formal occasions—although in Riyadh, women are nevertheless obliged to wear the black abaya over it.

The dancers gently swirled the fabric of their thobs and swung their long hair from side to side, as their garments enlarged the design of the dance. These performers were young and demure. Their amateur tentativeness enhanced the feeling that this was all about heritage, not a contest or any forbidden display. In the Hijaz section of the festival grounds, another set of dancers performed a dance from Medina, one, clad in white satin, representing a mother with her baby.

Predictably, on my return to the parking lot, the same young mutawa saved up some resentment and special comments for me. "Your skirt should be longer! Longer!" he yelled. My skirt was nearly to my ankles, but in the front it veered upward about two inches in a sort of innocuous ruffle.

"Are you my father?" I hissed back. "My brother?"

Later that evening, I told the story to a woman who in turn related her own mutawa tale, in which an elderly woman had been admonished for pushing her sleeves up. She had grabbed him, pointing to his long legs, exposed by his too-short thob. While he had attractive ankles, she told him, no one was going to take a second look at her forearms.

"Why don't the mutawain go after the men who don't pay child support?" asked progressive journalist Khalid al-Maeena, in a column in *Arab News* printed during my visit. "Why don't they go after the men who beat their wives?"

The abaya, particularly over an ankle-length skirt and long sleeves, is uncomfortably hot once the warm spring weather begins, and summer temperatures in Saudi Arabia can reach one hundred and fifteen degrees Fahrenheit. In 2006, I traveled from Riyadh to Jeddah, and as so often happens, the airplane was delayed on the tarmac, without any air conditioning. I felt faint, and my heart was pounding. I decided that as I was seated with men on each side (though I requested a seat next to a woman passenger), I could not remove the abaya. I wondered if anyone from Saudi Airlines would let my family know that I died because it was too hot, and I couldn't take the wretched abaya off?

Many women now wear hijab, a head scarf, and then don the abaya atop it. Quite a few women wear a black *niqab*, a face mask, as well. A journalist wearing the niqab came to my hotel to interview me the night I left the kingdom. She in her niqab and I in my abaya were unable to identify each other, though we were in the lobby simultaneously. I was settling my bill, and she was trying to figure out where I was, since I had no cell phone. By the time I realized which indistinguishable female figure was she, I had to leave for the airport, full of anxiety about whether I'd be harassed for traveling without a *mahram,* a male guardian. Sure enough, an airport guard loudly demanded to know the whereabouts of my mahram, just as soon as my friends walked back to their cars.

I have since acquired my own abaya for travel to the Gulf and Iraq, but on this trip I had borrowed my abaya from a friend in the United States. She is about an inch and a half taller than I, and with high heels I could avoid tripping but often stepped on the robe when I sat or moved. The scarf was constantly unpeeling, or blowing off and requiring readjustment, turning me into a clumsy Star Wars character. How could I feel like a professional swaddled in an abaya, unable to travel to any meeting without prior arrangements, and unable to call to my contacts? Yet wearing the abaya was a less significant impediment than not being able to drive or allowed to rent a cell phone. And naturally, women are excluded from the hotels' exercise facility, pool, and golf course.

My American colleagues have suggested I lecture in an abaya to illustrate my remarks about Saudi women. But for some audience members, a huge percentage of my intellectual credibility would vanish, while a weird, false authenticity would be established for a different portion of the same audience. What about lecturing or interacting with colleagues in the kingdom? Oh, I forgot. I would have no colleagues, because there are not yet women in the Foreign Ministry and no women in the military research units, so I would have no job! Or I'd have to shift back to a different area of academia. Women are permitted to be historians, or literary scholars, but they are not represented in policy making, international relations, the higher echelons of the military, or the type of political research and policy making that is my bread and butter.[1]

Does my veiling in order "to pass" bolster those who impose the veil on others? If the veil should be a matter of individual choice, as many Islamist women hold, why is it *obligatory* in the Kingdom of Saudi Arabia? If wearing the hijab fulfills the requirements of modest dress, then why the additional requirement of the abaya (or the *chadri* in Iran)?

The veil has multiple meanings specific to its country and context. It can mean, "I am Muslim and others around me aren't." It could signal modesty, or obedience to the rules, or, when a little hair shows, fairly daring liberalism. Some Saudi women complained that their acquaintances criticized them for not veiling their faces and marveled that, paradoxically, extremists could hide under face veils and yet recognize those of similar political views.

In Riyadh, the veil is as much a component of female behavior as are the cars and drivers that transport women, who are not allowed to drive themselves. But if the meaning of the cover is geographically specific, then why should Muslim women wear it in the United States? The aim of the practice, my own mentor once argued, is to NOT draw attention to yourself. The disagreement between Muslim women concerning the veil is that it was NOT required of ordinary Muslim women, in contrast with the Prophet Muhammad's wives, or that if it was, that represented a historical condition. Nearly all Islamists agree that all Muslim women must veil— as Islam is for all time and place—and heartily disagreed with the once more common attitude that veiling is not a *fard* (requirement).

In the field, women's (and men's) ideas were very different. Wherever the hijab has had overtones—political (as in Turkey) or sectarian (as in the Palestinian territories, or Lebanon)—they are not simple assertions of modesty or religiosity. In the late 1980s, sometimes to the dismay of their families, respondents for my book *Revealing Reveiling: Islamist Gender Ideology in Contemporary Egypt* had, by and large, made individual choices to adopt the hijab.[2] They described their decisions to begin wearing the hijab as rather solemn occasions, often preceded by dreams and a feeling of being "born again." One young woman who had dreamed of herself wearing hijab, took some time before making her decision, because she felt that it would be sinful to put it on and then cease wearing it. This was a step that once taken, would be irrevocable.

Those opposed to the Islamist movement argue that peer pressure is behind it all. This has proved to be partially correct, particularly among the young. For example, a dormitory monitor and older student at Cairo University stridently upheld the necessity of covering. One day, about ten of us had gathered to discuss the issue. A few of the young women refused to express themselves openly in front of this monitor, who they feared might formulate judgments about their characters and could damage their reputations. The young women who spoke to me when the monitor was not present were more forthcoming about their differing opinions of women's careers, covering, and political prospects.

Other unveiled women complained that men harassed them in the street, and that the verbal abuse and attempts to grope them seemed to have become more frequent, more pronounced, now that a larger proportion of Egyptian women wore hijab. The proportion has only increased since my fieldwork in the 1980s and residence in Egypt through the 1990s. In some areas of Cairo, the island of Roda, for instance, or in Imbaba, there are no unveiled women to be seen.

Damascus, Syria. The women in the rather conservative family I married into in the early 1990s wore a form of veil that I have also seen in Riyadh: the entire face is covered with transparent material; the wearer can see out, but no one sees in. My very young, unmarried sister-in-law, however, wore tracksuits, tight T-shirts, and really anything she wished. My clothes were not an issue. I could wear pants but mostly wore longer skirts because I traveled frequently outside the city on buses.

Yet my knee-length dress did not pass muster on my wedding day. "Can't you put a towel or something over your legs?" my bridegroom asked.

And later on: "If I asked you to wear hijab, would you?"

"If I asked you to wear a pink shirt every day, would you?" I replied. I attributed his attitude to the growth in the numbers of women wearing hijab in Syria at that time and realized from the way he had posed his question that he felt it was a rather ordinary request to make of one's wife. Maybe he understood from my response that I disagreed. Or maybe not. Our marriage dissolved so rapidly that this incident wasn't uppermost in my mind.

The "new" modest dress of a long raincoat and head scarf contrasted with the black garb and traditional headdresses of Damascene, Homsi, and Hamawi families (the Homsi and Hamawi headgear resemble horns). The few women working in the Assad National Library in Damascus— where I was carrying out research—tended to wear the overcoat variety of hijab, as did other women in the university or on the streets. I was told that Baath Party officials had spoken out against hijab wearing, because it was a symbol of the illegal Islamist groups and it countered the secularism upheld by the party. Once the reveiling movement had spread throughout the Muslim and Arab countries, this argument became hard to defend. Today, many more women wear hijab in Syria, Iraq, Lebanon, and Jordan, as well as Egypt.

In Lebanon, the northern portion of the Bekaa Valley is supposedly dominated by Hizbollah, the Party of God, which promotes modest dress for women. When I carried out research there in 1999 and 2000, I found that women who had traditionally worn a peasant style of head covering prior to the Lebanese civil war (1975–91) might still do so, but that younger women were split into two groups—hijabed and not. And within that distinction, some women wore hijab only outside their homes, while others wore it even in their homes.

The wives of religious officials also wore the Iranian-style chadri—a garment made like two long skirts sewn together—or black abayas, which are not native to Lebanon. Veiling wasn't an issue of much interest; people were primarily concerned with the dismal economic situation and Syria's influence in the countryside. At the Hizbollah-established hospital outside Baalbek, in the eastern Bekaa region, the guard would not let me enter with a bare head. I quickly tied on the scarf I had brought with me. "Mom," my six-year-old son complained, "You look weird. I don't like the way you look with that thing on your head." Once we left the hospital and went to visit the small surrounding villages, there was no need for the scarf. Hizbollah is not a governing force in all of these small hamlets, only in certain ones.

In one village, practically everyone came out to entertain us, including a darling little girl named Islam. She wore a sleeveless dress that exposed a huge wound on her arm, an accidental injury that was healing. Her father, the village schoolteacher, was a Palestinian who had lived there for years. I saw one young woman married wearing hijab, but most in their late teens did not. Later, I met another little girl in the *suq* of Fez, Morocco, not much older than Islam. She was wearing hijab, though she was a year or two too young for it. Many people say that the hijab should be worn

Figure 21.1. Six-year-old school-
girls in Kabul, Afghanistan, 2003.
Increasingly younger children are
wearing *hijab* (though one child
has let her scarf slip off her head).
Photo by Sheryl B. Shapiro.

from age nine, because some girls enter puberty then. And unlike tomboy-
ish little Islam dashing up and down the road, this child was begging for
money, not aggressively, but persistently, enough to make one wince at
the lessons in human relations she had learned in the streets (figure 21.1).

Wearing the hijab in Lebanon signifies sectarian membership, particularly in the big city—Beirut—where young or urban Christian women do
not wear any form of head covering. Outside a friend's apartment in
Beirut's southern Shi'i area, young neighborhood toughs yelled obsceni-
ties at me when I left without wearing hijab. I certainly had not needed
to wear it on the other side of town.

The communal meaning of the hijab can be stronger, as it was in Beersheba,
a big city in the south of Israel surrounded by a Bedouin population, where
it goes without saying that the garment distinguishes Arab from Jewish
women. Most Jewish women here wear no head covering at all, although
some Orthodox women wear long skirts and little hats that are quite dis-

tinct from the older Bedouin women in their embroidered dresses and white veils, or the younger ones in hijab. Here too, the hijab is a new form of dress that signals a continuing attentiveness to modesty, but also that the wearer is younger, possibly educated, and not as poor as the wearer of traditional Bedouin dress.

The Israeli Ben Gurion University of the Negev in Beersheba has admitted young Bedouin women and men into its mixed environment, so the hijab identifies these students who further mark out their own comfort zones, along the wall of the library and inside the building, tending to congregate away from other students' gathering areas. Not all Arab women wear hijab here, although most do. Some are not southern Bedouin, but from the northern Triangle area, and regard hijab as restrictive, signaling identification with religious or political groups like Hamas, which are distasteful to them.

The Israeli discourse about the Bedouin, including these young women, was somewhat alarming and confusing to me when I arrived in Beersheba for a year's stay. These women, the Other, are seen as proof of the Arab's retrogressive and oppressive tendencies. Some town dwellers blame the Bedouin for crime and petty theft; others trace the problem back to the government's enforced settlement scheme, in which the nomadic Bedouin were compelled to settle in seven towns with mixed results. Still other Israelis see their own isolation from this Arab community as counterproductive and try to bridge that gap where they can, through educational efforts, small meetings, or community groups. Even in these groups, however, the issue of women's rights, or women's adhesion to the honor code, divides the room in two—maybe because Israelis, like Americans, learn about these "rights" or lack thereof, in a theoretical form and are not very familiar with women's methods of resistance to or manipulation of the status quo.

On a trip in 2000 into the Wadi al-Sada, a high desert in the north of the Egyptian portion of the Sinai Peninsula, we turned off the dirt road to survey an old wrecked Ford truck near a canyon where the Bedouin camped. My friend, an irrepressible Arab Don Juan, uttered an audible gasp as the women served us tea. "She grew up since last year," he exclaimed, gesturing at a young woman, who was carrying a baby. Neither

her married status nor her veil deterred him from staring and flirting. "Look at her eyes," he sighed, "and see how she looks back at you, it's just like having sex."

Obviously the veil does little to discourage male lust, though it is supposed to. Nor does it dampen flirting from the female side. Is it merely habitual? Or is it a new way of displaying identity? Certainly it is many things to women, as to men.

Outside these field experiences—which to me, express the local meanings of covering—I am called upon, like many academics, to explain the "rules about Muslim women" in the classroom or to professional or general audiences. Americans frequently assume that any veil means that a woman is "religious," while other women who do not wear one are "Westernized." I caution them not to judge the book by its cover.

Muslims disagree about the "rules," as much as they do about the benefits of veiling. Thus, one consideration is whether or not it is helpful to think about all the formal restrictions of women's rights out of context. For example, the United States military has acquired its own knowledge of women's rights in a Muslim country through the media, academic presentations, as well as observation. The range of female dress, behavior, and attitudes in Iraq is often misunderstood. Not all women wear the abaya. Some wear dresses, or jeans and T-shirts, highlight their hair, and wear a lot of makeup. Campaigns by Islamist insurgents and Sadrists and others have intimidated women and promoted veiling all over Iraq. This is extremely troubling, even though there are reports that men are also targeted for wearing shorts or red or orange shirts, or for having their hair cut and beards shaved. Unveiled women have been murdered and girls who attend university are wearing hijab in response. In addition, women have been attacked, raped, and hundreds of women and men have been kidnapped and held for ransom.[3] Simply leaving one's home to go to school or work is a risk.

Such extremist attitudes and attacks on women have also taken place elsewhere. In Algeria, in the 1990s. In Afghanistan, after the Taliban's conquest in 1996. In the Sudan, in 1996, women demonstrators who wore trousers were sentenced to flogging. Islamic rules about covering were put in place after 1989 despite the fact that Sudanese women already have their own national form of modest dress, the Sudanese thob, which resembles the Indian sari.

And of course, the hijab has been required in the Islamic Republic of Iran since the revolution of 1979. The chadri is also compulsory there for certain public venues, such as the courts, where women must remove their makeup as well, before entering.

We can only hope that the range of women's rights that need to be addressed worldwide will go far beyond the matter of dress and accommodate those women who do as well as those who do not wish to veil. Despite my musings, as I travel from veil to veil, I suggest that we should not be obsessed with constant references to Muslim exceptionality. While we reflect on one veil or another, the ambiguity of its purpose and that of other Islamic rules deserves some discussion, but what women can achieve or have available to them, beyond their dress and initial circumstances in life, should be of interest as well.

Long ago, one of my Egyptian interlocutors—a member of the Socialist Labor Party, which was allied with the Muslim Brotherhood and thus included female party members who had adopted hijab—said to me rather defensively: "What's in a woman's head is a lot more important than what's on it."

NOTES

The views expressed in this essay are those of the author and do not necessarily reflect the official policy or position of the Department of the Army, Department of Defense, or the U.S. government.

1. Sherifa Zuhur, *Saudi Arabia: Islamic Threat, Political Reform, and the Global War on Terror* (Carlisle, PA: Strategic Studies Institute, U.S. Army War College, 2005), 33–34, available at www.strategicstudiesinstitute.army.mil/pubs/display.cfm?publID=598.

2. To understand Islamic arguments about veiling and other aspects of gender ideology, see Sherifa Zuhur, *Revealing Reveiling: Islamist Gender Ideology in Contemporary Egypt* (Albany: State University of New York Press, 1992).

3. Sherifa Zuhur, *Iraq, Women's Empowerment, and Public Policy* (Carlisle, PA: Strategic Studies Institute, U.S. Army War College, 2006), available at www.strategicstudiesinstitute.army.mil/pubs/display.cfm?publID=748.

Epilogue

The purpose of this book is to locate the veil in broader contexts than the stereotypes into which it has been boxed. To that end, these writers have pursued its history and import from diverse points of view, cultures, politics, and religions. We have explored the veil's layered meanings and poetics.

An overriding concern expressed in these chapters is the exploitation of the veil for political agendas. Veiling has been abused in many places, societies, and circumstances across time, but its misuse is especially virulent today with respect to the Muslim veil, which is seen by the West as a challenge to modernity and secular enlightenment and even as a terrorist threat. Simultaneously, it has become a symbol of Islamist solidarity and anti-Western sentiment. For generations, forced veiling and unveiling have been relentless—in the interests of colonialization or of decolonialization. Certain questions thread through this book, among them Who makes veiling a political issue? Why? And most important, What does politicizing the veil mean in terms of women's agency?

Neither legislation nor bombing will "solve" veiling. The veil does not need to be solved. The energy that has been expended on veiling, unveiling, reveiling, or deveiling by non-Muslims and Muslims alike has by now become downright preposterous and dangerous. Considering the real problems facing women, ideological battles about the veil are tragic wastes of time. They hinder feminist progress and blind us to the increasing feminization of poverty. The veil has become a subterfuge, diverting us from the fact that millions of women of all faiths and in all societies around the globe live in abject poverty. That millions are uneducated and unskilled and have no economic power. That millions are victims of HIV/AIDS and domestic violence. That millions die in childbirth (or their children do not live past the age of five). That millions are refugees. That millions are robbed and raped and held hostage by conflicts they did not invite and do not want. That women's disadvantages feed a destructive spiral of impoverishment, population growth, and environmental degradation worldwide.

To veil or not to veil is not the burning question. Not in Afghanistan—where beneath the *burqa* underfed, uneducated women, veterans of nearly three decades of continuous war, are barely clothed and where they shelter ragged, starving children. It is not the issue in Iran and Saudi Arabia—where the veil is mandated, but where the pressing problems are gender apartheid: women's rights to work, to divorce, to own land and other assets, to vote, to be represented in government, and to be treated as fully human. The first step is to end religious extremism and political religion of all stripes—whether Jewish, Christian, Muslim, Hindu, or any other creed—for it is women who pay the price for men's tickets to heaven. And it is an old saw, but sadly true, that men's wars are fought on the bodies of women (and their children). The veil is merely a distracting and detracting banner under which insufferable conditions are permitted to continue. This, finally, is the truth behind the veil.

Among the themes recurring in these pages—directly and indirectly—is that when women receive equal rights, veils will fall away *or* they will stay as simple matters of *choice*. What a woman *chooses* to wear on her head should be trivial to anyone other than that woman herself.

Each chapter in this book—whether based on history, politics, or memoir—owes its ballast on some level to the difficult and deep work of scholars. There is always room for further study about the veil, but it is my belief that most of what has needed to be said about veiling as liberation, subordination, resistance, tradition, or icon has pretty much been done. What's required now is to invest creative energy and scholarship—as well as hard work on the ground—on improving women's welfare, well-being, and equality, and on developing more histories of feminism that extract solutions to contemporary tragedies. Poverty has many dimensions and is difficult to measure, but according to United Nations statistics as of this writing, women are thought to comprise 70 percent of the world's poor. Although the figures vary—depending on who's counting and when—all concerned agree that the situation for women worldwide is growing worse. This, not veiling, is what must be solved. Soon.

This book operates on myriad levels. In addition to sociopolitical discussions of the veil, it brings to light multiple perspectives, many highly personal. For that is where the veil begins. And that is where it should end. It belongs only to the wearer.

Jennifer Heath

About the Contributors

KECIA ALI is Assistant Professor of Religion at Boston University. She received her PhD in Religion (Islamic Studies) from Duke University and has held research and teaching fellowships at Brandeis University and Harvard Divinity School. She is the author of *Sexual Ethics and Islam: Feminist Reflections on Qur'an, Hadith, and Jurisprudence* (2006) and the coauthor of *Islam: The Key Concepts* (2007). She has published in scholarly and popular journals and in various collections, including *Progressive Muslims: On Justice, Gender, and Pluralism* (2002) and *Taking Back Islam: American Muslims Reclaim Their Faith* (2003).

MICHELLE AUERBACH's work has been seen most recently in *Van Gogh's Ear, Bombay Gin, Xcp, Chelsea,* and *The American Drivel Review.* She is the author of the forthcoming historical novella *Alice Modern* (Excessive Poetics Press). She received her Master of Fine Arts from Naropa University in Colorado, where she is chair of Arts and Humanities at Front Range Community College.

SARAH C. BELL is a painter and comic book artist in San Francisco, author of *La Niña: Urban Fairy Tales,* a collection of autobiographical comix. She illustrated *El Repelente (or the Anti-Nuke Antics of Anabela)* (1995), a graphic novel by Jennifer

Heath, has created comix for numerous zines and newspapers, and has illustrated a variety of book and CD covers. Her work, for which she has been the recipient of five arts grants, has been exhibited in diverse venues—from alternative to mainstream spaces. The second volume of *La Niña* is forthcoming.

ALIDA JAY BOYE was Coordinator of the Mali Program at the University of Oslo in 1989–99 and is now Initiator and Coordinator of the Timbuktu Manuscripts Project at the Centre for Development and the Environment.

MEGAN BRUSCA grew up in St. Charles, Missouri. She graduated from the University of Missouri in December 2006 with a Bachelor of Science in Textile and Apparel Management. She has been drawing since she was a child.

BARBARA GOLDMAN CARREL is Adjunct Assistant Professor at the City University of New York. She received her Bachelor of Arts in Anthropology from the University of Pennsylvania, a Master of Arts in Anthropology from New York University, and a Master in Library Science from Drexel University. Her research on Hasidic women's dress combines scholarly investigations of fashion and ethnic dress in an attempt to reveal ethnic and religious significance in mass-produced fashion—how fashion is appropriated (both physically and ideologically) in order to promote ethnic and/or religious principles, distinctions, and identity.

EVE GRUBIN is the author of *Morning Prayer* (2005), a book of poems. Her work has appeared in *The American Poetry Review, The New Republic, The Virginia Quarterly Review,* and elsewhere. A group of her poems, introduced by Fanny Howe, appeared in *Conjunctions.* She teaches poetry at The New School and has taught poetry in the graduate writing program at the City College of New York, where she was also the Marvin and Edward Kaplan Lecturer in Jewish Studies. She writes for modestlyyours.net, and she is a fellow at the Drisha Institute for Jewish Education. She holds a Master in Fine Arts from Sarah Lawrence College and is currently working toward her PhD in English at CUNY's Graduate Center. She has studied Hebrew and Jewish texts at Midreshet Rachel v'Chaya College of Jewish Studies in Jerusalem.

ROXANNE KAMAYANI GUPTA, PhD, has been living, dancing, writing, and teaching between East and West since 1973, when she first traveled to India to study Indian classical dance and religion. She is the author of *A Yoga of Indian Classical Dance: The Yogini's Mirror* and numerous scholarly articles and chapters. She has taught Religious Studies, Anthropology, and South Asian Studies at several colleges in the United States and has led study tours in India. She is an initiate of both Kriya yoga and Sri Vidya tantra and has taught yoga since 1974. She currently teaches at her studio, Earthdance Centre for Body, Spirit, and Nature, in Romulus, New York.

JANA M. HAWLEY is Professor and Department Head of Apparel Textiles and Interior Design, Kansas State University, Manhattan, Kansas. She earned her Master of Arts from Oklahoma State University and her PhD at the University of Missouri. Her areas of research include textile recycling, e-commerce, and the Old Order Amish. She has published several manuscripts about Amish culture including their business practices and articles on their quilts. She served as an International Advisory for the Kyoto Fiber Recycling conference and serves as Vice President of Operations on the International Textiles and Apparel Association. She is a Fulbright Scholar to India, where she studied women artisans and their textile arts.

JENNIFER HEATH is an award-winning arts journalist, editor, and the author of eight books of fiction and nonfiction, including *The Scimitar and the Veil: Extraordinary Women of Islam* (2004); *Black Velvet: The Art We Love to Hate* (1994); *A House White with Sorrow: A Ballad for Afghanistan* (1996); *On the Edge of Dream: The Women of Celtic Myth and Legend* (1998); and *The Echoing Green: The Garden in Myth and Memory* (2000). She grew up around the world and is the founder of Seeds for Afghanistan and the Afghanistan Relief Organization Midwife Training and Infant Care Program.

VALARI JACK has been a portrait and documentary photographer for twenty-five years. Her work has always been concerned with capturing the mystery and possibility in people and their lives. Her photo "At Vespers" is one image from a project documenting the lives of a community of Benedictine nuns near Boulder, Colorado, in 1987–88.

JASBIR JAIN, Professor Emeritus Fellow at the University of Rajasthan, Jaipur, and director of IRIS, has worked extensively on epistemological and ideological issues in twentieth-century writing across languages and cultures. She is series editor for *Writers of the Indian Diaspora* (2001) and has authored several books, including *Beyond Postcolonialism: Dreams and Realities of a Nation* (2006) and *Gendered Realities, Human Spaces: The Novels of Shashi Deshpande* (2003). She is currently engaged in working on *Indigenous Roots of Feminism*.

MOHJA KAHF is an Associate Professor of Comparative Literature at the University of Arkansas and author of *Western Representations of the Muslim Woman: From Termagant to Odalisque* (1999) and "Braiding the Stories: Women's Eloquence in the Early Islamic Era," in *Windows of Faith: Muslim Women Scholar-Activists in North America*, edited by Gisela Webb (2000). Her poetry book, *E-mails from Scheherazad*, was a finalist in the 2004 Paterson Poetry Prize. Winner of an Arkansas Arts Council award, she writes fiction on MuslimWakeUp.com's "Sex and the Ummah" column. Her novel, *Girl in the Tangerine Scarf*, was published in 2006.

DÉSIRÉE G. KOSLIN holds a PhD in Art History from New York University and is currently Adjunct Assistant Professor in Fashion and Textile Studies at the Fashion Institute of Technology. In addition, she is an artist whose work has been exhibited at New York's SOHO20 Chelsea Gallery. Her many publications include entries in *Berg Encyclopedia on World Dress*, *Encyclopedia on Gender in the Middle Ages*,

Encyclopedia of Clothing and Fashion, and *Trade, Travel, and Exploration in the Middle Ages: An Encyclopedia,* essays in the *Journal of the International Association of Costume* and the *Catalogue of the Dubrovnik Synagogue Textile Collection,* Yeshiva University Art Museum, as well as articles in numerous anthologies, such as *Disentangling Textiles* (2002); *Robes and Honor: The Medieval World of Investiture* (2001); and *Sacred and Ceremonial Textiles, Proceedings of the Fifth Biennial Symposium of the Textile Society of America* (1996). She is coeditor, with Janet E. Snyder, of *Encountering Medieval Textiles and Dress: Objects, Texts, Images* (2002).

VIJAY KUTTY is a documentary filmmaker and photographer in Delhi. In the last few years he has shot several films in India and abroad with international collaborations. Some of these have been broadcast on channels like ARTE, ORF, and other European channels. He also writes travel pieces and his photographs have been published in magazines and newspapers, as well as corporate brochures.

LAURENE M. LAFONTAINE is a spiritual leader, educator, and social activist. Since graduating from Princeton Theological Seminary and being ordained as a Presbyterian Church USA minister in 1987, her work has reflected her commitment to peace and justice within the larger interfaith community. Most recently, she was the pastor of Highland Park Presbyterian Church in Denver, Colorado. She has taught courses in Advanced Placement European History, Twentieth-Century World History, Great Ideas in Religion, and coordinated the Community Service Program at St. Mary's Academy in Englewood, Colorado. She has served as the National Co-Moderator for Presbyterians for Lesbian/Gay Concerns and directed the *Voices of Faith* program for GLBT civil rights with Equality Colorado. After completing a two-year postgraduate internship and residency hospital chaplaincy program at Presbyterian/St. Luke's Hospital and the University of Colorado Health Science center, she founded and directed the AIDS/HIV Interfaith Network. She is the founding director of Simply Justice, a nonprofit organization focused on the integration of feminist spirituality, social justice, and progressive politics.

VIRGINIA MAITLAND is a highly acclaimed, award-winning abstract artist, living in Colorado. She graduated from the Pennsylvania Academy of Fine Arts, where she began with academic training in the tradition of Mary Cassatt and Thomas Eakins. There, under the influence of the 1960s art school experience, she soon moved toward abstraction, influenced by abstract expressionism, surrealism, and color field painting. Maitland's paintings seduce through the beauty of pure paint, vivid colors, and illusory spaces. The experience of light, space, and color in nature has been an enduring inspiration. Her work has been shown in solo and group exhibitions throughout the United States and is in myriad public and private collections. Her work can be seen on www.virginiamaitland.com.

SHIREEN MALIK is a multicultural dance artist and independent researcher, focusing primarily on traditions of the Middle East, Spain, Cuba, and Hawaii. A performer, instructor, and choreographer, she has received support for her work from the Colorado Scientific and Cultural Facilities District and Boulder Arts Commission. She is a graduate with honors from the University of California, Berkeley, with a degree in the combined fields of anthropology, psychology, sociology.

MALIHA MASOOD was born in Karachi, Pakistan. She came to the United States at the age of twelve and grew up in Seattle, Washington. Her essays and commentaries on Islam, gender, and spirituality have been featured in *Asia Times, Al-Ahram Weekly,* and several anthologies. Maliha appeared in and cowrote an award-winning documentary film, *Nazrah, A Muslim Woman's Perspective* (2003). She is also the founder of Diwaan, a cultural institute and theater collective addressing the American-Muslim experience. A graduate of Tufts University with a Master in Law and Diplomacy, Maliha has worked in her native Pakistan as a development consultant and continues to do independent research in human rights and Islamic law. She is the author of the travel memoir, *Zaatar Days, Henna Nights: Adventures, Dreams and Destinations across the Middle East* (2007). Her website is www.maliha-masood.com.

DAN PIRARO is a surrealist painter, illustrator, and cartoonist best known for his award-winning syndicated panel cartoon, *Bizarro.* He has received the National Cartoonist Society Panel Cartoon Award for 1999, 2000, and 2001, and been nominated for their Reuben Award several times. Since 2001, he has toured the United States with various forms of a one-man comedy show called *The Bizarro Baloney Show.* The show won the 2002 New York International Fringe Festival award for "Best Solo Show." His many books include *Bizarro and Other Strange Manifestations of the Art of Dan Piraro* (2006) and *The Three Little Pigs Buy the White House* (2004).

MARJANE SATRAPI was born in 1969 in Rasht, Iran. She grew up in Tehran, where she studied at the Lycée Français before leaving for Vienna and then going to Strasbourg to study illustration. She currently lives in Paris. She is the author of several children's books, and her graphic novels include *Persepolis, Persepolis 2, Embroideries,* and *Chicken with Plums.* The film version of *Persepolis* was released by Sony Pictures in 2007.

MAUREEN SELWOOD is on the faculty of the California Institute of the Arts, in the Experimental Animation Department, and is a leading figure in American Independent animation. Her latest works include a book, *Green Is for Privacy* (2007), and a large-scale installation, *Ombre dal Lupercale* (Shadows from the realms of wolves) for the 2007 summer solstice on the Tiber River in Rome. Her installation *As the Veil Lifts* uses animation and the voice of a woman performing a song of loss and suffering caused by the effects of war. Her latest film, *Mistaken Identity,* is an experimental narrative using archival footage from Robert Aldrich's noir *Kiss*

Me Deadly. She has been a recipient of grants from the John Solomon Guggenheim Foundation, New York State Council on the Arts, the Jerome Foundation, the American Film Institute, and the Rome Prize from the American Academy in Rome. Megan Cotts is Selwood's daughter and sometime collaborator.

AISHA LEE FOX SHAHEED is a writer-researcher with a background in history, emphasizing gender, (post)colonialism, and historiography. She is an active networker for the transnational feminist solidarity network Women Living Under Muslim Laws, which endeavors to create links among women and women's groups within Muslim countries and communities and to strengthen local and global struggles for social justice. She is currently based in WLUML's international coordination office in London. Her writing ventures from historical analysis to journalism, academic writing to spoken-word poetry, and beyond. As a person of many cultural and national backgrounds—and of many interests—she enjoys dividing her time between Canada, Pakistan, and England and is especially intrigued by representations of women that cut across various markers of identity. Her forthcoming publications include a chapter on storytelling as feminist historiography and an analytical overview of the status of women and women's activism in Saudi Arabia.

SHERYL B. SHAPIRO is a freelance photographer based in Boulder, Colorado. Her passion is photographing indigenous people living traditional lifestyles. She has traveled extensively in the developing world, including Afghanistan, Iran, Yemen, North Korea, Mongolia, Cuba, and Tibet. Her images reflect the humanity and dignity of her subjects. Her work has been published in *Practical Horseman,* the *Melbourne Herald Sun,* and the *Brisbane Sunday Mail,* among others. She teaches courses on independent third-world travel and presents educational presentations of her journeys for public and private audiences.

RITA STEPHAN is a PhD candidate in sociology at the University of Texas at Austin writing her dissertation on "The Family and the Making of Women's Rights Activism in Lebanon." She is a research fellow at the American University of Beirut and Notre Dame University, Lebanon, and a lecturer at St. Edwards University, where she teaches Women in the Third World, Islam and Race, Class and Gender. She is the recipient of the American Association of University Women's American Fellowship and P.E.O. Scholar Award. Her publications include articles in the *Women Studies International Forum,* the *Hawwa Journal of Women of the Middle East and the Islamic World,* and *al Raeda* Journal of the Institute for the Studies of Arab Women at the Lebanese American University.

PAMELA K. TAYLOR is a writer and public speaker of wide-ranging interests, director of the Islamic Writers Alliance, and cofounder of Muslims for Progressive Values. She has published numerous short stories, personal essays, poetry, news articles, and opinion pieces in the mainstream and Muslim presses. From poetry readings to storytelling sessions to presentations on Islam, she tries to show the human side of Muslims. She received her Bachelor of Arts from Dartmouth College and a Master of Theological Studies from Harvard Divinity School. She currently has a science fiction novel under consideration by DAW Books and is working on her second manuscript. You may find more of Pamela's writings at her blog, www.pktaylor.com/pksblog/warpedgalaxies.html, or at On Faith, http://newsweek.washingtonpost.com/onfaith/pamela_k_taylor .

ASHRAF ZAHEDI, PhD, is a sociologist and an affiliated scholar at Beatrice Bain Research Group at the University of California, Berkeley. She has taught at Boston University, Suffolk University, and Santa Clara University. She has conducted research at many universities including the Institute for Research on Women and Gender, Stanford University. She has served as the Commissioner of Human Relations of Santa Clara County, California, and chaired the Santa Clara County Network for a Hate-Free Community, which she initiated. She is the recipient of "Special Congressional Recognition" from the United States House of Representatives. She is a native of Iran.

DINAH ZEIGER recently completed her PhD at the School of Journalism and Mass Communications at the University of Colorado-Boulder and now teaches on the adjunct faculty in the University of Denver's Department of Mass Communications and Journalism Studies. She was a business reporter and editor for various newspapers and wire services in the United States and Europe for more than twenty years and most recently has published extensively as an arts critic.

SHERIFA ZUHUR is currently Research Professor of Islamic and Regional Studies at the Strategic Studies Institute of the U.S. Army War College. She has been a faculty member or researcher at various universities including MIT, University of California, Berkeley, and UCLA. She is the author of twelve books and monographs including *Revealing Reveiling: Islamist Gender Ideology in Contemporary Egypt* (1992); and *Colors of Enchantment: Theater, Dance, Music, and the Visual Arts of the Middle East* (2001).

Index

Text: Palatino
Display: Univers Condensed Light 47 and Bauer Bodoni
Compositor: Integrated Composition Systems
Indexer: Roberta Engleman
Printer and Binder: Thomson-Shore, Inc.